Magna Carta

IN 20
PLACES

Magna Carta

IN 20 PLACES

DEREK J. TAYLOR

The History Press

To Stan Revill

My history teacher – long gone, but still living in this book.

By the same author
A Horse in the Bathroom

First published 2015

The History Press
The Mill, Brimscombe Port
Stroud, Gloucestershire, GL5 2QG
www.thehistorypress.co.uk

British Library Cataloguing in Publication Data.
A catalogue record for this book is available from the British Library.

ISBN 978 0 7509 6229 2

Typesetting and origination by The History Press
Printed in Malta by Melita Press

CONTENTS

1 The Royal Exchange, City of London: *A magnificent myth* 7

2 The Fens, Cambridgeshire, England: *The barons on top* 17

3 Clarendon Palace, Wiltshire, England: *The flying monarch* 29

4 Acre, Israel: *Lionheart's legacy* 41

5 Angoulême, France: *The child witch* 53

6 Mirebeau-en-Poitou, France: *The warrior queen* 63

7 Château Gaillard, Normandy, France: *Lost!* 73

8 The Marches, South Wales: *Rule by vendetta* 87

9 Laxton, Nottinghamshire, England: *The serfs in the fields* 97

10 Lincoln, Lincolnshire, England: *The smell of money* 109

11 Temple Ewell, Kent, England: *A triumphant humiliation* 121

12 Bouvines, Northern France: *A battle for three empires* 131

13 Runnymede, Surrey, England: *The line-up* 145

14 The British Library, London: *The deal* 157

15 The Wash, Lincolnshire, England: *Agony in the wasteland* 169

16 Worcester Cathedral, England: *The man laid bare* 179

17 The Internet: *A bad press* 189

18 The Palace of Westminster, London: *A charter for all seasons* 197

19 Jamestown, Virginia, USA: *The gentlemen cannibals* 211

20 Washington DC: *Temples and tyrants* 221

21 Back to Runnymede: *Magna Carta's future* 235

Appendix: The text of Magna Carta 242

Index 251

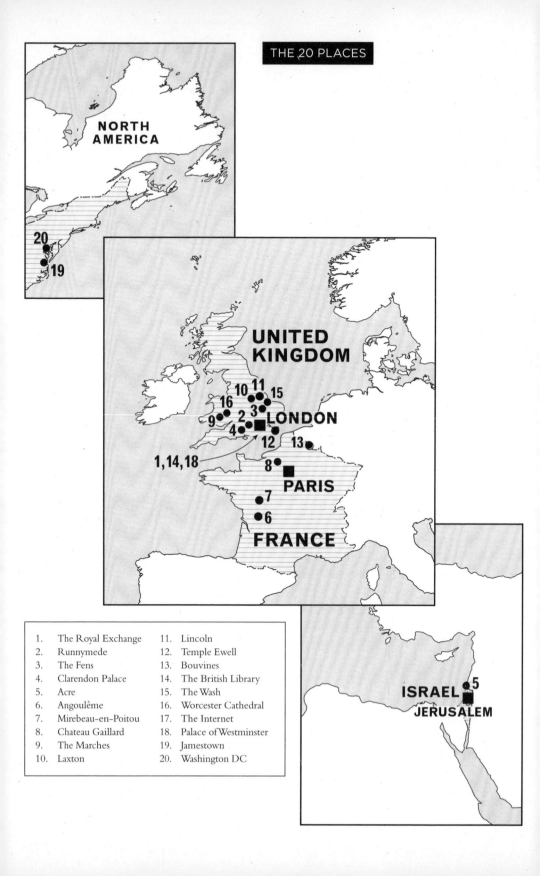

THE 20 PLACES

NORTH
AMERICA

20
19

UNITED
KINGDOM

10 11 15
16
9   2 3 LONDON
  4
    12   13
1, 14, 18
       8
       PARIS
      7
     6
FRANCE

ISRAEL 5
JERUSALEM

1.	The Royal Exchange	11.	Lincoln
2.	Runnymede	12.	Temple Ewell
3.	The Fens	13.	Bouvines
4.	Clarendon Palace	14.	The British Library
5.	Acre	15.	The Wash
6.	Angoulême	16.	Worcester Cathedral
7.	Mirebeau–en–Poitou	17.	The Internet
8.	Chateau Gaillard	18.	Palace of Westminster
9.	The Marches	19.	Jamestown
10.	Laxton	20.	Washington DC

1 THE ROYAL EXCHANGE, CITY OF LONDON

A MAGNIFICENT MYTH

cross the road from the Bank of England stands what looks like a vast temple with eight pairs of massive Corinthian columns along its front rising 90 feet into the air. You could imagine the entrance was built this high so that giants, or gods, could stride in without ducking. When TV economics correspondents want to 'go live' in the City of London and tell us on the six o'clock news about the latest GDP figures or the shrinking fiscal deficit, they ask their camera crews to set up so we'll see it in the background. The building exudes dignity and reliability. It says 'this is where weighty matters are decided.' It's called the Royal Exchange. And it makes the nearby Bank of England in Threadneedle Street look by comparison like a warehouse with a church on top, or a Las Vegas shopping mall pretending to be Grecian.

But the Royal Exchange isn't a temple, not in the religious sense, though you could argue that what goes on inside is a cult. There's a 10-foot-high statue of a crowned goddess at the top of its facade. She represents Commerce, and from the street we can see her right elbow leaning – implausibly – on the prow of a ship, while a beehive, positioned dangerously close to her left armpit, signifies how very busy her adherents are down below. Charles Dickens knew the Royal Exchange simply as The Change, and in *A Christmas Carol*, Scrooge sold debts here, and was taken by the Ghost of Christmas Yet To Come to see its merchants as they 'hurried up and down, and chinked the money in their pockets, and conversed in groups, and looked at their watches, and trifled thoughtfully with their great gold seals.'

But the reason we've come to the Royal Exchange is neither to trade nor to admire the architecture. We're here to look at a painting commissioned by the Exchange's governors at the end of the nineteenth century to commemorate the freedom without which the goddess Commerce couldn't function. The picture shows the birth, in the year 1215 on the banks of the River Thames at Runnymede, of Magna Carta, also known as the Great Charter of Liberties, when King John was backed into a corner by the mightiest barons of England

and forced to issue the document that's come to be regarded down the ages and over much of the planet ever since as the foundation of civil liberty and the rule of law.

✴✴✴

At the top of the wide flight of steps leading to the Exchange's entrance, I pass between the towering columns, then through a pair of glass doors. It turns out that, if the Bank of England is a solid institution that looks like a shopping mall, the Royal Exchange only looks like a solid institution but is in fact a shopping mall. The interior of the building is formed as a single room, that's 'room' in the sense that a cathedral nave is a room. It rises to a glass ceiling 80 feet above its marble floor. As shopping malls go, it's the uppermost of the upmarket variety. All along its sides, extravagantly lit windows between stone archways show off the sort of necklaces and watches royalty might wear on gala night at the palace. There are only two or three of these sparkling items in each showcase, which tells you all you need to know about their price. Discreet illuminated signs announce that Bvlgari, Tiffany & Co., Agent Provocateur and Lulu Guinness feel at home here. The whole floor of this well-ordered Aladdin's cave is filled with

The Royal Exchange, temple of commerce. Its governors commissioned Ernest Normand's painting of the sealing of Magna Carta in the 1890s.

small round tables and ladderback chairs, most of them occupied by men and women in sharp dark suits, leaning forward, neglecting their lattes and croissants, and looking intently at each other or at their laptop screens. I feel like an alien in my jeans and dark green thorn-proof country-style jacket. But I pull out my camera, zoom it back to a wide angle and have just snapped the glittering scene when the viewfinder is blocked by a blurred face which is speaking.

'Sorry, sir,' it says, 'photography is not allowed anywhere in the Royal Exchange.' It's a man in dark grey trousers rising to a buttoned-up black overcoat. His tie is golden. He points at the camera, and, perhaps assuming I'm a bumpkin, slow on the uptake, says, 'It's prohibited.'

'Why's that then?' I ask.

'Security,' he replies, and I'm expecting him to escort me from the premises. 'But you may walk around and look,' he concedes, just in case I think I've a right to order a cup of peppermint tea and sit down.

The Royal Exchange, as you might imagine, has been a target for jewel thieves. In one recent heist, two figures in motorcycle gear and armed with axes broke through the outer wrought iron gates on a Saturday night when the place was closed. They smashed display cabinets and snatched watches worth £300,000 (at a guess, that's about four watches). Their accomplices were waiting outside on motorbikes. They all sped off and lost their police pursuers. This particular mob were 'dubbed' (as tabloid newspapers put it) 'the Fagin's Kitchen gang', because the thieves, though not quite as young as Oliver Twist and the Artful Dodger, were teenagers.

I said the place is now an upmarket shopping mall, and so it is, but nevertheless it still serves its original purpose. The first Exchange on this site was opened by Queen Elizabeth I in 1570 as a meeting-place for merchants. That building burned down in the Great Fire of London in 1666, and its replacement too went up in flames in the early nineteenth century. The monumental structure we're visiting today was inaugurated by Queen Victoria in 1845 'for the convenience of merchants and bankers'. The merchants and bankers are still here, though nowadays they insist on fresh ground coffee and waitress service for their client meetings, in a place where, when the deal's done, they can blow their bonuses at Bvlgari or Tiffany's.

In some senses, Magna Carta itself, back in 1215, was a business deal. When hostilities had broken out between King John and the rebel barons earlier that year, the City of London – already a thriving trade centre – saw a commercial opportunity. The canny burghers of the city pitched their support behind the barons. It was a game-changer. It tipped the balance away from John, who now saw he had to reach an agreement with his opponents, if only to buy time. Charters granting certain concessions to towns were commonplace in the early thirteenth century. And in return for backing the rebels, Londoners got a neat little clause inserted into Magna Carta. It said that the city should 'enjoy all its ancient liberties and free customs, both by land and by water'. So we can see why the Victorian governors of the Royal Exchange would commission a painting of 'King John and the barons'.

✳ ✳ ✳

The picture of the momentous event that took place on the meadow at Runnymede is up on the mezzanine level, which runs like a wide balcony behind decorated columns around the interior of the whole building. There are twenty-four murals you can admire from the restaurant up here. They were produced during the 1890s to illustrate episodes in the history of England which were important to the Royal Exchange and to the City of London as one of the world's great trading centres. The paintings are all huge, approximately 12 feet high and 8 feet wide. When the Exchange's governors commissioned the one of Magna Carta, they decided they wanted something expressive, dramatic and colourful. And that's what they got. Truthful – well, that's another matter.

In the centre of the picture is King John, wearing his crown and sitting on a throne beneath swirling banners. The Archbishop of Canterbury at his left shoulder is advising him. Below, to the king's right, is a clerk holding a parchment, presumably the Charter. And in front of him are ranged the barons, some of them in battle dress, one leaning on a broadsword. In the right foreground of the picture is what looks like an old-fashioned printing press. In fact, it's the machine that was used to make an imprint of the royal seal in a lump of wax, which would then be fixed to a ribbon or cord appended to the bottom of the document. Contrary to popular notions, King John did not 'sign' Magna Carta. Not that he was stupid or illiterate. Far from it. But, just as he enjoyed food though wouldn't have dreamed of cooking it himself, so he could read and write, but usually had a man – or men – to do the manual work for him with pens and parchment. And anyway, the idea of authorising a document by writing your name on it in a distinctive way, i.e. signing it, was virtually unknown in the thirteenth century.

But what we're interested in is not whether the painting is an accurate record of the event. No handy contemporary sketch, or even detailed description of the scene at Runnymede, has come down to us. What is significant for our investigation is the way the artist has tried to manipulate our feelings by bringing out the character of the protagonists and their reactions to the momentous event in which they're participating. The painter was Ernest Normand, a notable Victorian who worked in the style of the Pre-Raphaelites. He completed the picture in 1900.

Most of Normand's other work is of sensual nudes or Old Testament scenes, all with characters whose emotions are conveyed through their ostentatious gestures. The wistful, the adoring, the betrayed, the angst-ridden, the lascivious are all revealed by a delicately positioned hand on the forehead, by yearning eyes, or a dissolute posture of the body. So Normand was the ideal choice to reflect on canvas the adoration, the pride, the hatred of tyranny which the story of King John, the barons and Magna Carta stirred in Victorian hearts.

Take the way he portrays the king, for instance. Beneath his golden crown, John has a furrowed brow. He's a worried man. Then his eyes, staring off stage left, are shown as cold and calculating. At the same time they're cowardly: he can't meet the stern gaze of the barons who have beaten him and now confront him. His full lips are those of someone who's more interested in the pleasures of the flesh than in the routine of good government. John doesn't sit upright as a monarch should, but is lounging like a sulky schoolboy. In a bizarre touch, Normand has given him what look like ballerina's shoes, perhaps to show that John is effeminate, not a rough, tough soldier like his brother Richard the Lionheart. The overall impression is not of a king – despite his crown – but of an untrustworthy, impetuous, shifty wimp who's abused his position of power, in fact a thoroughly bad lot who's rightly been brought to heel. The courtier just behind his right shoulder knows the game's up. He's doing what today's politicians on media-handling courses are taught never to do: move your eyes sideways while still facing the camera. It makes you look devious and uncertain.

Contrast this image with those of the barons. There are four of them visible. Unlike the slouching king, their backs are all ramrod straight. The one at the front has his left foot planted on the steps leading up to the king's throne, as if to show that he's not cowed by the trappings of an unworthy king. He's gripping his sword and looks like a man who will use it if necessary. But most striking, his facial expression is one of steely determination. He's not to be trifled with. He knows he has right and the weight of history on his side. He's a man you'd trust to lead you in the battle against the forces of tyranny. Behind him are two other barons. One is in full mail, with what looks like the hilt of a battleaxe tilted at the ready over his shoulder. The other is an older man, with white hair and beard, but again his back is firm and straight. It's clear the wisdom of old age is also on the side of the barons. All three of these opponents of the king are skewering him with undeviating glares. They don't trust him an inch. The fourth of their colleagues is turning, as though to look back at an unseen host of mighty men following up, ready to do what's right.

In the background of the painting, at the side of the king's tented pavilion, we can just see what appear to be the heads of hundreds of men crowding forward. The nation is watching, perhaps waiting to be liberated.

When Normand painted the picture, he was reflecting mainstream opinion. The great Victorian historian William Stubbs wrote of John that he was, 'the very worst of all our kings, a faithless son, a treacherous brother, polluted with every crime'. Stubbs saw John's father Henry II as a good and strong monarch, and King Richard the Lionheart, John's brother who followed Henry, as a brave soldier. By contrast, John was tyrannical and cowardly. And the barons who rose up against him were regarded as early champions of civil liberty, battling on behalf of all the people of England for democracy, freedom and justice, principles thus enshrined in Magna Carta.

This uplifting picture has been guaranteed to stir hearts in England and wherever in the world there are folk who love freedom and abhor dictatorship, and are prepared to fight for what they know is right.

The trouble is that, in almost every respect, it's wrong. It's a myth.

The true story is rather different.

King John, according recent evidence, wasn't entirely the 'bad' monarch of popular imagination. One renowned historian has described him as 'a ruler of consummate ability'.

The rebel barons are even less like Normand's picture of them. They weren't the straight-backed, look-you-in-the-eye, idealistic, altruistic Honest Joes that he would have had us believe. As far as we can generalise, they were a self-serving bunch led by manipulative thugs.

And the commonly held view that Magna Carta is the guarantee of everything we in a free and democratic country hold dear is even wider of the historically accurate mark. It's a view, however, that does have a long and respectable tradition. In the eighteenth century the British Prime Minister William Pitt the Elder described Magna Carta as 'The Bible of the English Constitution'. A hundred years later, Stubbs could make the sweeping statement that, 'The whole constitutional history of England is little more than a commentary on Magna Carta.' And in the twentieth century, US President Franklin D. Roosevelt declared in his inaugural address to the American people that, 'the democratic aspiration is no mere recent phase in human history … It was written in Magna Charta [sic].' In 2012, a poll of British adults carried out for the *Daily Telegraph* found that 85 per cent of us have heard of the Great Charter; of those, 60 per cent believe it guaranteed the rule of law, half think it safeguards our right to trial by jury and 38 per cent are convinced that without it there'd be no democracy.

But the plain fact is that Magna Carta, as sealed by King John in 1215, was not what later generations made of it. For a start, it contains no high-sounding statement guaranteeing freedom, justice and democracy. Most of its clauses deal with the technicalities of thirteenth-century feudal law, and were largely aimed at protecting the rights of the upper classes: 1 per cent or less of the population.

In 1215 the Charter wasn't even regarded as being particularly important. It's called Magna, or Great, only because it was written on a piece of parchment slightly bigger than that of another charter issued soon afterwards. It might even have been consigned to the dustiest archives of history and forgotten if King John had managed to survive its birth by more than a year or so and re-establish his control over the country.

The Great Charter was not an early constitution. It wasn't a proclamation of universal freedom under the law. And it certainly wasn't the foundation of democracy. That's a myth.

But of course, this is not the whole story. Far from it.

Myths have always been important throughout the history of humankind. Great nations are often founded on them. Take the United States of America, for instance, often said to be founded by the puritans arriving on the *Mayflower* to establish a country with freedom of worship. A myth because these early settlers wanted nothing of the sort. Yes, they were fleeing persecution back in England. However, their dream was not of a nation based on religious liberty, but of a country where the only sect permitted would be theirs. Or take ancient Rome, founded on the myth of Romulus and Remus suckled by a she-wolf. Not true in itself, but a sign that Romans were brutal, relentless fighters. Though its facts may be jumbled, a myth will have a golden thread of truth running through it. So it is with the story of John, the barons and Magna Carta.

The Great Charter couldn't have exerted the power over our minds that it has for eight centuries if there were nothing to it but a list of feudal customs. It's true the majority of its sixty-three clauses were just that. But through much of the document there's a whiff of something different, something which hinted that ideas about freedom and justice have a vital role to play in the way that people living together organise themselves. Something that later generations could seize on and develop, so that the Great Charter could become a powerful, all-enduring watchword for our most cherished political, legal and civil rights. It deserves our reverence, though not for the reasons that Ernest Normand presented to us when he painted his picture of John and the barons at Runnymede in the year 1900. The real story of Magna Carta is what we shall pursue on our journey.

★★★

Back outside the Royal Exchange, on the triangle of pavement in front of the towering columns, there are no BBC reporters today testing their microphones. Instead there's a tight-packed bunch of kids in their mid teens gathered halfway between a statue of the Duke of Wellington on his horse and another – rather less arrogant – stone figure with his raincoat over his arm, a Mr J.H. Greathead, according to the plaque, inventor of the 'travelling shield' which enabled tunnels to be cut for London's underground railway. There's something odd about these schoolkids. As they huddle against the cold, in beanie hats and anoraks and strapped into small rucksacks, I suddenly realise what it is. They're all listening. Whatever the small, bald bespectacled chap in their midst is saying, presumably their teacher, it has grabbed them. Nobody's chatting or giggling or fooling about. I edge closer. It sounds like he's speaking Russian, or some other Slavic language. He opens his shoulder bag, and pulls out a sheaf of £20 notes. They look crisp, straight out of the Mint. He hands them out among the students closest to him, then holds one up where they can all see it. At first I think he's showing them the picture of the queen on the note, but then realise it's the image next to her that he's pointing to. I hear him say something like 'Banka z Anglie' several times, and I seize on the few seconds' silence that follow, to tackle him.

'Excuse me,' I say, 'could I ask where you're from?'

I quickly realise that I should have opened up with a softer approach, something about the weather maybe, because the chap steps back, his eyes wide in fright. So to put him at his ease, I assume an excessively broad smile. And as his expression changes from that of a man facing a secret policeman to one dealing with a lunatic, he replies, 'We are here from the Czech Republic. It is our first visit,' then he turns and marches off down Cornhill, with his obedient brood at his heels. I make a mental note to remember that freedom from oppression is a relatively new concept to some of our East European allies.

And it's time we set off on our journey too. It will take us to the places where the ghosts of those who made Magna Carta, or who worshipped it later, still lurk. In palaces and villages, around the streets of bustling towns, in the shadows of ruined castles and the nooks of ancient churches, along desolate mountainsides and remote shorelines. To reach them, we shall travel through England and Wales, via France and the Middle East, until finally we arrive in the United States of America and discover that the Great Charter's long and glorious – though often misrepresented – story isn't finished yet.

One of the delights of Magna Carta is that its real history is much more engaging, exciting and surprising than any simple fairy tale of good defeating evil. On our travels, we shall see how lawlessness, violence, betrayal and the smack of firm government led to the birth of the Great Charter of Liberties in 1215. And we shall try to discover why Magna Carta, for all the misunderstandings about it (or maybe because of them), has continued to inspire its later followers to risk torture, imprisonment and death for what they believed it represented – through civil war, the fight for parliamentary democracy, and the colonisation of 'new worlds' – until today, 800 years later, people have even been known to brush away a tear when they speak of it.

✯ ✯ ✯

Our next destination is an isolated spot in eastern England seventy-two years before King John sealed Magna Carta. Trouble between king and barons was nothing new in 1215; the tug of war between them had started decades before John came to the throne. In the mid-twelfth century, the balance of power was so heavily weighted in the barons' favour that any form of effective central authority had collapsed and there was a near total breakdown in civil order over much of the country. Historians have called this period quite simply 'the Anarchy'. In the Cambridgeshire Fens, where we're heading, the lawlessness and savagery – both arbitrary and calculated – were so terrifying that ordinary people conjured up a diabolical image to describe their sense of helplessness. They said that Christ and his saints slept.

2 THE FENS, CAMBRIDGESHIRE, ENGLAND

THE BARONS ON TOP

Anywhere less anarchic today than the first villages we come across on the edge of the Cambridgeshire fenlands would be hard to imagine. Little places with names full of old English charm like Abbots Ripton, Wennington, Kings Ripton. They must be a roof thatcher's cash flow paradise. The ancient cottages here are all kept exquisitely pretty. Their reed-thatched roofs, thick and neat, patterned with chevrons and semicircles, droop like monks' cowls around the faces of tiny upstairs windows. Below the eaves, smoothed plaster walls are coloured soft pink or a light shade of fresh buttermilk. In Wennington, all is serene. A patriarchal gentleman, with trimmed moustache, tweed jacket, knotted tie and upright stance – a veteran soldier perhaps – is walking his spaniel. A middle-aged woman with shopping bag approaches him, and he touches his hat with old-time courtesy. Some of the house-owners here have got so carried away with the cuteness of it all that they've had their thatchers model from reed a fox or a pheasant to grace the rooftops of their homes. No dwelling here is spoiled by the faint damp stains, hairline cracks or raggedy moss that you expect on old cottages. These dwellings are so perfect – set off by a well-mown lawn and a shady fruit tree or two – that they don't look real. They have the rounded, sugar candy appearance of fairy-tale houses in Disneyland.

But imagine. Eight and a half centuries ago, Wennington, Kings Ripton, Abbots Ripton and many surrounding villages and towns were the scene of some of the most savage, unchecked gang violence ever seen in England.

Sudden outbreaks of widespread lawlessness were endemic in the hierarchical structure of medieval Europe. Feudalism didn't work. Not as a means to a peaceful society anyway.

The system was based on contract. The greatest men in the land – the barons or the tenants-in-chief, as they were also known – swore allegiance to the king and were obliged to provide him with a certain level of military support. In return, the king, who received his authority from God, granted them title to their lands and offered his vassals a degree of protection. That at least, in a nutshell, was the theory. The reality was often very different.

Since the Norman Conquest in 1066, the relationship between king and barons had been a continual power struggle. On the one hand, the barons' constant objective was to run their own territories as independent fiefdoms, as free as possible from royal interference. And the more aggressive of these aristocrats would seize any opportunity – a weak king, or one distracted by an overseas war or a disputed claim to the throne – to try to minimise any governmental or judicial role for the monarchy in their own vast and often remote territories. The king, on the other hand, was constantly worried that, if enough of the barons got their way, he would be reduced to no more than a symbolic figurehead: a monarch with God's blessing, but with very little real power beyond his own castles and their immediate surrounds. So if the king wanted to prevent this, he had to assert his royal rights throughout the realm whenever and however he could. The result was often what amounted to a bare-knuckle contest and no quarter given. Whenever tensions rose, the king would attempt to suppress his baronial opponents, calling them traitors. And they in turn would hit back claiming that he was overstepping the mark laid down by tradition, and would accuse the king of abusing the office granted him by God.

By the time John came to the throne, cataclysmic events over the previous seventy or so years had rocked the system. Both sides had challenged the other's feudal status. Magna Carta can be understood only in the context of the violent swings in the balance of power between monarchy and baronage during the reigns of John's immediate predecessors. And in the middle of the twelfth century, sixty years before John came to the throne, the man who called himself king was distracted by civil war and frankly was not very bright. A weak king was an opportunity for barons to feather their nests, fortify their castles and, for some of them, to run amok. This was what happened in the Cambridgeshire fens.

The most violent episodes began in the year 1143 with the arrival of one man, Geoffrey de Mandeville.

For eight years, following the death of Henry I, the country had been torn by a civil war between competing candidates for the throne: King Stephen, who was William the Conqueror's grandson, and the Empress Matilda, who was the late king Henry's daughter. Stephen was king solely by virtue of getting himself crowned first ahead of his rival. Contemporaries wrote that, apart from his prowess as a fighter, he 'was almost an imbecile'. Matilda, described as haughty, tactless and grasping, was called empress because she was the widow of the German ruler of the Holy Roman Empire (which cynics have observed was neither holy, nor Roman, nor an empire). Stephen and Matilda were each desperate to win over to their own cause as many of the barons as they could. They did this by creating lordly titles and then handing them out, with the appropriate lands, to anyone with a decent army of knights and bowmen who had come over to their side. Before the civil war began, England had seven earls. Seven years later the number had shot up to twenty-two. For the barons, this was a winning game. The past master at it was Geoffrey de Mandeville.

De Mandeville at first backed Stephen and was given the earldom of Essex as a reward. But when the king was defeated at the Battle of Lincoln in 1141, he figured the empress was a better bet and switched sides. Then, as her fortunes declined, he swapped back to the king's camp. Each of these shifts delivered him more high-flown ranks, land and cash till he ended up in control of the counties of Middlesex, Essex and Hertfordshire as well as the City of London. But he then got to be a bit too clever for his own good and, while publicly supporting Stephen, he began plotting in secret to put Matilda on the throne. By now, de Mandeville was himself almost as powerful as a monarch.

At this point, even the king stirred from his imbecility and at last got wise to de Mandeville's double dealing. In 1143, while the royal court was at St Albans, Stephen decided to arrest him. But the job was botched. The king's men tried to jump de Mandeville in the street; there was a scuffle, during which one of the king's supporters, the Earl of Arundel, was rolled on the ground, horse and all, and almost drowned when he fell into the abbey's sacred pond. De Mandeville managed to make it to the altar of the nearby chapel, where he claimed sanctuary. But Stephen's men ignored the earl's claim to God's protection, dragged him out, bound his hands and hauled him before the king. Stephen accused him of treachery, and offered him a straight choice: either regain his freedom by surrendering all his castles including the Tower of London, or be hanged.

De Mandeville was beaten. He had no option but hand the lot over to Stephen. However, once freed, he exploded with rage, gathered together a couple of loyal relatives and their men, and headed for Cambridgeshire. There, he chose as his headquarters the Benedictine abbey in the little town of Ramsey. It was now December, and de Mandeville and his gang burst into the monastic house at dawn. They grabbed hold of the monks – some at prayer, some in bed – and threw them out into the fields with nothing more than the clothes they had on. De Mandeville stabled his horses in the cloisters, plundered the church of its sacred treasures, and then set about fortifying the abbey. A chronicler wrote that he 'made of the church of God a very den of thieves'. But this was only the start. Ramsey was to be the base from which he would terrorise by robbery, rape and torture every living person, rich or poor, cleric or lay, young or old, for a distance of 30 miles around.

★★★

Ramsey today, in its buildings and people, still reflects a range of class, age and faith, though now according to twenty-first-century definitions.

A sign on the road as you enter welcomes you to 'Ramsey, Historic Fenland Town'. But apart from a row of bleak-looking houses called 'Abbey Terrace' and a building called 'Abbey Rooms', which has all the charm of a 1950s municipal swimming baths, there's not much historic about the town centre itself. You could be anywhere in middle England. I step off the narrow pavement to make way for two young women in tight jeans pushing buggies. At the street corner, a couple of bent-backed older citizens in flat caps leaning on sticks nod to me and say, 'Morning. Not a bad day.' The Bengal restaurant is opposite the Indiaana ('Banquet Night, 5 Courses for £10.95'), which is next door to Chilli Hut. The fact that Ramsey is surrounded by some of England's prime agricultural land is reflected in a shop boasting 'rural pest solutions ('rat and mice bait' says a sign in the window near a stuffed rabbit hesitating at the gate of a humane trap), and also in the East European accents I hear outside the Three Horseshoes pub. Vegetable pickers from Poland, Romania or Bulgaria, I guess.

At the end of the High Street, around and beyond the church, however, it's a different tale. Several grand mansions look out on to Church Green, where mallards are pottering about on the pond and shaking themselves beneath its fountain. Across the road by a broad gateway a sign announces 'Abbey College' within, and warns us against entering unless authorised. The original abbey was torn down when Henry VIII dissolved the monasteries in the mid-sixteenth century. The building that replaced it was put up a hundred years later and is now a school.

But if we're looking for old stones that we could stroke and say with a wistful look, 'Ah if only these things could talk …', there are plenty that fit the bill. The ruined masonry of the old abbey was re-used to build the mile of wall that now surrounds Abbey College. But more central to our story, the medieval gatehouse of the ancient abbey has survived: the faces of its lichen-encrusted and wind-worn gargoyles sneer down from alongside intricately decorated windows. Although this facade was added three centuries after Geoffrey de Mandeville and his thugs arrived here, behind it the ancient stonework, propping up the structure, is still intact. One of its sides has been sheered away, and looks much as it must have done when Henry VIII's demolition men finished their job and moved on to dissolve the next religious institution. They left a shattered line of broken pillars and blocks, with the mighty guts of the original wall exposed. It's 10 feet or more thick, and although the top has been smashed off, the ruined gatehouse still reaches up 25 feet above the road. It must have made an impregnable lookout post for de Mandeville and his henchmen.

But for evidence of the real military advantages that Ramsey gave to de Mandeville's operations, we need to drive out of town. Our route takes us along its wide main street, called 'the Great Whyte', which incidentally used to be a navigable canal, may even have been in existence in de Mandeville's day, and continued to serve this purpose until the 1850s, when the water was channelled underground into a tunnel, and shops and houses were built on the dry stretch of land left behind. Today, the Great Whyte is the road to Tesco, and then on out into the countryside. The land around Ramsey is flat. It's flat in every direction. This is the fens, vast primeval East Anglian marshlands. The ground is so level that at no point is it more than a few inches higher than the North Sea 30 miles east of Ramsey. From the walls and pinnacles of its abbey, de Mandeville's men would have been able to see an enemy approaching 10 miles away.

Even in the twenty-first century, there are few trees and no hedges to obstruct the low, distant vistas. The reason is that over the centuries, farmers have dredged out long straight ditches to drain the land and turn the fens into arable land. Now, thousands of fields, all filled with endless rows of green sugar beet plants, are divided one from another, not by fences or hedges, but by these long, deep drainage channels. So here, a mile outside Ramsey, I can see the land stretching away – just as it has always done – until it merges into the distant, misty sky. The only difference today is that the blurred line of the horizon is broken by a clutch of wind turbines. Locals reckon that when the wind's in the east, it blows straight in from the Ural Mountains of Russia, over the Baltic Sea, the Danish marshes, the North Sea and on to the fens with nothing in its way to slow it down.

Our route today takes us alongside the River Nene, as unbending and neat as you'd expect from what is in fact a man-made canal where there's neither rocky outcrop nor the hint of a hillock to be skirted. Occasionally, a few houses huddle at the roadside. One such hamlet is called Ramsey Heights. It must be a Fenland joke, because Ramsey Heights is barely a thumb's width higher than the sugar beet fields that surround it. Today, half its couple of dozen little houses – of a more 1960s humdrum variety than the ancient thatched ones in King's Ripton – have 4-foot-high, pinky-mauve UK Independence Party posters in their front gardens.

For de Mandeville, the fens – as well as revealing an enemy hours before he reached you – offered another military advantage. While the area was still swampy in the twelfth century, would-be attackers had to pick their way along the few man-made causeway roads built up a few inches higher than the surrounding treacherous marshland. No opponents, therefore, could advance on a broad front. They would arrive, a few at a time, along the narrow trackways and would be easy meat for the waiting defenders.

So in 1143, the stone walls and gatehouse tower of Ramsey Abbey sitting in the middle of the fens were a perfect look-out post, as well as a redoubt, hard to attack, and a perfect launch pad for marauding outrages against a defenceless local population.

★ ★ ★

Geoffrey de Mandeville began by capturing all other strong points in the area, such as the castles on the nearby Isle of Ely – isles here are not islands as we know them, they're just bits of land once slightly higher than the surrounding swampland. Word of what de Mandeville was up to soon reached the southern and midland counties of England. Lured by the prospect of robbery and rape on a grand scale, hordes of mercenaries and other lordless soldiers began to turn up on their steeds at the Ramsey Abbey gatehouse. Within a week or two, there were enough of them to begin major operations.

The first target was to be the town of Cambridge. The citizens there had got wind of trouble and hurried to stash their cash and other valuables in the church. But de Mandeville – the man who had tried to rely on God's protection by flee-ing to the altar in St Albans – ordered his men to take axes and smash down the church door. They carried off all they could find inside, then went out and set fire to the town.

The attack on Cambridge was a model for other raids. And the gang systemati-cally plundered every village church and religious institution in the surrounding fens. Apparently, when the men were getting merry after a hard day's looting, they used to sing a song, which went:

I ne mai a live
For Benoit ne for Ive

Which boasted how they had pillaged the abbey of Benoit – that was St Benedict's at Ramsey – and the abbey at St Ives. The message was clear: God could not pro-tect you from the scourge of de Mandeville and his thugs. And the pickings were easy in the fens, where ecclesiastical booty was plentiful. The area was known as the 'Holy Land of the English' because of the large number of churches, abbeys and monasteries here.

At this point, King Stephen decided enough was enough. He marched a small army up to Cambridgeshire with the aim of seizing de Mandeville in order to restore order and put a stop to the gangland rule that had made a large tract of eastern England a no-go area. But the defensive strength of the Fenland was too much for Stephen. The best he could manage was to occupy a few castles around the outside of the marshlands in the hope that this would box in the marauders. But the area of the fens controlled by de Mandeville was so extensive that his activities were hardly cramped, and so the king retreated to get back to his war with Matilda.

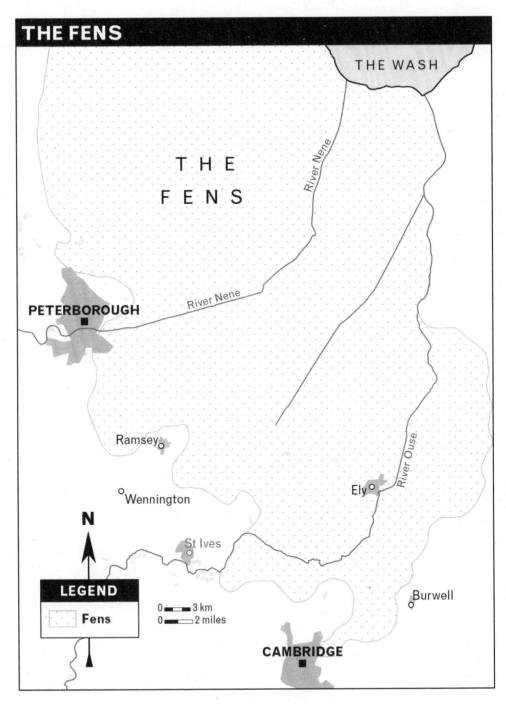

Geoffrey de Mandeville's area of operation in the Fenlands of Cambridgeshire.

The gang next turned to extortion, at which they proved to be as well organised and violent as the mafia in 1920s Chicago. The victims were the Fenlands' better-off citizens. Once a promising grand mansion had been picked out, some of de Mandeville's men would swap mail and leather battle dress for a few torn and filthy rags. Then, merging into the background as humble beggars, they would case the joint, checking out the homeowner's movements and what security measures were in place. Next, usually in the middle of the night, the rest of the gang would arrive, tooled up and mob-handed, to break in. They wouldn't waste time searching the premises. Instead, they would head straight for the sleeping quarters of the master and mistress, haul them, terrified, out of their beds, drag them off and throw them in front of de Mandeville himself. In order to extort all movable wealth from these hapless folk, he had them tortured. According to a contemporary chronicler, he employed ingenious and diabolic methods of inflicting pain, until the hiding place of every item of value was revealed.

Then came a bizarre development. King Stephen, furious that he couldn't bring de Mandeville to justice, put the blame for the Fenland lawlessness on the Bishop of Ely. The bishop had actually been away in Rome when de Mandeville first showed up, and his monks, mistakenly believing the renegade earl would be their protector, had invited him into the abbey. Stephen, in his impotent rage, seized all the abbey's surrounding lands. By the time the bishop got back from seeing the Pope, he found that de Mandeville had – of course – plundered all the sacred treasures from inside Ely's abbey walls, while King Stephen had stolen everything the monks owned outside.

Meanwhile, across the fens, the Abbot of Ramsey itself, a devout man named Walter, decided that he too would go to Rome, in order to seek there the highest spiritual help on earth against the cohorts of the Devil who had turned Ramsey Abbey into their fortress. The Pope gave Walter his support, and the abbot duly trekked back across Europe, now fired up, we are told, with the Holy Spirit. Walter turned out to be a man of steely nerve, if somewhat naïve. Back in Ramsey, he marched – alone – straight into de Mandeville's camp, grabbed hold of a flaming torch and set fire not only to the robbers' tents but also to the abbey's gatehouse, which by now was a fortified barbican. He then went from one man to another formally laying on him God's curse. Walter was lucky to escape with his life. The enraged bandits threatened to kill him on the spot and brandished their swords and knives in his face.

The Anarchy now hit its most terrifying depths.

Walter, weary, miserable at his failure, and homeless, wandered the fens and saw for himself the dreadful plight of the common people. There was barely a plough left anywhere. All provisions had been carried off. No one was tilling the land. At nearby Ely, there was famine for a distance of up to 30 miles. Not a single ox was left alive. A small sack of grain was being sold for the huge sum of 200 pence. Thousands of people were dying of starvation. One chronicler said that the corpses of the dead lay unburied in the fields, 'a prey to beasts and to fowls of the air'. Villages were in flames. De Mandeville's men would drag the peasants from their hiding places, and, said the chronicler, 'in the mad orgy of wickedness, neither women nor the aged were spared'. Ransom was wrung from the quivering victims by a thousand refinements of torture.'

And it was now that people openly spoke those spine-chilling words which at any other time would have been regarded as blasphemy: 'Christ and his saints are sleeping.'

Even allowing for bias in the account of the religious chronicler, it's clear this was a hideously fearful time. It was, he wrote, a fulfilment of the prophecy of St John: 'In those days shall men ... desire to die, and death shall flee from them.' The very walls of Ramsey Abbey were sweating blood – the archdeacon of nearby Peterborough said he had witnessed it with his own eyes. But then a different kind of vision was reported. Something that implied a little hope. Some said they had seen the finger of God. It was whispered that maybe the end would come soon.

Final justice for Geoffrey de Mandeville didn't come from the king. And it didn't come from the Pope, though the monks of Ramsey saw it as divine intervention. De Mandeville's death was delivered by the strong arm of a common soldier.

On a hot August day in 1144, de Mandeville led a band of his men to lay siege to a fortified post in the village of Burwell, 20 miles south-east of Ramsey. This fort would have been nothing more than a simple stockade surrounding a wooden tower. A troop of the king's men had managed to seize the place. De Mandeville couldn't afford to have royal soldiers nesting on his patch, so he circled the place to find the weakest point where he could attack it. Sweating in the heat, he stopped to loosen his mail and for a moment removed his helmet. A bowman on top of the wooden tower, who must have been a fine shot, or just lucky, saw his chance, and loosed; the arrow hit de Mandeville in the head.

At first, it seems, he shrugged it off as no more than a scratch. But within days he fell ill, and then, realising he was going to die, began to pray for salvation. The religious chronicler noted with satisfaction that at the end there was no one there to grant him absolution. Geoffrey de Mandeville's soul was bound for hell.

And so it was that his savage rule on earth collapsed, and his followers melted back into the surrounding countryside.

But that wasn't the end of his tale. According to Church law, the body of a man who had died unshriven – that is, who had not been granted absolution for his sins – couldn't be buried. So his corpse was put into a lead coffin and removed to the City of London. There it was hung from a gnarled fruit tree. And it remained so for nineteen years, mocked and despised by Londoners, who hated him for the way he had oppressed them in his earlier years. Then one day in 1163, de Mandeville's son arrived at the gatehouse of Ramsey Abbey, not as his father had done to turf out the monks and make the holy place a thieves' den, but as a humble penitent to beg forgiveness on behalf of his dead father. And when he had made atonement to the monks of Ramsey, Pope Alexander III granted post-mortem absolution to the arch-brigand. Whereupon, presumably, Geoffrey de Mandeville went to heaven, to sit at the feet of Christ and all the saints who had slept during the worst of his sins.

★ ★ ★

The brutal Fenland reign of Geoffrey de Mandeville was an extreme example of the way the barons of England behaved during the civil war between Stephen and Matilda. But it wasn't unique. Two years later, the Earl of Chester, similarly deprived of his castles by Stephen, also plunged into an orgy of plunder and ferocious violence. And what these mighty men did on a grand scale scores of lesser nobles and lordless knights repeated over smaller territories all across England, robbing and terrorising their weaker neighbours. Their behaviour had nothing to do with supporting the cause of either the king or the empress. These titled-men-turned-bandits acted entirely out of selfish opportunism.

Although there were many barons who weren't Geoffrey de Mandevilles, either great or small, and although there were parts of England that didn't collapse into anarchy, the reign of King Stephen was undoubtedly a period when baronial power was at its height. The barons who decades later opposed King John and obliged him to issue the Great Charter of Liberties, would have been brought up on family stories of the time of King Stephen, not long past, when a baron might do as he pleased, largely free from royal interference. One way of seeing Magna Carta is as just another tug – from the baronial side – in the centuries-long tug of war between English kings and their mightiest subjects. The balance of power could swing violently from one side to the other. After the baronial supremacy during Stephen's reign, came a radical shift back towards the crown under his successor.

The war between Stephen and Matilda drifted into stalemate. But though Matilda had failed to win the crown herself, it was her son who, on Stephen's death in 1154, became King of England as Henry II. And from him the Angevin dynasty was born.

Henry II was an altogether different ruler from his royal predecessor. He was clever and he was energetic. And he was determined to re-establish the authority of the monarchy. We could choose a hundred places in England to tell Henry's story, because he was forever on the move, enforcing royal justice in towns and villages throughout the land. It was an age when a criminal trial often meant being thrown into a pond and proving one's innocence by sinking to the bottom. Henry had other ideas about justice. To find out how he contributed to Magna Carta, we're going to one of his palaces, a place where notions of justice and central government were changed for ever.

3 CLARENDON PALACE, WILTSHIRE, ENGLAND

THE FLYING MONARCH

Imagine the opening scene of a post-apocalypse movie. It's many years since a meteor hit wiped out 99.9 per cent of humanity, and the descendants of the few survivors wander among the wreckage of a lost civilisation. The ruined walls and collapsed roofs – all that's left of the vast and sumptuous buildings of the old world – are now meaningless. And the lives of the ancestors who once lived in these places are long forgotten.

That's what Clarendon Palace feels like. Once the finest residence of medieval kings, where queens presided over chivalrous courts, through whose gates archbishops set off hunting, where courtyards bustled with the clatter of knights' horses, and where foreign monarchs were once imprisoned in the dungeon below its towering great halls, Clarendon is now a forlorn ruin, lying half hidden in a tangled wood somewhere in southern England.

Even though I knew what I was looking for, I had trouble finding it. I'd read that the remains of the palace are located 4 miles east of the small cathedral city of Salisbury. I'd assumed there'd be plenty of road signs. And I'd deliberately chosen a weekday so there wouldn't be too many picnickers or ice cream-toting kids, and there'd be no problem joining a guided tour without an advanced reservation.

So I drove east from Salisbury, and after 10 miles decided I was on the wrong road. I retraced my steps to the village of Laverstock and stopped to ask a young chap who was jogging. No, he had never heard of any *palaces* round here, but the Clarendon Estate was over that way. And he waved vaguely beyond a sign that said Queen Manor Road. After a few hundred yards this turned into a bumpy dirt track that looked like it doubled as a stream bed in wet weather. After a further ten minutes' worrying about the car's suspension, I passed between a couple of corrugated iron farm buildings – without a farmer to consult – and then the track suddenly narrowed to walkers-only width. I got out and padded on between high hedges until I reached the top of a low hill. A palace-less valley stretched before me. So it was back to the car, and after a ten-point turn, I bounced a slow return journey with the distant spire of Salisbury cathedral now ahead of me.

Suddenly there was a cart-track rising off to the left, and on a whim, I swung the car on to it. A slow half-mile later, I again abandoned the wheels in favour of feet, and tramped a sunken pathway beneath an arcade of birch tree branches. As luck would have it, I happened – just happened – to glance over to the left where a gate was set back among the elder trees. Beyond it was a clearing, and in the middle I saw the remains of a towering broken stone wall.

So now, here I am.

At least, I'm guessing I am, because once through the gate I spot a small sagging metal sign with a warning engraved on it:

Ancient Monuments Act
1913 and 1931
Any person injuring or defacing
this monument will be liable to
prosecution according to law
– Ministry of Works

Now, the old Ministry of Works was wound up in 1962, so it seems that Clarendon Palace may have been forgotten even by the twenty-first-century bureaucracy of conservation.

But I'm not disappointed.

The ruin before me is scattered in all directions around what looks like a central shattered tower. I wander on up to the broken stone walls, packed by the medieval masons with knobs of flint rubble. I rub my hand over the giant base of columns that once supported the vaulting roof of the palace's great hall, and stagger down the cracked steps that now lead to nothing but a grassy hole, somewhere near where Kings David of Scotland and Jean of France were once held prisoner. And a sense of excitement starts to creep up my spine. After all, it's not often you can experience – just a little – of what Howard Carter must have felt when he discovered the tomb of Tutankhamen.

I say 'just a little', because – to be fair – it's not as if I'm the first person to stumble on this place. But it's sufficiently hidden away, with no one else around, to make me feel like I'm the first person to stumble upon this treasure for many a year. There are a couple of English Heritage information boards with some helpful plans of the old palace. But even these notices, their words barely decipherable beneath a thick mottled covering of algae, look like long-neglected historic relics

✷ ✷ ✷

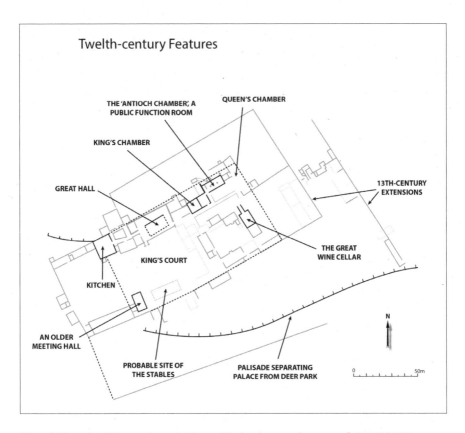

Plan of Clarendon Palace as it was in Henry II's day. It covered an area of over 175,000 square feet. John and Henry III extended it even further during the thirteenth century.

One of the many reasons why Clarendon Palace is so remarkable is that, unlike most sizeable stone buildings constructed in the Middle Ages, it was nothing to do with either of the two great 'Ws' of upper-class medieval life: war and worship. It was neither a castle nor a church. It was erected for the enjoyment of kings in their time off from the these two more serious occupations. It was originally a hunting lodge. By the time Henry II ascended the throne in 1154, Clarendon had grown into a palace, and soon became the new king's favourite haunt. He had, it's said, an 'immoderate fondness' for chasing and killing deer, and for riding with a hawk on his fist ready to swoop on a scampering rabbit. Clarendon Palace was at the centre of the largest deer park in medieval England.

I head for the highest point on the site, by the tallest surviving piece of masonry – still 30 feet high – not a tower it turns out but the end wall of what was once the great hall. From here, I can see out over trees to the surrounding countryside. There are earth ridges, the remains of the old deer-proof embankment that ran for 13 miles around the park. There are tracks criss-crossing the fields below, much as they did 850 years ago. And there are small square scars on the hillside, where archaeologists have discovered outbuildings dating back to the twelfth century.

But Clarendon was much more than a pleasure palace for Henry. In an age when kings were constantly on the move around their kingdom, it was the closest anywhere in England came to being his administrative base, his headquarters.

Henry, like Richard the Lionheart and John, the two sons who succeeded him to the throne, was forever restless. His energy tired those around him. He might be at Clarendon one day, then at short notice he'd be off to Woodstock or Oxford or trekking off to Scotland. The vast courtyard at Clarendon immediately inside the now collapsed gateway is a reminder of the size of the king's entourage, not just the finely dressed earls and their consorts, but the hundreds of ordinary people whom the court required for its smooth – and often apparently not so smooth – functioning. Henry's secretary, Peter of Blois, has left behind a vivid account of what it would have been like here in this yard on a typical morning. As well as being energetic, Henry, it seems, was unpredictable. Peter writes:

> If the king has promised to stay for the next day – and particularly if he's instructed that his herald announce his intention publicly – he's sure to upset all the arrangements by departing early in the morning. Then you see men dashing around like mad things, beating their packhorses, as their carts bang into each other – in short giving a lively imitation of Hell. If on the other hand, the king orders an early start, he's certain to change his mind ... Then you'll see the packhorses loaded and waiting, the carts all ready, the courtiers dozing, traders fretting and everyone grumbling. People go and ask the maids and door-keepers what the king's plans are, because they're the only ones likely to know the secrets of the court.

One of the chroniclers described Henry as 'a human chariot drawing everything after him.' Even in church, he was forever doodling or whispering to his courtiers. And if you managed to get an audience with him to plead your case, he would as like as not be sharpening his hunting knife while you talked. When the King of France learned that Henry had suddenly turned up in Normandy, he exclaimed that the English king 'must fly rather than travel by horse or ship'.

✷ ✷ ✷

Henry was only 21 when he came to the throne, but he was in no doubt about the job before him. Initially he concentrated on getting rid of the most obvious evidence of the independence the barons had won for themselves during Stephen's chaotic reign. He forced them to tear down the castles that they had built without a royal licence. It seems he was helped in this by a good deal of war weariness among the barons. They wanted a period of stability to consolidate the gains they had made during the civil war. But they misjudged what 'stability' meant to the new young king. It meant the imposition of royal authority. It meant a wider attempt to impose order, something which was to bring Henry up against both church and barons.

The anarchy of Stephen's reign had brought misery, violence and anxiety to all ranks of English society but perhaps most of all to the average family near the bottom of the social scale, who lacked any means of protecting themselves. There'd been an unchecked increase in crimes such as theft, rape and murder. And this in an age when normal levels of crime throughout England would have made the drug-racked inner cities of our own time seem idyllic pastures by comparison. It's difficult for us to imagine today how frightening life must have been in the twelfth century, when there was little resembling a professional police force either to prevent or detect crime. It has been calculated, for instance, that in medieval Oxford – and there's no reason to believe Oxford was any more or less violent that anywhere else – one person in 1,000 was murdered annually. To get that into perspective, if the population of England and Wales today suffered a murder rate that high, then the number of us getting stabbed to death, shot or otherwise slaughtered every year would be over 56,000. In 2013, the actual figure was 551. Or consider Lincoln at the start of the thirteenth century, where one judicial session alone dealt with over 100 murders, nearly 90 robberies and 50 rapes, as well as numerous other offences. All this for a city with a population of less than 8,000 – a smallish market town by today's standards. And of course we don't know how many other crimes never came to light.

Nor was the judicial system organised in such a way as to discourage crime. Much of what we know about life in the mid-twelfth century can seem bizarre to our eyes, but nothing more so than the way crime and criminals were dealt with. Apprehending a suspect was the first problem. In towns the sheriff's officer, the sergeant, was supposed to keep the streets and lanes crime-free. But the few such officials there were could often be bribed by their social inferiors or be leant on by their superiors. To beef up their efforts, everyone was deemed an amateur policeman. So when someone was seen in the act of committing a crime, the whole community was supposed to chase and apprehend the alleged criminal – an action known as a 'hue and cry'. If these ordinary folk failed to lay hands on the offender, they themselves could be punished. Otherwise, when the crime was discovered later, it was often up to the victims or their families to make a sworn accusation against an alleged wrongdoer. The trouble here was that if the accused was found to be innocent, then the accuser was punished for laying a false charge.

But it was the trial that followed which would have seemed most strange to us. There were several methods available for testing guilt or innocence, all no better than a lottery, and most involving physical brutality.

Take, for example, trial by battle. In this, unless either accused or accuser was old or disabled, they had to fight it out. To the death. It was believed that God would only allow the innocent to win, so the loser must be lying. If your weapon broke, you were required to battle on with hands, fists, nails, teeth, feet and legs. And if you were defeated but by any chance were still breathing, you were usually hanged. However, if you were a member of the baronial class, trial by battle was not so dire. You could employ a strong, agile professional fighter to stand in for you. Equality under the law was an alien concept in the twelfth century.

The more usual method of proving or disproving a case was by the ordeal of cold water. The accused had his hands and feet tied tightly and was taken to a nearby lake or other stretch of deep water. The priest, who was paid a fixed sum for the job, then blessed the pool, and the accused was lowered in. If he sank, as his lungs presumably filled with water, he was pronounced innocent. If he bobbed gaily on the surface, he was guilty, the theory being that the consecrated water had rejected the sinner. Any modern idea we may have that in the Middle Ages this kind of treatment was reserved for witches on ducking stools is wide of the truth. In fact, in the twelfth century, women accused of a crime were let off being trussed and dumped in water. Instead, they had to carry a piece of iron that had been preheated in a forge until red hot. If they dropped it too quickly, they were guilty. As with trial by battle, both of these ordeals, water and iron, were thought to be foolproof because they relied on God's decision rather than the evidence of mere mortal witnesses.

The other common method of trial was less physically risky, but only marginally more reliable. It was called compurgation. An accused had to round up as many friends as possible and get them to swear to his or her innocence. So, for instance, according to the records a woman in Bedford was accused of the crime of cheating her customers by using a false measure for the beer she sold. She was cleared when eleven of her fellow citizens supported her on oath. Reasonable evidence of her innocence, we might think. Of course, if her husband had happened to be a much-feared local bully, it might be otherwise.

Another problem was that the administration of this whole process – if administration is not too flattering a word for it – was usually in the hands of the local baron, or more likely of his corrupt junior official. So to a criminal trial based largely on superstition, you have to add the complication of bribery and bias.

If the justice system down here on earth offered little deterrence to crime, the threat of an excruciating and everlasting fiery fate in the hereafter, we might assume, would be a more effective guarantee of good behaviour in an age when

Christian belief was, the chroniclers tell us, universal and absolute. Unfortunately not, because priests taught that no matter what evil you inflicted on your fellow creatures during your life, provided you confessed your sins before you died (or, in the case of Geoffrey de Mandeville, if you had a son who asked later for forgiveness on your behalf), then you would be saved. So hell was little deterrent either.

And the Church's role in this whole rickety structure of justice didn't end there. The bishops claimed an exclusive jurisdiction over all those ordained in holy orders. In other words, a priest accused of any crime had to be tried by an ecclesiastical court. In case you think this must have been a rare circumstance, it's worth noting that during the first eight years alone of Henry II's reign, over a hundred homicides were perpetrated by men of the cloth. And there must have been many more that went unreported. What's more, just about anybody – anybody male, that is – could become an officer of the Church. Bishops demanded no minimum standards of either education or morality when they appointed the thousands of priests. And the Church was expanding its ambitions. It had always claimed that certain offences committed in the community at large could be tried only in ecclesiastical courts: incest, for instance. But now the bishops were spreading their jurisdiction even wider by asserting that any crime where a contract was involved should also be tried in a Church court, because it required an oath before God.

The heart of the problem was that the punishments available in ecclesiastical courts were disproportionately trivial. The Church, according to its beliefs, could not impose on a convicted felon any 'sentence of blood', such as hanging or the chopping off of a hand, which were common penalties in lay jurisdiction. Those convicted in a bishop's court could be jailed, but this seldom happened because Church administrators begrudged the cost of running prisons. So the only punishments available were either a penance – reciting Hail Marys or going on a pilgrimage, for instance – or, in the case of a criminal priest, being defrocked.

So, adding together the lack of any real policing, the risks involved in making an accusation and getting it wrong, the bloody lottery of criminal trials, a corrupt administration of justice, and the Church's example of punishing murderers with a slap on the wrist, it's not surprising that in mid-twelfth-century England, crime was out of control. And this is not counting the impact of the nineteen anarchic years during Stephen's reign, when most criminals had found it especially easy to evade what few traces of justice the system could throw up.

✶✶✶

So how did Henry II, Clarendon Palace and Magna Carta fit into this sorry, corrupt and dangerous mess?

Henry had two motives for trying to improve matters: duty and money. All medieval kings, as part of their coronation ceremony, swore to maintain peace among their subjects. It was a primary function of royalty to do what was necessary to maintain an orderly society. And it's fair to say that Henry took this responsibility seriously. Happily for him, it also coincided with a more immediately selfish cause. There was a medieval proverb, much loved in contemporary alehouses frequented by lawyers: '*Magnum emolumentum justicia est*', which we might translate as 'Justice is a nice little earner.' For the king, that meant offering a judicial process administered by competent, objective royal judges, a more attractive alternative to that run by corrupt and biased local officials. And for this popular option, the king would be able to charge a fee. It was not a universally popular idea, because the more that royal justice spread, the less judicial power would be left in the hands of the barons and the Church.

And this is where Clarendon Palace came in. It was to an assembly here, on two separate occasions, that Henry summoned the country's mightiest subjects, before issuing the two most important royal edicts of his reign, designed to implement his plan to overhaul the country's legal system.

At the first of these gatherings, he tackled the Church and the growing powers of the ecclesiastical courts. In 1164, the king was joined at Clarendon by over 1,800 people. It's difficult to imagine that scene as I sit today alone on the broken walls of the old great kitchen, looking out over the long-since flattened courtyard, with no more noise in my ears than a blackbird's song interrupted by the occasional rasping caw of a crow in the old oak tree below. But on a frosty morning in January 1164, it would have been bedlam here. Servants running among the smouldering courtyard campfires, shouting and arguing as each tried to organise breakfast, wash clothes, find extra bedding or get whatever their own master or mistress was demanding. And inside the great apartments of Clarendon, the two most powerful figures in the land were themselves squaring up for a fight that would end in death for one of them.

The drama of Thomas à Becket has been told many times, in books, on the stage and in films, the story of a man with a driving compulsion to play to the full whatever part he was given. As Henry's chancellor, he had been an outstanding administrator, advisor and diplomat, as well as a splendidly dressed courtier who loved to go hunting in the park at Clarendon. Most of all he had been a loyal friend to the king. So, when Becket became Archbishop of Canterbury, Henry thought he could rely on him to push through the reforms to the Church's own judicial system. How wrong the king was.

During the several weeks of the assembly at Clarendon, Henry and his archbishop clashed in ferocious arguments, the churchman rejecting any attempt by Henry to interfere in the running of the ecclesiastical courts. We don't know exactly where the confrontations took place. It wouldn't have been in the great hall whose remains can be seen today – that was built in the following century. But it has been suggested that the dispute between the two leaders blew up in the old hall that then stood on the same spot. Becket lost the fight – for the moment anyway – and a document was issued in the king's name, known as the Constitutions of Clarendon. Among other clauses, it required 'criminous clerks' – criminal priests, in other words – after they had been tried and convicted in the bishop's court, to be handed over to a royal officer who would then administer an appropriate punishment much more severe than anything the Church would have handed out.

The Constitutions of Clarendon had dramatic and unexpected results.

It began a train of events that brought about the murder of Thomas à Becket. Becket didn't drop his opposition to the Clarendon statutes, and when Henry one day expressed his exasperation in public, he unwittingly triggered four over-enthusiastic royal knights to believe they were acting in the king's name when they killed Becket within the cathedral at Canterbury. Henry was forced to undertake a humiliating barefoot walk to the scene of martyrdom where he had to ask forgiveness. And Becket was made a saint within two years.

The Constitutions of Clarendon ensured that the rights and liberties of the Church remained a hot issue. So when Magna Carta was negotiated fifty-one years later, it was the then Archbishop of Canterbury who brokered the deal. He got his reward. He made sure the opening clause of the Great Charter guaranteed the independence of the Church.

✳ ✳ ✳

In 1166, two years after the argument between Henry and Becket at Clarendon, this great palace was the scene of another massive assembly. This time the result was a document known as the Assize of Clarendon which tried to tackle head-on the crime tsunami in wider English society, and to bring some logic at the same time to the settlement of civil law disputes.

By the Assize of Clarendon, an order was sent throughout the country that in each district, twelve selected freemen were to investigate all murders, robberies and thefts committed since the beginning of Henry's reign twelve years earlier. And the investigators had to name anyone suspected of these crimes and anyone who might have harboured the suspects. This must have been a mammoth task, and one can't help but admire the king's ambition. At the same time, he dispatched scores of travelling judges – known as 'justices in eyre' – to tour the country, to hear the results of these investigations, and to try those accused before a royal court. The twelve investigators were known as a 'jury of presentment,' and they were the origin of the Grand Jury, which is still used in the legal system of the United States today.

We shouldn't jump to the conclusion, however, that the Assize of Clarendon was an immediate revolution in criminal justice. Though compurgation – trial by oath-helpers – was abandoned, trial by being trussed and dipped in cold water continued. But clearly the king saw the shortcomings of such a process, and the Assize stated that if the twelve investigators thought a suspect was really guilty despite having passed the water ordeal then they should banish him and declare him an outlaw anyway. This was a long way short of what we would know as trial by jury, but it was the first hint that guilt or innocence might be decided by twelve of the accused's peers.

In civil law, Henry also made some fundamental changes. Methods of settling such disputes – such as who was the rightful owner of land, or who should inherit an estate – had been little better than the old criminal justice system, and had largely ignored what we in the twenty-first century might call 'facts on the ground'. Henry's reforms enacted here at Clarendon Palace changed that. For instance, in a case where someone had recently occupied a piece of land and there was a dispute over who owned it, the assize of *novel disseisin* – meaning 'recent dispossession' – stated that twelve knights, who should be 'sword-girt' – i.e. they must be fit and of fighting age – should decide who was right and who wrong. And significantly, they should do so 'upon their own knowledge'. This *was* a revolution. There was no question of relying on bizarre methods of interpreting God's will with cold water, hot iron or in a sword fight. Facts on the ground were starting to figure in justice. Provided, of course, that you first paid the appropriate fee to the king to get the benefit of *novel disseisin*.

One important impact of these changes was that an individual could now appeal over the head of his baronial master, to his master's master, the king, or in practice to one of the king's judges. In effect, the new system, when it applied to the middle and lower ranks of society, bypassed the barons. The king, or his judges, were dealing directly with the barons' tenants, which was contrary to the traditions of feudalism. Perhaps the strangest thing is that the country's leading barons were well represented here at Clarendon Palace when the Assize of 1166 was drawn up, and the wording of the document makes it clear that they consented to it. Why was that? Perhaps they didn't fully understand how their own judicial powers would be undermined. Or, more likely, they felt that on balance the Assize of Clarendon, by bringing some element of peace and stability, might be to their benefit. And when it came time to draw up Magna Carta half a century later, the barons did not seize the opportunity to overturn what was in effect a powerful extension of royal authority. There would be much they liked about the new legal processes set in train by Henry at Clarendon Palace, so much so that – as we shall see – they tried in several clauses of Magna Carta to clean up abuses of the new royal judicial system.

So, here's where truth comes crashing into myth. Who did more for the development of English common law? The barons who extracted Magna Carta from King John? Or King Henry II? Anyone with a well-developed sense of irony might enjoy arguing that Clarendon and its 1166 Assize are more important symbols of freedom under the law than Runnymede and Magna Carta. History has shown us that they aren't, of course. But it's a mischievous thought.

As I muse on this, sitting on the knee-high remains of the palace's western gatehouse, there's suddenly a terrific crack that fills my ears and echoes through the trees. A gunshot. Someone is out in the nearby woods popping away at rabbits or a pheasant. And from behind the towering broken wall of the great hall, a deer prances out, freezes and stares at me. Or I think it's a deer, just for a moment. Then I see it's more like a sheep on stilts. It's a llama. Two others hop out to join it. Let loose here, I suppose, to keep the grass down. I rather like the idea of such mythical-looking beasts roving the place where a medieval king once debated the relative merits of superstition and fact.

★ ★ ★

From Clarendon Palace, the administration of justice in England had started on a new more modern journey. And that meant more effective royal government, with new sources of cash for the king's treasury. And something else was born here, an administrative machine that could drive itself even in the king's absence. In 1189 Henry II was succeeded by his son. King Richard the Lionheart was to spend 95 per cent of his ten-year reign overseas. But royal justice was still dealt out, and fees to the crown were still collected. Richard was not cut out to argue the finer points of the law or to be the head of the civil service. He didn't need to be. He could leave that to the teams of professionals put in place by his father's new system, and could instead devote himself to what he loved, adventuring and soldiering in France and in the Holy Land 2,000 miles away.

The Holy Land is where we're heading next, to the little port of Acre in modern-day Israel. It was the scene of Richard's finest hour, which did much to earn him the title Lionheart. However, Acre's story also epitomises other, less savoury aspects of the new king's character. His reputation as a military hero is what has echoed down the ages. But he was also an impetuous man whose spendthrift ways were to leave his brother John with some discontented barons back in England.

4 ACRE, ISRAEL

LIONHEART'S LEGACY

This morning, thousands are on the march in Acre beneath a scorching sun. An army, you might say, divided into what seem like regiments, each denoted by their uniforms, red, blue, beige and green. The bellow of trumpets and the crash of drums kick back off the harsh grey walls of the ancient city. A woman with white headscarf pulled tight around her face peers down through the metal bars of an upstairs window, the green conical minaret of a mosque rising over the rooftop above her. An old man, sitting in the canopied shade of a ragged sheet, stares vacantly at the parade. He takes a pull on his shisha pipe, then blows the smoke out through his nose. A small boy dressed in a red cape with a gold cross sewn into the back jogs on his father's shoulders as if he's riding a horse, and he's prodding the air with a long pole like a jousting knight.

Acre, on the north coast of Israel, was known in the days of Richard the Lionheart as St Jean d'Acre, because the Knights of the Hospital of St John made their headquarters here. Throughout its long history, foreign armies have often marched through its narrow little streets flaunting their victories. The ancient Greeks, the Romans, the Egyptians, the Armenians, the Persians, the soldiers of several different Muslim caliphates, the crusaders, the Muslims again, the crusaders again, the Mamluks, the Turks of the Ottoman Empire – though not Napoleon, who in 1799 was defeated by its thick old walls and had to retreat – then the British army during the Mandate in the early twentieth century, and finally, following the war of independence in 1948, the Israelis trooped into Acre.

This morning's army, however, is a peaceful one, carrying nothing more dangerous than musical instruments. Its marchers aren't old enough to be soldiers. They're mostly in their mid teens. They are in fact boy scouts and girl scouts, each group of thirty or forty in a different coloured beret, neckerchief, sash and jacket. They're having fun, laughing and waving to each other whenever they stop, which is often because they can't squeeze quickly enough through the narrow lanes and alleyways of old Acre.

'They're Israeli Arabs,' says Amar, my guide. 'This is their big day. They've come here from all over the country. There are over a million and a half Palestinian Arabs in Israel,' he explains, 'twenty per cent of the population. They're mainly Muslim, and some Christian.'

Amar is a well-built young man in tight blue t-shirt and jeans. He announces his information at each stop we make with a note of pride in his knowledge. He calls now – in Arabic, I guess – to a man at a wayside stall selling cardamom pods, vanilla sticks, ginger roots and lots more exotic pink, yellow and green spices. The man shouts back to him, laughing. I ask what they were talking about.

Amar replies: 'I just greeted him in Arabic, and he said, "I took you for a tourist. How come you speak my language?" I told him, "My father is Arab." He thought that was funny.'

'So, how many languages do you speak, Amar?' I ask.

He pauses, adjusts his wrap-around dark glasses, and holds up his hand to count them off on his fingers. 'Hebrew, from my mother, who's Jewish. Arabic from my father, who's Muslim. Georgian, because that's where they both grew up. Russian, from my ex-wife. And Spanish, that's from an old girlfriend who was Mexican.'

'And English,' I add.

'Yes, I forgot that. I couldn't work with tourists if I didn't speak English.'

More scouts come around the corner, a mixture of boys and girls, this time playing bagpipes. The girl in the front rank has a shock of ginger hair. All her companions have jet black locks. It's said that in the Middle Ages the crusaders, some of whom came from Scotland and other parts of northern Europe, inter-married with local Arab women, and that their red-hair genes still sometimes re-emerge many centuries later.

✷ ✷ ✷

Acre in the late twelfth century was the second biggest city after Jerusalem in what the crusaders called Outremer, literally, 'Beyond the sea'. According to con-temporary accounts, the city was an immoral and dangerous place. Not only was it the medieval equivalent of Bangkok – any form of sexual pleasure could be bought here – but the city was also the murder capital of the Holy Land.

Violence is not unknown in Acre's twenty-first-century streets either. From time to time, tension between Jews and Arabs rises. On one side, young men from the mainly Arab population of the old city cover their faces, burn tyres and throw rocks. On the other, the Israeli police use tear gas, water cannon and fire stun grenades.

This morning though, deep inside the dark lanes of its souk – the market-place – it's a picture of peaceful commerce. A young woman in jeans and kaftan, clutching several flimsy plastic bags, is bartering with the owner of a stall piled high with peaches, bananas, plums, grapes, apples, lemons and melons. Opposite, at the fishmonger's, a small boy, just tall enough to get his chin on the marble slab, is peering at the sweet-smelling sea bream and slushy octopus. Next door there's a shop bursting with ivory chess sets, worry beads, mandolins, shisha pipes and CDs of popular Egyptian female vocalists.

Little remains these days – above ground, at least – of medieval Acre. The Mamluks, who drove the crusaders out of the city (and at the same time out of Outremer entirely) once and for all in 1291, smashed the old city walls to the ground. There are some magnificent columned halls surviving from the hospital of the Knights of St John, though these were built decades after King Richard and the knights of the Third Crusade were here. Soon though we should be able to see something of twelfth-century Acre, when archaeologists complete a major survey recently begun in the ancient city.

Most of the old buildings and fortified walls visible today were built by the Ottomans in the fifteenth and sixteenth centuries. However, for those of us who want to experience and understand the place as it was when Richard arrived here in 1191, all is far from lost. The Ottomans constructed their fortifications and their roads on the foundations of the medieval town. So Acre's defensive layout today is just as apparent as it was in 1191.

Acre sits on a roughly triangular peninsula. A stout defensive wall, in medieval times studded with towers and defended further by a deep ditch, separates the town from the plain to the landward side. The eastern seaboard of the Mediterranean forms the second side of the triangle, while the third is made by the harbour facing the Bay of Haifa.

Amar now guides us through the warren of narrow streets down to the quayside. This morning it shelters a couple of dozen small yachts and motorboats, strictly for pleasure, as well as several fishing smacks. Overlooking the harbour at one end of the quay is a stone archway, over which two large red Coca-Cola badges frame the words 'Abu Christo'.

'It means "Father of Christ" in Arabic,' explains Amar. 'It's a Christian-owned restaurant.'

The wharfs and walkways of the little port are skirted by a high stone wall built by the Ottomans for extra protection against attack from the bay. In the crusaders' time, they relied for defence here on a massive tower built out by the harbour entrance. From the southern of the two jetties, I can still see its remains: a black square rock sticking up from the calm blue waters and surmounted by the ruins of the old tower's walls. The high structure that used to rise up here dominated the approach from the Bay of Haifa. It was known as the Tower of the Flies, for the gruesome reason that in earlier times it had been a place of human sacrifice and the rotting corpses had made it a paradise

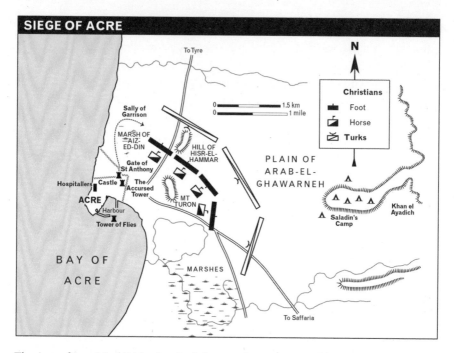

SIEGE OF ACRE

To Tyre

N

0 ———————— 1.5 km
0 ———————— 1 mile

Christians

▬ Foot

Horse

Turks

Sally of Garrison

MARSH OF AIZ-ED-DIN

HILL OF HISR-EL-HAMMAR

Gate of St Anthony

PLAIN OF ARAB-EL-GHAWARNEH

Hospitallers

Castle

The Accursed Tower

ACRE

MT TURON

Harbour

Tower of Flies

Saladin's Camp

Khan el Ayadich

BAY OF ACRE

MARSHES

To Saffaria

The siege of Acre. Until Richard arrived, the crusaders were trapped between Saladin's army and the town. The huge numbers of men and military equipment brought by the English king tipped the balance in the Christians' favour.

for insects. In the crusading era, the crossbowmen and catapult operators up on its battlements had a clear advantage looking down on any ships attempting an attack from this quarter.

From the port, Amar leads us through an ancient Turkish warehouse, then after weaving around more drummers and buglers, we cross Salah ad Din Street, past a modern clean stone building that proclaims itself the 'Knights' Youth Hostel and Guest House', and then on through the ancient Gate of St Anthony. We're now outside the old city. To the west from here the wall runs in a straight line to the sea, where the second side of the triangle is today a long stretch of sand. In the Middle Ages, before the days of motorised assault craft, there would have been no practical way to land enough men quickly enough to take on a waiting army of defenders.

We head in the other direction, to the right, across a car park – what would have been the edge of the open plain in the twelfth century, and is now part of a modern suburb – until we come to a sharp corner of the old wall. There are flying buttresses here and a flight of worn stone steps leading up. We climb to the top and peer down over the battlements. One way, to the south, we can see a tiny fleet of sailboards bobbing just beyond the Tower of Flies rock. To the east and north, the apartment blocks of modern Acre dominate, though I can just see open country and hills beyond. The point where I'm standing on the bend in the old wall is where another important defensive tower once stood. It was known as the Accursed Tower, because it was said that Judas's thirty pieces of silver were minted here, though for the Muslim defenders when King Richard arrived, it might have been cursed for another reason, as we shall see.

$$\star\ \star\ \star$$

The first crusaders had captured Acre in 1104. In 1187, the great Ayyubid sultan Salah ad Din, known in the west as Saladin, retook it along with Jerusalem itself. Saladin left a garrison of troops in Acre, while he himself returned to Jerusalem. The loss of the site of Christ's crucifixion and others of the most holy of Christian places to the infidel prompted Pope Gregory VII to summon Europe's nobles to arms once more, on a third crusade.

When Richard succeeded his father, Henry II, as King of England two years later, he had one overriding ambition: to win military glory in the Holy Land by answering the Pope's call – with a good chance of a place in paradise thrown in. Richard was already the most renowned soldier and military strategist of his day. If John has been miscast as all villain, his brother Richard has, just as unfairly, often been raised to the status of an English national hero. His is the most prominent statue, for instance, outside the Houses of Parliament in London.

Soldiering was something of an obsession with Richard. For a start, he looked the part, which, then as now, helped. He was 6 feet tall, which in the twelfth century would have put him above all but a few of his subjects. His eyes were a striking blue, his limbs long and straight, he had a weightlifter's chest, and his hair was a mix of red and blonde. He was a champion jouster, showed the appropriate courage when needed, and could be generous, though just like his father and his brother John he had a violent temper.

It was John's misfortune to follow the most accomplished soldier-king England had then ever seen. In the twelfth and thirteenth centuries, the nobility could forgive a lot in a ruler with the traditional attributes of a warrior. By comparison, John's performance on the battlefield was to be pathetic. And this was undoubtedly a factor in strengthening the rebel barons' resolve a decade and a half later in the run-up to Magna Carta.

Richard, immediately put his crusading plans into action. He would need a large army, and he would need it for several years.

According to feudal tradition, a king could call upon the great barons of his realm to provide him with the services of so many knights for so many days a year. The downside of such a system is obvious. What happens when your knights and their followers announce their time is up for this year and head home mid campaign? The result was not necessarily too serious, because the same limitation applied to both sides. And, by gentleman's agreement, the two opposing armies would often suspend killing each other over winter as well as at spring crop-sowing and autumn harvest when manpower was needed back on the farms.

But this kind of hobbyist mentality was anathema to Richard's professionalism. And so, to the dismay of his enemies – as well of his vassal barons – he would often break with tradition and take to the battlefield in all seasons. To do this he depended to a great extent on men who would muster whenever he needed them and who wouldn't skip off back home on a fine autumn day. He needed soldiers who would fight for pay. The term 'mercenaries' encompassed a range of military humanity, from landless junior noblemen and skilled carpenters who could build a siege engine, down to the *routiers*, a rabble of often criminal thugs who provoked fear and hatred wherever they turned up.

There was nothing new about a king using mercenaries, but Richard made them the mainstay of his army, and that was an unpopular innovation with his leading subjects, who saw themselves deprived of their traditional, privileged position at the king's right hand. Of course, Richard needed to find the wages for a mercenary army. And he did it partly by demanding cash from the barons in lieu of their traditional days of military service. But that wasn't nearly enough. He was fortunate that his father Henry II had not only stocked the royal vaults with a vast number of barrels full of silver pennies, but had also devoted much of his reign – as we've seen – to building and refining an efficient governmental administration, capable of collecting taxes throughout the English realm.

When it came to planning his crusade, a campaign which took soldiers away for several years rather than a few months, Richard anticipated rightly that the costs of warfare would rise exponentially. Henry II's silver pennies didn't last long, and the tax gatherers were sent out to squeeze more cash from the king's subjects. So when Richard set sail on crusade in 1190, he left behind in England a kingdom many of whose citizens were resentful of the heavy financial burden they had to bear. And so, contrary to the popular notion that Magna Carta was a personal attack on 'bad' King John, it was in fact a reaction against a system of heavy taxation instituted by King Richard to fund a mercenary army.

★★★

The English king found himself joint leader of the Third Crusade alongside King Philip Augustus of France. Though traditional enemies, they made a non-aggression pact before setting off – neither would use the other's absence in the Holy Land to gain an advantage back home – and they agreed to split fifty-fifty any spoils of their crusade.

The principal objective of the expedition was to retake Jerusalem and liberate its holy places for Christendom. First, however, control of Outremer's chief port, Acre, would have to be secured. There was no question of attempting a head-on attack against it from the sea. The Tower of the Flies did its job there as a deterrent. So Richard, after a long, circuitous and politically tumultuous journey through the Mediterranean, made landfall north of Acre and marched south. He arrived on the plain outside the city's gates on 8 June 1191. He was late at the party. Philip Augustus had arrived two months earlier, but his army was said to be so pathetically small that it had actually put new heart into the Muslim garrison inside Acre. The French king's assaults on the walls of the city had achieved nothing.

The siege of Acre had in fact been going on for almost two years before Philip Augustus and Richard showed up. The advance party of Christian assailants were led by Guy de Lusignan, and they had had a grim time of it.

First, they had come up against a hitherto unknown weapon. The Muslim defenders inside Acre's sturdy walls had discovered a spectacular and extremely painful way of tormenting the besieging army. They mixed oil and gunpowder, which they showered on the crusaders with lethal effect.

Then Guy, his fellow noblemen, their knights and soldiers, who had camped in an arc to the north and east of the town, found themselves in the position of besiegers besieged. Saladin himself came up from Jerusalem and arrayed his forces on the plain outside Acre so that he could harass the Christians from the rear.

Finally, Guy and his men starved. In the winter of 1190–91, they were reduced to eating grass. Disease followed – scurvy, gingivitis, the plague – and the Duke of Swabia, the Count of Flanders and many more of the crusader leaders were among the dead. The Muslim defenders inside Acre fared little better. It was stalemate. The only victories the crusaders claimed in this period were, frankly, scraping the bottom of the glory barrel. An infidel urinating on a crucifix atop Acre's outer wall was brought down by a crossbow bolt. A Christian sergeant was saved when an arrow loosed at him hit a metal badge on his chest. Slim pickings indeed.

So Richard's arrival with an estimated 10,000 men and several siege engines was salvation, a cause for celebration in the crusading ranks. Guy's men got so excited that they proceeded to get drunk and dance the night away (the chroniclers do not specify the choice of partners).

Events then moved quickly. Richard suddenly became ill. He almost died. But, like the hero of his reputation, he insisted on being carried to the front line on a litter to direct operations. Day after day, assaults were mounted against the Accursed Tower. It was from here that the enemy controlled any approach to the landward walls. It had to be taken or undermined. But day after day the crusaders' assaults on it were beaten off. Finally, though, it seems there was an accumulation of damage to the great tower. The continual battering from Richard's siege engines and catapults gradually weakened it, and by the time the English king recovered his health, the masonry had crumbled so much that suddenly a huge breach opened up, large enough to allow the besiegers to pour through.

The defenders, who were aware of the English king's huge force of knights and infantry, decided their continued resistance was futile, and on 12 July Saladin surrendered Acre and its garrison to the crusaders.

It was the Lionheart's finest hour. He had achieved in five weeks what others had failed to do in twenty-two months.

All, however, soon turned sour. Richard accused Saladin of breaking the terms of the surrender. In retribution, he marched 3,000 unarmed Muslim prisoners on to the plain of Acre and, before the eyes of Saladin and his soldiers, ordered his men to commence the slaughter. It was an orgy of slashing and stabbing whose brutality was shocking even by twelfth-century standards.

And it was not just his enemies whom Richard affronted. He managed to outrage one of his key allies too. When Acre fell, and the victorious Christians marched in to trumpet their victory, one of Richard's companions in arms, Leopold, Duke of Austria, raised his own standard on the walls. On seeing the flag of his social inferior fluttering over the battlements, the English king, was furious. His kingly honour had been insulted. He ordered his soldiers up the stone staircase to where Leopold's standard waved in the wind. They tore it down and hurled it into the ditch below. It was a typically rash and jealous act on the Lionheart's part, and one which was to have far-reaching consequences.

Relations between Richard and Philip Augustus also became strained and the French king departed, leaving his English counterpart sole commander for the rest of the campaign. Richard went on to take Jaffa further down the coast, and was never defeated in the field by Saladin. But although he came within a dozen miles of Jerusalem, the king failed in his objective of recapturing the Holy City, and in October 1192 he too set off home.

★★★

Richard's route took him through the territories of that same Duke Leopold of Austria whom he had so insulted at Acre. By the time he got close to Leopold's domains, he realised the risk and disguised himself in the drab robe of a monk with drooping cowl covering much of his face. But acting was not the king's forte, nor that of his courtiers, it seems, and he and his royal party were soon spotted by some of Leopold's men. The duke, no doubt with glee, took the king hostage. Leopold was a canny operator, and decided he didn't want the bother of a prolonged negotiation for Richard's release. So instead – like Somali pirates in the twenty-first century – he sold his valuable royal package on. The buyer was Henry, the German ruler of the misnamed Holy Roman Empire.

Henry was in luck. As soon as he put Richard up for ransom, he found himself with two competing bidders. In addition to Richard's own ministers and the queen mother Eleanor of Aquitaine, who were scrambling to raise the necessary cash, Philip Augustus dropped all pretence of comradeship and decided he would put in a bid himself. If he could make his arch-enemy his prisoner, Philip hoped to extract significant territorial advantages in return for Richard's release. How the Muslim defenders of Acre must have laughed when they heard of their erstwhile enemies at each others' throats.

The emperor was demanding an astronomical ransom for Richard: 150,000 marks. It's impossible to measure the exact size of this sum in today's terms, but to give some idea, in 1205 a royal administrator bought 4,000 fine quality plates and 500 cups for just 4 marks. Talks between the emperor, the French king and Richard's representatives in England dragged on.

It was now that Richard's younger brother Prince John saw his chance. He threw in his lot with Philip Augustus, then sped off to England with the intention of fomenting civil war. On the death of his father, Henry II, John as the younger brother had found himself in noble poverty, which earned him the nickname Lackland. Richard, however, had shown his generous side, and granted John various titles and territories. But they were not enough for John, who, in his brother's absence, now had his eye on the crown itself.

John had reason to think that the barons of England harboured enough resentment against the king that they would join his rebellion. When, on top of several years of detested taxation to fund the crusade, came demands to meet the huge ransom for the king, it might be thought the barons would say 'enough is enough' and back John's uprising. He even improved his chances of success by hounding William Longchamp – the hated chief taxman Richard had left behind – out of office (he was intercepted trying to flee the country disguised in women's clothes, when – it was said – a randy Dover fisherman made a pass at him).

However, despite all John's efforts, the barons did not flock to his cause. Why? It was partly because some of them, despite the weight of taxation, had done well for themselves under Richard. As part of his holy war effort, the king had raised cash by selling off whatever he could. 'I would have sold London,' he declared, 'if I could have found a buyer.' Everything from castles to earldoms had price tags on them. And by snapping up the bargains, some of the barons had bolstered their power.

But in addition, the barons' loyalty to Richard was undoubtedly due in part to the survival of an ancient tradition that a king needed to be a tribal warrior leader. John couldn't compete on that score. Richard played to this sentiment from his comfortable captivity at Henry's court, remarking, 'My brother John is not a man to win land for himself by force if there is anyone to put up a mere show of resistance.' In the end, the barons were smart enough not to back a loser.

Meanwhile, the tax collectors in Richard's lands raised a first instalment, and Henry agreed to release him. Philip Augustus got word of this and warned his failed ally, John: 'Look to yourself, for the devil is loosed.' John fled. The newly freed king stripped him of his titles. John was Lackland again.

★ ★ ★

With his ambitions for crusading glory behind him, Richard now turned his attention to his possessions in France and in particular Normandy. Philip Augustus had the military strength to threaten the duchy, and it was a priority for Richard to block that ambition. In 1196, therefore, the English king embarked on a great building project. High on a crag overlooking the River Seine, at the gateway to Normandy, he built a castle. It was his pride and joy. Once it was complete, Richard looked on it and declared, 'Behold my fair daughter, how beautiful she is! What a saucy castle!' A strange choice of adjective for a brutal, forbidding fortress. He used the Norman-French word 'gaillard', and that's how it got its name, Château Gaillard. But like many beautiful daughters, Gaillard was expensive. By the time the masons had tapped the last stones into place, the whole duchy of Normandy was bankrupt, and England again was having to foot the bill.

Château Gaillard was to be a scene of disaster for Richard's brother John, and we shall return to it later on our journey.

It's a delightful irony – for us at least – that money, which in life Richard had made the servant of his military ambition, in death came back to bite him. In the winter of 1198–99, a ploughman near Limoges, 200 miles south of Château Gaillard, turned up a hoard of Roman coins. Richard felt he had a claim to the treasure. Unfortunately, so did a local lord, and the king marched off to sort him out. The lord's castle at Chalus was a dilapidated wreck, an ugly little thing compared with Richard's own cherished Gaillard. The garrison was a mere forty men. As the king plotted its inevitable downfall, he decided to take a relaxed evening ride around its palisade. He didn't bother with full armour, but just grabbed his helmet and picked up a shield. He spotted a lone sniper on the enemy ramparts. The man cut a ridiculous figure. He was waving a cooking pan as his only protection against missiles from below. Richard gave him a cheer. But a moment later the man shot his crossbow, and the bolt ripped into the king's left shoulder. Richard stayed calm, and back in his tent tried to pull out the barb himself. But it broke, leaving the iron tip embedded in his flesh. His surgeon managed to hack it out in what must have been an excruciating operation. The wound festered and turned gangrenous.

In great pain, the king died ten days later.

Richard the Lionheart, sometime English national hero, had spent only six months of his ten-year reign in England, and had regarded the country as little more than a cash cow. The weight of taxation he had heaped on the country's nobility, much of it arguably in pursuit of his personal glory, would still be strong in the minds of the barons when they agreed the wording of Magna Carta sixteen years later. Richard avoided any such revolt himself, partly because some of the barons had benefited by purchasing land and honours from him, and partly because of the traditional respect for a warrior king. John had no such weapons in his armoury. And Richard had done him no favours.

★★★

So John was now king. But he had little time to relax and glory in that title. The territories he inherited from his brother were in a dire state, stricken by a decade of crippling demands for money and military support. And what's more, as ill luck would have it, his new lands were being devastated by famine, their crops destroyed by some unidentifiable disease. Times were so bad that priests were preaching that the anti-Christ had been born in Egypt, and the apocalypse was nigh. Even John's title to his territories was in dispute. His nephew, Arthur of Brittany, was laying claim to them. At the same time, the new king found himself embroiled in a war – unresolved by Richard, despite all his military genius – against Philip Augustus of France.

Extreme measures were needed. And John took them. The French king was the one man who could give real weight to Arthur's claim. John decided to neutralise him. He concluded a peace treaty with Philip Augustus. Those of John's opponents who had admired Richard's often less subtle methods saw it as caving in without a fight, and gave John a new nickname: 'Softsword'.

But the treaty gave John breathing space, which he used to bring his lordly French vassals to heel. He criss-crossed his western French territories at the head of a great army in a grand demonstration of his power. The explicit threat did the trick, and the local counts and dukes of his territories acknowledged his authority, without any necessity for John to draw his sword in anger. He and his soldiers marched and rode over 1,100 miles in under three months during the summer of the year 1200.

Towards the end of this marathon tour, John arrived at the city of Angoulême. And that's our next stop. For John, it was where sex and politics – as ever in the history of the world – came together.

5 ANGOULÊME, FRANCE

THE CHILD WITCH

I n cities across Europe, you'll often find street signs that are enough to make the unsuspecting amateur historian salivate. They say something like '*Au vieux quartier*' or '*La città vecchia*', '*Die Altstadt*', or in the UK usually 'To Historic Centre', all designed to lure us into thinking that just around the corner there awaits a flavour of life in medieval Nantes, Bologna, Heidelberg or York. It's a con, of course. Because 'historic' usually means not much more than narrower streets, an old church, and a small plaque announcing that 'On this site once stood a candlemaker's workshop'. What you usually do get more of is picture galleries, gothic lettering on shop fronts and maybe a handful of ancient houses clustered around a venerable church. These so-called old quarters are often so unremarkable that you can find yourself back in the modern part of town without realising you've wandered out of the old bit.

Angoulême in south-western France is different; not because its old city doesn't have its fair share of the quaint and the arty – it does – but because of its geography. In some ways, Angoulême is like Jerusalem, in that both places have a clear demarcation between the ancient and modern. In Jerusalem it's the old city wall that does it. In Angoulême, you can't accidentally stray out of the old town because you'd fall off a cliff. The city was founded – centuries before King John and Magna Carta – on a tabletop hill with steep sides falling away on all sides. This meant that when, hundreds of years later in the early nineteenth century, the population of industrialised France ballooned and people flocked from the countryside to cities looking for work, Angoulême couldn't, like other great towns, simply spread sideways. Hence, the modern city of Angoulême lies clustered around the old town's feet, like a wedding dress that's been hastily unzipped and dropped to the floor.

One result is that there's an element to old Angoulême that's unchangeably medieval. If we look outwards from its precipitous edges, we can instantly understand the city's strategic importance in the Middle Ages. When the newly

The intricate Romanesque facade of Angoulême cathedral still looks today much as did when John married Isabella here in 1200.

crowned King John came here in 1200, Angoulême, then as now, was mistress of all she surveyed for scores of miles on every side.

But the city in 1200 was also home to another mistress, a 12-year-old girl – some contemporaries even wrote that she was only 7 – named Isabella. John saw her and instantly wanted her. His desires were to land him in trouble.

★★★

It's Sunday morning when I arrive in Angoulême's old city. The little main square La Place Francis Louvel is an odd mix. At one end, a flight of steps leads up to a huge, grey, stone colonnaded building. 'Palais de Justice 1896', it says across the top. It looks like a monument to bureaucracy. In contrast, the other three sides of the square are packed with bright little bars, restaurants and family hotels. Right now however, they have that eerie abandoned feel to them that all places get on the morning after a party. The square's only occupants are a wiry terrier scratching itself and yawning, and a middle-aged man, shaped like a pumpkin with thin legs, coffee cup in one hand and cigarette in the other, standing outside the Café de Saint-Germain.

The debris from last night's action is telling, partly by what's not been left behind. There are no polystyrene burger boxes, vomit or beer glasses all over the pavement, which I'm ashamed to say might be the case in some UK cities on a Sabbath morn. It's true there are a few empty bottles here, one of them broken, but they're not scattered about, an offence to the eye and a danger to limb. These Saturday night leftovers have been arranged into a small impromptu work of art, mounted on a low wall outside one of the bars. In the middle of the composition is a litre glass water-bottle, on its side, smashed and jagged like a nasty weapon in a bar-room brawl. But in its neck at the other end there's a little bouquet of purple and red flowers. It's flanked on each side by two beer bottles, one of which holds its own spray of delicate red blooms. Around the outside, large shiny leaves have been arranged, and on the left there's a breathalyser kit (all motorists in France were briefly required to carry one) squashed flat. Now, call me a romantic, but this *oeuvre* makes me imagine that Angoulême's Saturday night drunks weren't yobs ranting incoherently into their mobile phones, but philosophy students and arts graduates, mellowed by alcohol into musings about the inadequacy of conceptualism as an existentialist tool, or whatever.

The little streets that lead away from La Place Francis Louvel are standard 'old city' thoroughfares. They're narrow and cobbled, with lantern-style street-lights fixed to the walls next to second-floor balconies, from which the occupants – if they wanted to – could lean out and swap croissants with their neighbours across the way. This morning, from the open windows, sounds drift down, of a woman calling, to her kids maybe, and of a church service on TV.

But in the next street, there's something non-standard. On the stone wall, a large hole apparently opens into a dark room within the building. Through it, two larger-than-life faces, men in 1950s brimmed hats and dark glasses, are peering out at me. It's a *trompe l'œil* mural painting. One of the faces is saying to the other, via a speech bubble, '*Alors? Vous voyez quelque chose?*' ('So, can you see anything?'). A few feet along the wall to the right is another picture. The fake, but realistic-looking hole is now bigger, and one of the men seems to be leaning through to get a good look at our side. He says, '*Mmm, c'est bien ce que je craignais!!!*' ('Hmm, it's just as I feared!'). His mate replies, '*Quoi? Encore un infra-monde?*' ('What? Another underworld?'). I hurry on to find how the story ends. And now the two men staring out at me look worried, and the second one is saying, '*Pire que ça! C'est la réalité!!*' ('Worse than that! It's reality!') Next to the line of pictures is a battered metal door, a real one, over which a sign has been fixed: *Réalité. Sortie de secours* ('Reality. Emergency exit').

Angoulême has a special place in twenty-first-century culture. Every year it hosts the International Comics Festival, that's 'comics' as in strip cartoons. It's the biggest such festival in the world after a similar event in Japan. As befits the unreal chaos of the comic world, no one is quite sure how many people pack these narrow little streets for four days each winter – comic happenings pop up and disappear all over the place. But it's reckoned to be several hundred thousand.

From the Rue de Beaulieu, I turn right into the Rue de l'Évêché. I can just see the tower of the Cathedral of St Pierre above the roof tops, rising in tiers like a grubby wedding cake. For fans of Romanesque decorated churches, Angoulême's cathedral is the equivalent of a first edition of Batman to a comic aficionado. And in fact the comparison isn't so far-fetched, because the cathedral's west facade could count as a page of medieval cartoons, but carved in stone. It has over seventy pictures. There's a tangled strip of figures in a half-circle over the door. Dragons leap out at unsuspecting young women, gigantic weird birds feed on human flesh, mounted warriors clash in the sky with alien-like demons. Elsewhere on the cathedral front, good guys are getting tortured, while others are preparing to fly to the rescue. And at the very top, the caped crusader himself (Jesus, for traditionalists) is, as always in the end, victorious. All that's missing for the cathedral to win the Grand Prix at the annual comics festival is a few WHAMMM!! KERPOW!!! bubbles.

But when it comes to the test of time, the cathedral is in a different league. Comic strips – in their pure modern form – go back fewer than eighty years.

But the facade we've been admiring had already looked more or less as it does now, for seventy years by the time King John came to Angoulême in 1200. The sheer size and the artistic magnificence of the west wall were designed to inspire reverence for the power of God in his battle with the forces of evil.

★★★

On the day that John first looked up at the cathedral's elaborate facade from somewhere near where I'm standing now, the city all around was buzzing with excitement. Noblemen and noblewomen, the peach of south-west France's chivalric society, were gathered here. The streets were crowded with their servants scurrying too and fro to organise food, shelter and all the daily necessities demanded by their masters and mistresses. The cathedral itself was being decked with banners and flowers.

There was to be a wedding, the most magnificent the city had seen for many years. Two families who had been at loggerheads for decades were to be united. Hugh le Brun de Lusignan was to wed Isabella of Angoulême. By their union, a block of territory would be formed stretching from the Atlantic Ocean in the west to the borders of the land directly ruled by the French king in the east.

Isabella – she it was who may have been only 7 years old at the time, or 12 at most – was considered by contemporaries to be a stunning beauty, a description of a child that we in the twenty-first century might consider inappropriate. By some accounts, John's first sight of her was on the great day itself, as she was being led up the aisle of the cathedral by her father. What happened next must have near traumatised the little girl waiting at the altar, while it enraged the Lusignan family gathered at the front of the nave, and gave the rest of the congregation a story to tell until their dying days. As soon as he set eyes on little Isabella, King John – it was said – stepped forward and held up his hand. He stopped the ceremony there and then. He marched up to the altar steps, and by his authority as overlord to the bridegroom, Hugh de Lusignan, ordered him out of the way. And he married the girl himself. Isabella didn't have a say in the matter.

This at least was the commonly told account at the time. And although we can't be sure of its complete accuracy, it probably wasn't far from the truth, because what is certain is that the wedding between John and Isabella came only days after the king arrived in Angoulême. The religious chroniclers said that she had bewitched him, not in the sense we might use the word – that he had fallen head over heels in love with her – but that she had consorted with the devil, and was a sorceress who had cast a wicked spell on him. They even accused her of incest. 'She should have been named Jezebel,' said one sniffy monk, 'rather than Isabel.'

So what do we know of John's motives? Given the couple's age difference and the lightning courtship, it's a safe bet there was no meeting of minds – rarely a reason for marriage among thirteenth-century nobility anyway. On the other hand, we can't exclude sex as at least part of the drive on John's part. We also know that he was looking for a wife. He had just had his first marriage to Isabel of Gloucester annulled, and had been in the process of lining up the King of Portugal's daughter via an exchange of ambassadors when he called in at Angoulême. But perhaps the strongest, long-term reason for his marriage to Isabella was staring him in the face when, with the little girl on his arm, he stepped out of the west door of the cathedral into the August sunshine.

★★★

The cathedral stands at the very edge of the ancient city, immediately above the rampart wall. Today, when we put ourselves where John would have stood at the cathedral door, and turn to the left, there's a sheer drop less than 50 yards away. It's the edge of the old city's ramparts, and beyond we can see the horizon 30 miles away. The city – now, as in John's day – dominates all routes in mid-western France between the central mountains and the sea.

Angoulême is known as 'the balcony of the south-west'. And for anyone taking a stroll round its ramparts – as we'll now set off to do – that's exactly what it's like. Imagine a huge grand old house with a balcony on its second floor, but this balcony doesn't just jut out from a bedroom or two, it encircles the whole place so that you can admire the ever-changing view as you wander round until you land up back where you started. On Angoulême's ramparts balcony, it's 1½ miles on a circular route back to the cathedral.

The ramparts road is narrow, like the other streets in the old city. On the left there are fine houses restored to the original glory of an indeterminate period, some with shutters swinging loose this morning in a gentle breeze. A little further along, there's a château disguising a museum and a local government office. All these buildings have wonderful views out from the ramparts, over nineteenth-century red-tiled roofs, down to the bending River Charente where little cargo boats seem frozen, over treetops in parks and along boulevards, and on to distant hills and fields.

The locals, however, seem to have got used to the privilege of such a sight on their doorsteps and this Sunday morning are taking it for granted. An elderly woman, all in black, bustles along the pavement in the direction of the cathedral. A man, with mournful moustache and sagging cardigan, pauses to smile a '*Bonjour, Madame*' at an elegant young woman in high heeled boots and a shawl, watching her dog sniff at the plinth of a long-dead French president's statue. It must be obvious to them that I'm a stranger, from the way I'm staring to the right, taking in the view over a waist-high wall along the edge. An occasional flight of steps leads down to that world, though they look too narrow and slippery to tempt me today.

A hundred feet below the ramparts, a modern wide road circles the old city like a flashy cheap necklace. Once a year, it becomes a racetrack, although – as if in deference to the gentility of old Angoulême – a sedate one for vintage cars taking part in Le Circuit International des Remparts d'Angoulême. For a weekend, the little upper road where we're walking now is crammed with spectators. The balcony makes a perfect grandstand from which to watch the veteran vehicles jostling for first place. This morning the impromptu racetrack is quiet. At intervals, traffic lights change needlessly at junctions where roads head out into the sharp green of the countryside, bound for Limoges, Bordeaux, Poitiers or Cognac.

When King John looked down from up here, ancient Roman roads were still used on most long-distance routes through France, and a network of them had their centre at Angoulême. He must have breathed a satisfied sigh as he stood on the ramparts while his courtiers congratulated him. A child bride and a strategic coup, both clinched in one deal.

But he'd have done well to pay attention too to the furious scowls of the slighted Lusignan family. Trouble was brewing.

✷✷✷

There is no doubt that the most immediate threat John faced in 1200 on his grand tour of western France was from the Lusignan–Angoulême marriage. For the security of his French holdings, he had to stop it. His action in elbowing Count Hugh – whether literally or metaphorically – off the altar steps broke up a power bloc which would have threatened his rule in Aquitaine. But – either blinded by passion for the child beauty, or overconfident with the success of his grand tour – John seems to have overlooked or ignored the fact that his hasty action would turn the Lusignan clan into bitter enemies.

As we shall see, John often had the motives of a wise ruler, but it was the way he set about things, stepping on toes (if that's not too mild a phrase for what sometimes involved humiliation and brutality), that was to play such a large part in provoking the rebellion that led to Magna Carta.

John didn't stop at stealing Hugh de Lusignan's bride. He also seized some of the family's territory and instructed his officials to carry out raids on land held by another Lusignan, Count Ralph, ordering the royal servants 'to do him all the harm they could'. The Lusignans appealed for help to King Philip Augustus.

The French monarch was in a delicate position: he may have welcomed the chance to undermine John's hold on territory bordering his own, but he had a peace treaty with the English king that couldn't be ignored. However, it was John himself – through his arrogance – who solved Philip Augustus's quandary. First, the English king stepped up his attack on the Lusignans by accusing them of treason. And he invited them to try to prove their innocence by fighting judicial duels – as usual to the death – against his own professional warriors. After that, he snubbed the French king, a man to whom, by the technical rules of feudal law, John owed allegiance as overlord of his continental territories. John refused to appear before Philip Augustus when summoned to do so. That was enough to open the gate for the French king. The peace treaty was dead, and he joined forces with the Lusignans against John.

Philip Augustus had yet another trump in his hand. At the town of Gournay, in July 1202, his courtiers assembled with great pomp to witness a chivalric ceremony. The king was to knight a new ally. And that ally was the 15-year-old Arthur of Brittany, the rival claimant to John's domains. Arthur was an insufferably pompous youth, we're told. With due ceremonial, Philip Augustus recognised the youth's right to rule over John's territories on the French side of the Channel, with the exception of Normandy. That duchy – united to the English crown since 1066 – the French king aimed to take for himself.

So John had let a great opportunity slip through his fingers. He had done it by kicking a powerful vassal and his family when they were down, and then treating his own overlord with disrespect. So now he faced all-out war against three allies: the French king, the Lusignans and his nephew Arthur.

According to one chronicler, John was later to tell his young bride Isabella that his wedding with her had cost him Normandy. That wasn't entirely accurate, but the decision he took on the altar steps at Angoulême cathedral and his subsequent assault on the Lusignans were the cause of other disasters that befell him. His treatment of the Lusignans was, arguably, the single biggest political mistake of his reign. In the short term, it helped forge a powerful coalition which would bring him to his knees. And more than that, fourteen years later, the family would still harbour the bitterest resentment against him. In 1214 they would desert John on the eve of battle; the result would be a defeat which would leave him vulnerable to the rebel barons back in England, with all that meant for the encounter at Runnymede and the sealing of Magna Carta.

But these events are for later on our journey. For now, at the start of his reign, we must follow John 130 miles north of Angoulême. Fate dealt him one more chance to overthrow his enemies, and he very nearly did it. But in the end, he blew it again. It happened at a village called Mirebeau-en-Poitou. That's our next stop. There, we shall see in action the inconsistencies that often seemed to make up John's character. And we shall meet his mother, one of the most remarkable women of the Middle Ages. Was the example she set for her son to blame for his wayward character? If Eleanor of Aquitaine had been a virtuous, mousy woman, would John have been a more compliant king? Would there then have been no Magna Carta?

6 MIREBEAU-EN-POITOU, FRANCE

THE WARRIOR QUEEN

In the fenlands of eastern England, it's sugar beet. In Iowa, it's corn. In China's Yangtze river valley, it's rice. Around Mirebeau-en-Poitou in western France, it's sunflowers. I don't know whether this is Europe's most important sunflower-growing region, but as I drive north from Angoulême it looks like it. Endless tracts of countryside on both sides of the road are packed with them. You might be picturing a mass of yellow petals and golden brown seed-pads dazzling me whenever I glance sideways. But it's early autumn, and the blooms are withering. The sight of them is nevertheless spectacular. It's more subtle than the gaudiness of summer, and even a little unnerving in what it suggests. I stop the car for a closer look.

Imagine a ragtag army of beggars, all in torn and dirty clothes, who have been rounded up and forced to show reverence to their queen. As one, they all bow their heads in the same direction, line upon line of them, rank upon rank of them, fearful of looking up to where they might catch a glimpse of her. That's what these fields of dying sunflowers look like. A slight breeze shuffles their heads as though they're a single creature, and sets up a dull, respectful moan in their midst.

Suddenly, the ones nearest me at the roadside start to twitch. It's a downpour. Heavy raindrops are bombarding them and me. I scoot back to the car, and five minutes later I make out, through thrashing windscreen wipers, a cut-out placard of a cartoon foot soldier. He's bright blue with brown cross-gartered leggings and is clutching a sword. He's been stuck on to what looks like an old city wall. This must be Mirebeau.

Mirebeau-en-Poitou has been described as one of the prettiest villages in France. By the time I reach its Place de la République, the rain is hammering on the car roof and 'pretty' isn't the word that springs to mind. I park by the church and hurry over to the Bar-Tabac de l'Hôtel de Ville, where there's an empty table on the pavement in the dry beneath an awning. After a shudder of cold and an unsuccessful attempt to catch the attention of the waiter, I take stock of the scene. The two couples at the next table are English. I hear an embarrassed 'Mercy bo coo' from a middle-aged woman in a padded fleece, followed by a discussion of how difficult it is to persuade the children to bring the grandchildren over to stay. Beyond, in the square, it's market day. Bedraggled, striped canopies are trying to keep the rain off flower stalls and slabs lined with fresh fish. And steam is rising like geyser vapour from the roof of the barbecue van. No one's buying. The few *Mirebalais* (that's what the citizens here are called) out there aren't hanging about.

Les foires, fairs or street markets, have been held in Mirebeau for centuries. There's an old saying here, *Qu'il en passe plus qu'il n'en reste*, which – even to the French – doesn't make much sense unless you know the story behind it. In 1569 during the Wars of Religion, a troop of protestant soldiers attacked Mirebeau. But just in time, the *Mirebalais* were alerted by the braying of donkeys in the village, and so were able to rally together and see off the assault. Strangers to Mirebeau then started to make fun of the inhabitants by calling them the donkeys. The word can also mean imbecile in French. The *Mirebalais* decided to get their own back. Donkeys had come and gone in Mirebeau for years. They were brought from all around to be sold in the village market, and then taken away by their buyers. So, whenever an outsider started on the old joke about the donkey folk of Mirebeau, the villagers would wink at each other and nod towards the visiting stranger, saying, *Qu'il en passe plus qu'il n'en reste*, which meant there are more donkeys that just pass through than stay here.

Markets would have been held in Mirebeau's central square, where the rain is now tipping down, long before the village suddenly figured in King John's life during the summer of 1202.

He came here to rescue his 80-year-old mother.

And he went away with an even more valuable prize, but one which turned to wormwood in his hands.

★★★

Eleanor of Aquitaine had twice been queen. First she had married King Louis VII of France, and then John's father, Henry II of England. The result of these two unions was ten children. The sixth was Richard the Lionheart. John was the last one. But it was not as a filler of royal nurseries or as an adjunct to royal men that she's remembered. She was a ruthless and mighty politician in her own right, who several times rode to war at the head of an army.

Eleanor was pitched into the limelight at an early age. She was 15, or possibly 13 (we can't be sure what year she was born), when her father the Duke of Aquitaine died. With no brothers, she was heiress to vast territories covering the whole of present-day south-west France. The French king, known by the unenviable title of Louis the Fat, stepped in smartly and married off Eleanor to his

17-year-old son, also called Louis. Within months, Louis the Fat died of dysentery, and Louis junior succeeded him. Eleanor of Aquitaine was Queen of France.

Louis and Eleanor made an ill match. At the court in Paris she grew into a feisty woman, who later described her husband as more monk than king. She had a quick tongue and a sharp mind for the subtleties of court politics. He on the other hand had fixed opinions often based on religious teachings. Though he adored her, his passion was more like a schoolboy's crush than the love of an enthusiastic bed-mate. After seven years, she had produced no heirs. And when finally, in 1145, she did give birth it was to a girl not a future King of France.

At Christmas in that same year, Eleanor's husband made an announcement that offered Eleanor the chance of adventure. He would go on crusade. Such an expedition in the twelfth century was a daunting prospect, even if you were a fit young athlete like Richard the Lionheart, never mind a monkish bookworm like King Louis. There were mountain ranges to cross and raging rivers to ford, through snow in winter and searing heat in summer, with non-existent hygiene in field kitchens that daily threatened food poisoning and disease without remedy or treatment. And then once in the Holy Land, a crusader must face the strong possibility of death or maiming at the hands of a skilled and merciless enemy.

Eleanor declared that she would go on crusade too.

It was a disastrous venture. By the time Louis's army reached Mount Cadmus in present-day Turkey, Eleanor and her retinue were in the leading contingent and wandered too far forward. As result, Louis wrongly believed the way ahead was safe. The men in his main contingent, wearied by the icy conditions, were ambushed in a narrow gorge. Soldiers, horses and baggage were forced over a cliff and toppled into the chasm below. The king escaped only under cover of darkness. It was almost a year since he and his army had left Paris 2,000 miles away. Now he and his queen and the battered remnants of his army limped into Antioch on the east Mediterranean coast.

The ruler of Antioch, as it happened, was Eleanor's uncle, Raymond of Poitiers. He was a worldly, generous and charming host, described by one chronicler as 'the most handsome of the earth's princes'. When King Louis announced that he'd had enough and now planned to return home, Raymond was appalled, and the two men had a falling-out. But there was another, more domestic, motive for the row. Eleanor revelled in Raymond's company. The two were often seen in long, intimate conversations, laughing together. Scandal was in the air. The rumour that their relationship was more than might be expected between uncle and niece spread back across Europe. The gossip was fuelled by Eleanor herself, who started to press her husband for a divorce, or in fact for the twelfth-century equivalent, which was to get the union annulled on grounds of consanguinity, the argument being that the couple were in some way related.

In the end, after Eleanor and Louis had returned to Paris and she had borne him another daughter, she got her way; by 1152, she was a free woman again. She was a prize catch, of course, with her powerful base in Aquitaine, and within months she had remarried. Her new husband was heir to the English throne, and within two years became Henry II, the flying monarch whom we met at Clarendon Palace. For the second time, Eleanor was queen.

Henry was an altogether different character from husband number one. He was energetic, wilful and intelligent. In fact he and Eleanor were peas in a pod. But two such strong personalities made for a union that was just as ill-matched as Eleanor's first marriage. Though she fulfilled her role as a baby-making machine – she bore Henry eight children, including five sons – the couple clashed more and more. Henry didn't like to be crossed. His tantrums were famous. He once dropped to the floor screaming and tearing the stuffing out of a mattress with his teeth. So by the time Eleanor was in her mid 40s, with her childbearing years behind her, the couple lived apart. She was back in Aquitaine. And when her 14-year-old son Richard – the future Lionheart – was enthroned as its duke, she in effect was its ruler.

The following year, something happened that, according to certain bishops, shook the very foundations of society. Henry faced open rebellion. Not from some ambitious nobleman in his territories, which was an almost annual event, but from his own sons, Richard and his younger brother Geoffrey. But this wasn't what upset the world order – there was nothing new about members of the same royal family turning their swords on each other, and this was to become particularly frequent among the Angevin monarchs, Henry II, Richard and John. This time there was something much more shocking to thirteenth-century sensibilities. Given that Richard and Geoffrey were aged only 15 and 14 respectively and hardly capable of mature political calculation, and given that they were under their mother's supervision at the court in Aquitaine, it was clear that Eleanor was the driving force behind the revolt.

The speculation at the time was that the queen betrayed King Henry, her actions driven by a furious jealousy of his mistress, a renowned beauty named Rosamund Clifford. She was the 'Fair Rosamund' celebrated in a later ballad:

Most peerlesse was her beautye founde,
Her favour, and her face;
A sweeter creature in this worlde
Could never prince embrace.

When Rosamund died three years later, it was said she had been poisoned on Eleanor's orders. True or not, Eleanor had other, political reasons to defy her husband. She wanted to rule her beloved Aquitaine without his interference. But whatever her motives, for a wife to foment rebellion against her royal mate was without precedent. So the Church stepped in and accused her of turning the world upside down.

But Eleanor was not to be cowed by such allegations. She continued drumming up armed support among the barons of Aquitaine. However, luck was not on her side. One day when travelling in disguise, dressed in men's clothing, along a country road – as it happened only a dozen miles or so from the village of Mirebeau – she ran into a troop of soldiers loyal to her husband. They recognised her, and delivered her to their master. When the uprising collapsed, Henry forgave his sons. But Eleanor got no such indulgence.

For the next fifteen years – during which Richard, joined now by the king's youngest son, John, again took up arms against their father – Eleanor was out of the game. She remained a prisoner until the day her husband died in 1189.

Richard's first act on becoming king was to set his mother free. She was in her mid 60s, and she wasn't going to retire yet. While Richard went off on crusade, he left his mother in England, 'with the power to do whatever she wished in the kingdom'. It was an unofficial regency. She went on a grand tour of the country, extracting oaths of allegiance to her son and turning the spotlight on abuses by local officials. And despite her advancing years, she undertook several missions on behalf of Richard that involved long arduous days on horseback, twice over the Pyrenees and back, and on another occasion across the Alps. And when John stirred up rebellion against his brother, it was Eleanor who put pressure on him to make peace.

In 1194, Eleanor decided to retire to the comfortable luxury of Fontevraud Abbey in the Loire Valley. But her life, her energy and her influence were far from exhausted. When Richard was killed in 1199, and her youngest son John faced opposition to his inheritance, Eleanor decided she needed to throw her prestige behind him. Though now in her mid to late 70s, she mounted her horse, rode out of the abbey gates, and placed herself at the head of an army loyal to John. In the next few months she covered almost 1,000 miles before yet again crossing the Pyrenees mountains on a mission to the Castilian court. Then, her work done, weary and in ill health, she again withdrew to Fontevraud.

But even now, at the age of 80, Eleanor didn't stay in the wings long. It was almost as though she became bored with life off the world stage. In 1202, as the war between her son John and her grandson Arthur of Brittany ground on, it suddenly looked as though John was losing control of Aquitaine to his rival. Eleanor couldn't sit back and let that happen. She again summoned up what strength she had left, got back on her horse and abandoned the comforts of her court at Fontevraud. Accompanied by a small force of soldiers, she set off to muster support for John among the barons of Aquitaine.

But she didn't get far. She had reached Mirebeau, 30 miles to the south, when suddenly she found herself facing an army led by John's archrival, her own grandson Arthur. Eleanor's meagre forces were greatly outnumbered so she led her troops to relative safety inside Mirebeau castle. Arthur's army soon swarmed over the village's outer ramparts and occupied its little streets. It's likely he set up his headquarters in the market square right in front of where I'm now sitting. Eleanor was surrounded and trapped. But she didn't surrender.

✵ ✵ ✵

This morning, it's one of those days when the rain is not only heavy but it doesn't stop. It's clattering on the café's awning over my head, and it's splattering off the sides on to the pavement with such a racket that my neighbours, the English group, are having to shout to be heard. The waiter takes one look at the stream of water now running down the street, grins at me and mouths, '*Merde!*' which is my cue to mime a cup of tea at him, which he delivers a few minutes later.

I've got a map of Mirebeau that I printed off the internet. It's got a little cartoon church marked Eglise Notre Dame, and there's a cartoon city wall marked Les Remparts close to where I arrived along the Boulevard Foulque Nera. Foulque Nera was the Count of Anjou who first built Mirebeau's castle in the early eleventh century. But nowhere on the map can I see any little picture to denote the location of his fort, where 190 years later Eleanor was besieged. I do find, lost in the modern outskirts of the village, a Rue Aliénor d'Aquitaine (Aliénor being old French for Eleanor), which seems a bit of a come-down for our redoubtable heroine. So, inspired by her example, I decide not to be daunted by a few drops of water, and leaving behind a couple of Euros for my tea and the comfort of the café, stride out beneath my umbrella to the Maison du Tourisme across the other side of the square.

There I meet Madame Godard, who too is not downhearted by the rain. She explains with a chuckle that Mirebeau's glorious castle was almost entirely demolished in the seventeenth century on the orders of '*le méchant* Cardinal Richelieu'. Though I'm charmed by the idea of a naughty (or is it nasty?) cardinal, I can't help showing my disappointment at his vandalism. Madame Godard comes to the rescue. 'Ah,' she explains, 'but the hill that Count Foulque had built to support his castle is still there, and from its top, you can appreciate Queen Aliénor's situation during her captivity in Mirebeau.' And with that she gives me another map, and puts a cross by the words '*Emplacement de l'ancien château dit La Cuve d'Anjou.*' *Cuve*, I later discover, means vat, as in large wine barrel, which presumably was what the circular fortress looked like from a distance until Richelieu got his hands on it.

The ancient city wall at Mirebeau. The castle where Eleanor of Aquitaine was besieged stood immediately behind.

So I bid Madame Godard, '*Merci,*' and, '*Adieu,*' and off I go to get lost. This is because I can't see much through the rain hitting my glasses, and because her map in my non-umbrella-holding hand has gone soggy. I do make out, opposite the church of Notre Dame, a sign saying Aliénor Immobilier, and wonder if this is a clue. But it turns out to be an estate agent who's hijacked Eleanor's name. Finally after attempts to interview several scurrying *Mirebalais*, who pause only long enough to wave vaguely in the direction I'm supposed to go, I find myself walking past a couple of *tricolores* dripping outside the Hôtel de Ville, and on down the Rue Nationale, which is nothing like as grand as it sounds. I spot the words *Motte Féodale XIe*, roughly translated as 'Eleventh-century feudal mound', on a brown sign with an arrow pointing into a farmyard. This is it. Once off the road, the choice of route is either straight on through a steel gate where a miserable-looking black horse is giving me the evil eye, or to the left along a grassy, puddled alleyway by some ancient stone buildings. I vote with my feet for the latter.

I can't see the castle mound anywhere. There's an open cellar on the left housing what looks like a rusty olive press and an old mangle. To the right, beyond an ivy-sprawled stone wall, giant weeds and broken trees block the view. The path itself curves gently around, and it's only after I've completed a semi-circle that I realise I'm in fact skirting the site of the old fortress. I can see now where it is. Beyond the undergrowth on my right, the ground rises steeply. And after some scrabbling about, I find some crude steps made from small logs. This morning they're shiny and slippery, and by the time I reach the top, my knees are muddy and I'm out of breath. I can understand why it would be no

69

easy task for a besieging army to storm the place. The mound is roughly the height of a three-storey house, with sides only slightly less sheer. But Eleanor would know that she was safe up here only until her grandson Arthur brought up siege engines and sappers to smash and undermine the castle's walls.

The top of the mound is flat. It's like a field in the sky. There's an occasional small tree, and the grass has been freshly mown. I spot some remnants of a rocky wall, presumably overlooked by Richelieu's demolition men. Its stones are icing-sugar white – from some kind of fungus – and with the flat of my hand I stroke their sides, greedy for some tangible vestige of Eleanor's entrapment here.

I'm discovering a strange psychological phenomenon on this quest for the roots of Magna Carta. The less a place looks like it did when a Queen Eleanor, a King John or a humble crossbowman visited it, the more my mind works over-time to picture them on the spot where I find myself. Of course, it's wonderful to look on the facade of Angoulême Cathedral just as John himself saw it. But there's still something … immediate (I can think of no other word) about places which nature and the human hand have changed. Unless we stand where once an ageing queen denounced her grandson, or where a common soldier lost his last spurt of blood, there's a danger our brains will simply sort these people into the same box as the characters in *Game of Thrones* or *Downton Abbey*. But they weren't the simple folk of fiction. They were as complex as you and me. And it's only yester-day (in cosmic terms) that they trod where we do now.

Suddenly the rain stops. A distant drumroll of thunder announces its retreat. And within minutes the mist lifts. From up here on Foulque Nera's castle mound, I can see over the scarred pantiles of the farm buildings to the spire of Mirebeau's church and the little market square. This was the view that Eleanor had each morning. She would have seen her grandson Arthur's standard flying over his tented pavilion down there, smoke rising from cooking fires, and on all sides a jumble of snorting horses and bustling men. But she would have needed to be careful. Snipers with crossbows would have been on the lookout for a target, a face, an arm, fleetingly exposed at any gap in the castle's wall.

From the opposite side of the mound I can see only a few yards away the rear of the fortified wall that I saw when I first approached the village. In 1202, there would have been a similar construction surrounding the whole of Mirebeau, though then it would have been an earth rampart with a crude stone structure running along the top and with a double ditch along its outer edge. The nearness of her fort to this rampart offered Eleanor a chance of salvation. Not for her to escape that way; it would have been too risky and too arduous a scramble for an 80-year-old. But she knew that her only hope lay with her son John, whose army was camped 120 miles north at Le Mans. So within a few days of being trapped up here, she chose one of her most enterprising followers and dispatched him on a mission. He clambered at night out of the castle where it butts on to the rampart here, making his way down precipitous drops, till somehow he managed to slip past Arthur's sentries. The price of being caught wouldn't just have been death, but a horrible, slow one in full view of the queen and her small troop of bodyguards to deter anyone else from such a venture. But Eleanor's man got through. He reached open countryside, where presumably he stole or bought a horse and rode off to the north.

Now, John wasn't the heroic, determined military genius that his brother Richard had been. But Mirebeau was *his* Acre, his finest hour. As soon as the messenger arrived with news of his mother's plight, he gave orders for an immediate advance. It was a forced march, with only brief pauses for rest. His troops covered the last 80 miles in just forty-eight hours, reaching the gates of Mirebeau as dawn broke on 31 July, just sixteen days after Eleanor had first taken refuge in its castle.

The action now shifted to the narrow streets and market square of Mirebeau. I climb back down the log steps (not making a fuss, when I remember Eleanor's messenger), walk past the suspicious gaze of the black horse, and back into the village.

Perhaps the biggest surprise about what happened next that early summer morning in 1202 is that Arthur's sentries failed to raise the alarm in time, and that his scouts – if he had any – gave no warning of the fast-approaching enemy. John's army swarmed through the town's gates, and the first that Arthur and his men knew of the attack was when they woke to hear horses' hooves clattering through these little streets. John's men met almost no resistance. One of Arthur's key allies, Hugh de Lusignan – head of the family that John had so offended with his marriage to Isabella of Angoulême – was seized in the middle of his breakfast, a tasty dish of pigeons, we're told. But there was an even bigger catch. Arthur, Duke of Brittany, John's nephew, was seized. He was now his uncle's prisoner.

✮ ✮ ✮

Eleanor was freed. After celebrating victory with her son she decided enough was enough, and with her immediate retainers, she made a slow progress back to Fontevraud Abbey. There she took the habit of a nun, her eye no longer on earthly power but on the world to come. She died twenty-one months later, at – by thirteenth-century standards – the quite extraordinary age of 82. Her career had been unmatched in medieval Europe. In an era when noblewomen were usually expected do no more than please their lord and master and to bear his children, or at most to run his household while he was away, she had ridden at the head of armies, had done the unthinkable and led a rebellion against her husband, was rumoured to have poisoned a rival, had survived years of imprisonment, had ruled a kingdom in the absence of her son, and had continued to exert her will for many years beyond when she might have expected to be infirm or dead. She had done this by means of an extraordinary strength, in both body and mind.

It would take a psychologist going back in time eight centuries to analyse the complex impact on John of being brought up in the presence of such a mother. And too, of course, under the influence of a father who one minute was throwing childish tantrums, and the next was hurling his energy into building Europe's most effective governmental and legal system. One thing is certain. Whether by nature or nurture, John was – in every sense – Eleanor's and Henry's son.

★ ★ ★

The story of John at Mirebeau – winning a stunning victory by decisive action and rescuing his mother in a daring dash – is one that chivalric balladeers might have celebrated in song. 'Might have', but didn't. It was John's bad luck that, unlike his brother Richard at Acre, he didn't have a loyal chronicler with him to tell posterity about every cut and thrust of his heroic adventure. But there's another reason why the names John and Mirebeau are not forever romantically linked. And that's not down to ill luck, but purely to ill judgement on John's part. He managed to throw away the advantages he had won where another man would have built on them.

First, he offended the two military allies who had won the Battle of Mirebeau at his side. Aimery de Thouars and William des Roches wanted a say in the fate of the prisoners of war, many of whom were their neighbours. John refused, and the two men turned their forces against him. Perhaps that was no more serious than his brother Richard's insult to Leopold of Austria at Acre.

But the serious damage to John's position came from what happened to his nephew Arthur. The young man was imprisoned in Rouen Castle. There, by some accounts, John, in a drunken rage one night, killed him by bashing his head in then throwing his body into the Seine. According to other reports, the king didn't murder his nephew himself, but was present when one of his henchmen did it. We can never know the truth. But many at the time believed John was responsible for Arthur's death and the story spread the length and breadth of England, Wales and France. In considering its impact, we have to remember that this was an age when political rivals were commonly disposed of by whatever means, violent or otherwise. Nevertheless, accounts of Arthur's murder would unnerve John's allies, be exploited by his enemies, and would play a key role in driving the barons of England along the road to Magna Carta.

That part of John's and the Great Charter's story is for later. Meanwhile we need to return to his brother's masterpiece, Château Gaillard. John may have taken Arthur out of the reckoning, but in 1203 his war with King Phillip Augustus of France was far from over, and Château Gaillard was where it would come to a head.

7 CHÂTEAU GAILLARD, NORMANDY, FRANCE

LOST!

igh on a precipitous rock above a wide bend of the River Seine in northern France stands the now part-ruined fortress of Château Gaillard, an aged, savage beast, hunched and battle-scarred, surveying its territory. Centuries after Richard the Lionheart oversaw its construction at the end of the twelfth century, poets and painters would come to see Château Gaillard and be inspired by its lonely magnificence. Historians would come too, to investigate the clever construction of its walls and declare Gaillard a revolution in military architecture.

It remains beautiful and ingenious. It was a spectacular failure.

Château Gaillard was said to be impregnable. It was not. Gaillard was a bitter legacy from Richard to his brother, and it was to be the start of John's undoing.

✳ ✳ ✳

From afar, the castle these days looks so inaccessible to us mortals below that it's not immediately obvious how we reach it. There are road signs in the middle of Les Andelys, the little town on the bank of the River Seine at the foot of the château's rocky platform. But on the day I make the trip, even these signs seem like a plot to lure me off course. I set off from the little market square, where the remains of a funfair – dodgem cars and painted wooden horses – are being packed away. The car is soon zigzagging up a long, steep hill through a thick wood. Then we're in the open, and the road ahead drops down again. This is a puzzle because the castle obviously isn't lower than the road. Maybe we're lost. There's a flat area of grass on my right, so I stop and get out to look around. It's then that I see it.

Château Gaillard, in all its broken glory, high on a hill across the other side of a small valley. But just as much as the castle itself, its backdrop is what makes me grab my camera. Beyond Gaillard and 300 feet or so below it, the blue waters of the Seine curve beneath limestone cliffs before embracing a green, tree-covered island, opposite the quaint and undisturbed houses of Les Andelys. The route to the castle is on down to the bottom of the valley and then up the other side.

When planning this trip, I'd got hold of a DVD – made by the Les Andelys tourist office – all about Château Gaillard and its history. The film's message was simple. Gaillard was the site of a famous French victory won by King Philip Augustus over the English, i.e. the army of King John. This slightly ignores the fact that kings of England at that time held just as much territory on the French side of the Channel as on the English, being Dukes of Normandy, Counts of Anjou and Maine, and Dukes of Aquitaine, and it overlooks the fact that many of John's soldiers were Flemish mercenaries rather than true-blooded Englishmen. Added to which, the King of France didn't rule what we know as France, but had direct control only over Paris and its more immediate surrounds.

But still, as I edge closer to Château Gaillard, I'm expecting to find this *monument historique* shown off to its maximum nationalistic advantage, maybe with some fancy virtual reality displays in a kid-friendly museum, and perhaps a gift shop selling model Gaillards with the '*tricolore*' on top, and certainly a discreet but ample car park for the hordes of patriotic French who are bound to flock here. So when the car comes to a stop on a muddy bit of gravel behind a hedge, alongside no more than half a dozen other visitors' vehicles, I again think I must have taken a wrong turn. The castle has disappeared somewhere over the hill.

A family, all in stout boots, marches around the corner. I approach them and stutter: '*Excusez-moi, est-ce que le Château Gaillard est pour ici?*'

Which doesn't sound quite right, but the patriarch of the group gives a little laugh, and replies, '*Mais oui, bien sûr,*' and points to a steep goat's path leading up the hillside a couple of yards to my right. With a self-deprecating chuckle (implying, '*Les Anglais, huh!*'), I murmur, '*Merci,*' and off I stride.

It's a good job I brought my hiking stick, because my feet are soon slipping and sending pebbles skittering down behind me. But I'm not complaining. After all, this is the real thing. Who wants twenty-first-century tarmac and railings when you can experience the trials of a thirteenth-century foot soldier on an assault party (without enemy arrows raining down on your head, obviously)?

Soon, the castle's curtain wall starts to appear above the brow of the hill ahead, and I can make out what's regarded as one of the most original of Richard's architectural innovations. The high wall of the inner fort isn't flat with right-angled corners, as it is in many castles from this period. Its surface is a series of shallow convex curves, to give it a rippled effect. The idea was that heavy missiles, usually massive rocks shot from giant catapults down below, would hit the wall – nine times out of ten at an oblique angle – and skid away, so causing far less damage than if they had smashed square-on against flat masonry.

The wall of Château Gaillard's inner ward, with its series of convex curves, was an innovation in castle building. Missiles shot at it were likely to bounce off at an angle, causing less damage than they would against flat masonry.

When I reach the top of the path, I'm in for a surprise. Far less of the original building seems to have survived than appears to be the case from a distance. I am of course used to medieval buildings being reduced more or less to ruins: Clarendon Palace, for instance. But in the outlying area where I've pitched up, away from the rippled wall, there are little more than ragged, unrecognisable stacks of shattered flint-stone and the occasional jagged remnant of a wall. The reason is that the castle drifted into a distinctly unheroic end. By the turn of the seventeenth century, it had become the squalid lair of criminal gangs. And once they had been flushed out of the place, the French king decided to dismantle parts of the castle so it would be no use to bandits again. Fortunately, much of the great fortress, including the rippled wall surrounding the main courtyard – the inner ward – and the towering keep inside it, have survived.

The path, now on the level, passes a small circular wall. It's exactly what it looks like, a well. If you lean over to peer down into it, there's nothing to see but black emptiness below weeds sprouting from its crumbled sides. But this is a true marvel of engineering. If you were a thirteenth-century defender of Gaillard, you'd need to be ready to withstand a siege that might last for years. Most of all, you'd want fresh water. And the nearest source for the garrison of Château Gaillard was the

Seine, 350 feet below. So to reach the river's water table, the labourers hacked out a borehole down through the solid limestone. Now, digging a 350-foot-deep well, 7 to 8 feet wide, through rock, before the invention of mechanised drills is an astonishing feat, not only of primitive engineering, but also of physical strength, endurance and courage. An archaeologist with a bent for mathematics has calculated that 814 tons of stone had to be hewn out and hauled up on pulleys to the surface. It apparently took twelve to fifteen men five months to reach the first signs of moisture at the bottom of the pit. They worked, we are told, 'with the protection of a shield'. This presumably was something like a wooden board that might stop the odd loose chip from landing on their heads, though it can't have been much defence against a more substantial rockfall. It's not recorded how many workers were seriously hurt or met a terrifying death down there.

★★★

To get some idea of the brilliance of Château Gaillard's design, we'll make our way to its south-eastern extremity. Earlier castle-builders in Europe had usually got their labourers to throw up a more or less circular mound on which a fort would be built, with a bailey – or enclosed courtyard – around it. Even if the castle were to be sited on a natural, rather than a man-made, hillock, a similar plan would apply and the builders would make sure it had a precipitous approach on all sides. Gaillard's location was novel, in Europe at least. It sits, not on a round hill, but on a long, narrow spur of rock, linked to the nearby hills. This land bridge was what made Gaillard's positioning different. The idea was that it would look like the castle's Achilles heel, the vulnerable spot where it could best be attacked. It's where we're standing now. If we think of ourselves as attackers, we can see the towering keep – our military objective – about 300 yards away, within the ripple walls of the inner bailey. So let's start the assault.

We first find ourselves having to stumble along a rocky isthmus, so narrow that no more than half a dozen of us could advance shoulder to shoulder. Eight hundred years ago, from the top of the tower ahead of us – where today weeds are sprouting – archers and crossbowmen would have us clearly in their sights. If we manage to survive that deadly rain of missiles, we somehow have to smash through the 40-foot-high tower or through the curtain wall, which runs – inconveniently for us – alongside a steep drop. Today we can step around the jagged remains of the tower, but then have to imagine ourselves trapped in a courtyard, within range of more bowmen above, only this time on both flanks. For the defenders, killing us would be like shooting fish in a barrel.

If we succeed in fighting our way across the open space, we then face a deep moat. This has been partly filled in over the years, so nowadays it's an easy job to walk down the dip and up the other side to where our predecessors of eight centuries ago would have to penetrate yet another massively thick wall. Through that, we're now surrounded by the solid stone barrier of the inner ward, and exposed to the same rain of missiles as in the last courtyard. By this stage our morale is taking a dive, because ahead of us, we can see that our next obstacle is the most impenetrable wall of all: Richard's innovative, and massively thick, rippled masonry, particularly resistant to battering rams, which of course somehow we have to have lugged along with us.

But anyway those in the vanguard of our assault can see there's also a deep moat in front of it. We can peer down at its sludgy bottom 15 feet below. Today of course there's a handy footbridge and rather fewer and less fearsome defenders to face, i.e. three ticket-sellers who demand, not a price in blood, but 3 Euros from each of us. So assuming, back in our role of castle assailants, that somehow we got across the moat and through the 11-foot-thick barrier of cement and flint, we're now in a smaller courtyard. Here we face our final task: to storm the last bastion, the inner keep, the tallest tower of all, which has some especially nasty treats in store. At the top of its walls are overhanging slots, called machicolations, from which the now desperate defenders – with no choice but to do or die – can hurl down stones, boiling water, red-hot iron bars, hot sand and quicklime on to our by now exhausted and probably wounded bodies.

This was the theory of Château Gaillard's defence. We can see why it was thought to be impregnable.

★ ★ ★

After John's victory at Mirebeau, his war against Philip Augustus drifted on for two years with neither side gaining much advantage. The French king's chief objective was to take the duchy of Normandy, which had been tightly tied to the English crown since 1066. John's brother Richard had built Château Gaillard to defend the duchy, and it was here that King John and King Philip Augustus finally squared up to each other, almost face to face. It was like a jousting tournament on a grand scale, with Normandy as the prize.

The castle itself was under the command of Roger de Lacey, one of John's most loyal barons. John himself was late on the scene, and by the time he arrived the first bloody action had already taken place. The French king had led his army up to the riverbank right opposite Gaillard, and set up camp in full view of the castle's garrison. Today from inside the inner ward we can look down through one of the large openings in the furthest stone wall. The experience is not for vertigo sufferers. It's the sort of view twenty-first-century air travellers get three minutes after take-off, except here you're not enclosed. But if you can relax enough to cringe forward across the 10-foot-wide windowsill, the picture below – apart from a couple of miniature tennis courts and a toy barge creeping down river – is much as the one that met garrison commander de Lacey's eyes when he looked down on the army of King Philip Augustus in the late summer of 1203. To the right, 100 yards downstream, we can see a small island, which back then formed the midpoint of a bridge spanning the River Seine in two hops. Philip's first objective was to take this bridge. And so the campaign began.

De Lacey packed the bridge's wooden structure with his soldiers and they readied themselves for the French assault. A terrifying struggle followed. The French king's chaplain, William the Breton, has left us an eyewitness account of what happened both on that day and in the months ahead, and while we should allow for his bias in presenting the heroism of the French troops, his is probably as accurate an account as we'll find anywhere of the bloody squalor of medieval warfare. Describing the bridge assault, William wallows in the suffering of the French soldiers. 'One falls with gushing entrails,' he writes, 'one with his throat cut, there a thigh is shattered by a staff, here brains are scattered with a club. One man's hand is shorn off with a sword, another forfeits both knees to an axe.' We should remember that in the thirteenth century, when treatment at a field hospital amounted to no more than swallowing some herbs or an amputation with a dirty knife, any half-serious wound was likely to be fatal. The chaplain tells us that none of Philip Augustus's men escaped without some injury, and the French attack against the bridge was repulsed.

Philip, however, immediately looked for an alternative strategy, and in this he was helped by a hero in his ranks, a man who, if he had fought in the Second World War, would have been attaching limpet mines to the hulls of enemy warships. This intrepid fellow swam across the river underwater, towing a barrel, inside which had been sealed some red-hot coals. He landed unseen at the little village of Les Andelys far below Gaillard's rocky heights, and he set fire to the wooden palisades installed there by the defenders to hinder the approach to the castle's mount. The flames rapidly spread to nearby houses, forcing the villagers of Les Andelys to flee. They took refuge inside Château Gaillard. John's commander, de Lacey, had been taken by surprise, and as his men on the bridge were thrown into confusion, Philip seized his chance and ordered his men to mount a second attack on the bridge; within a short time his forces occupied the ground on the Gaillard bank. It was first victory to the French, and they celebrated with a tournament of jousting, wrestling and suchlike soldierly games. Philip put up the prizes, at a handsome total of £1,000 a day.

At this point, John arrived and decided that what the castle garrison needed most were supplies, of both food and armaments. His next move was clever, if overambitious. Under cover of darkness, he sent seventy boats loaded with provisions up the

Seine, while at the same time ordering a land attack against the French army as a diversion. But it all went wrong. The rowers found themselves struggling against a strong current and fell behind schedule. As a result the French were able to see off the two threats one at a time. It was carnage. The river, it was said, ran thick with blood.

John did not renew his attempt to relieve the siege of Gaillard. Instead he left the scene to turn his attention to Philip's allies in Brittany, and after some desultory burning and sacking there, which achieved little, he crossed the Channel back to England. Was this ignominious retreat the result of John drinking away his nights and lying abed all day, as the chroniclers alleged? Probably not; the real cause was treachery. The barons of Normandy seemed to regard a French victory as inevitable, and they deserted John. There was now, in effect, only one obstacle to Philip Augustus's capture of the duchy: Château Gaillard.

Gaillard was now under blockade on all sides. And it was clear that the battle was going to go the way that struggles for castles usually went. It would be a death-or-victory war of attrition. John's commander, de Lacey, realised that his strongest defence was no longer the crossbow. It was food and water. There was plenty to drink inside Gaillard, thanks to Richard's wells drilled down through the rock. And John's predecessor had also provided cool, dry cellars within the castle where food could be stored. There is still today a hole – around 5 feet square – dropping down into the ground of the inner ward. We can clamber down a flight of fearsomely steep, stone steps and find ourselves in a set of man-made caves, with stone columns holding up the roof. Here salted meat would be kept in barrels, dried beef could be hung from the ceiling, and grain stacked in sacks. A paradise no doubt for rats, though of course cooked rat was a welcome source of protein when other forms of hunting were out of the question.

But de Lacey knew that these stores couldn't be replenished. Losing a few mouthfuls to vermin was one thing, but daily food for crowds of non-combatant humans was another altogether. In the first days, before Philip's noose had been tightened around the castle, the civilian refugees from Les Andelys had been useful to the garrison. They would slip out at night and smuggle food in. But now this was no longer possible, and de Lacey calculated that if he reduced the garrison down to just those who were capable of fighting he would have enough supplies to hold out for a year. That left another 1,200 souls whom he categorised as 'useless mouths'. He rounded them up and forced them out through the gates, leaving them to scramble down the steep slopes surrounding the castle.

William the Breton blamed de Lacey for what happened next. The castle's commander, he says, 'had no doubt he was sending these wretches to their deaths, nor did he care what fate overtook them provided he could save the fort for a short time'. However, the French king too showed no compassion, not at first anyway. He gave orders to open fire on the hapless villagers, who found themselves the target of javelins and darts. Philip evidently wanted the civilians back inside the castle, where they would eat up the defenders' food supplies and so bring the siege to a quicker end. But when the refugees made a rush for the safety of Gaillard, they found the gates locked against them. They were stranded in the ditch, in no-man's-land. They had neither shelter nor food. As winter set in, their plight became so appalling that when some died, their corpses were promptly eaten by their fellows. William the Breton – loyal chronicler that he was – tells us that his master, the king, then showed mercy. On one of his inspections of the front lines, the starving people surrounded him, begging for bread and a safe passage, both of which the French monarch now granted.

With the arrival of spring, Philip Augustus found himself in a dilemma. His feudal men-at-arms were getting itchy feet. They were anxious to get back to their farms. And his mercenaries wanted their pay. So the French king couldn't afford to sit it out much longer, waiting for the castle's garrison to be starved into submission. He needed a quick win. So he decided he would have to crack the toughest military nut in Europe.

His first objective was to take the outer ward. But he didn't get lured into the trap laid for attackers by Gaillard's architect, King Richard. Philip didn't approach the triangular fortification from the south-east corner – as we did in our mock assault – where the huge tower had been positioned. Instead, he decided to go for the eastern side, somewhere close to where I'd scrambled up the goat's path to reach the castle from the muddy little car park. It was a hopeless obstacle for siege engines and monster catapults. So he set his men to fill in part of this ditch with tree trunks, earth, rocks and other debris. Not an easy task in close range of the defenders' cross-bow snipers. But the French king's labourers put up wooden shields and eventually managed to construct a kind of roadway across the ditch, right up to the castle wall. This let them bring up crude wooden towers, known as 'belfries', even higher than the curtain wall of the outer ward. Now neither side had the advantage in the daily sniper exchange, and any defender who showed himself on the battlements or at a slit in the castle walls risked a crossbow bolt in the face.

But it was the miners who held the key to the outer ward's capture. In the gloom of candlelight and with a constant risk of being crushed to death by a tunnel collapse, Philip's sappers slowly dug down and gouged out a cavern beneath the castle wall. When the job was complete, they packed brushwood at the farthest point, and set it on fire before scrambling back out to see the result. The heat inside became more and more intense, and eventually there was an echoing crack, and a huge fissure split the wall. William the Breton takes up the story: 'It produces a great roar as it collapses,' he writes; 'a cloud of smoke whirls upwards in a twisting vortex with mixed flame and smoke, and the ruin belches out a great dust cloud that mushrooms out above.'

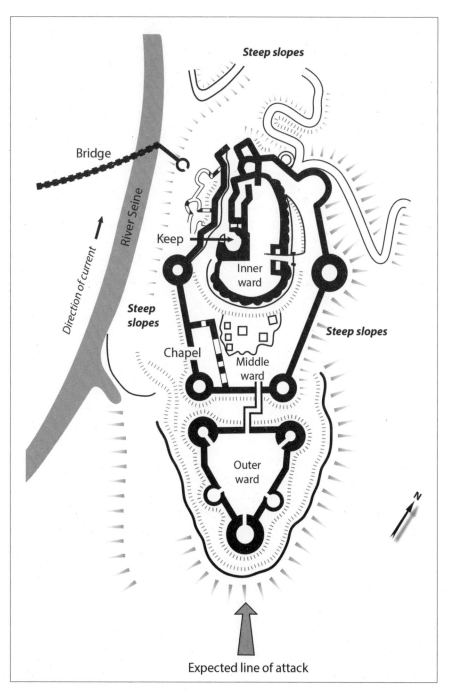

Château Gaillard's design assumed an enemy would attack along the spur of land from the south. In 1204 King Philip Augustus of France ignored this temptation and instead breached the walls across the ditch to the east.

With loud shouting and blowing of trumpets, Philip's men poured through the breach. The defenders didn't put up much of a fight, probably not through any lack of nerve. Richard had designed this outlying part of the castle, now occupied by Philip's men, to be little more than a delaying obstacle to any attackers. De Lacey probably felt he would need as many fighters as possible for the more crucial battle to come. So he gave orders for them to set fire to anything in the outer ward that might be useful to the enemy, and then to retreat to the next line of defence, the middle ward.

It was a second victory to the French king. But he knew, just as well as de Lacey, that capturing the middle ward, with its deeper moat, and its higher and thicker walls, was going to be an altogether bigger challenge.

★★★

Among the French king's men was a particularly resourceful common soldier. We even know his name, or rather his nickname: Bogis, which in some forgotten local dialect meant 'little nose'. In our day, he wouldd be the sort of tough and fearless soldier who would lead a special ops force. Bogis reconnoitred the walls of the middle ward and spotted a chink in its armour. On the ward's south-western side there was a drain coming down into the surrounding ditch from the crypt of the chapel up above. This place of worship had been added to Richard's original design for the castle by John himself on an earlier visit. Unseen by the castle garrison's sentries on the battlements, Bogis and five of his mates crawled up inside the foul drainpipe, which brought them to a window in the chapel. They climbed through, the idea being that they would kick up a commotion in the hope of creating a diversion while their comrades outside stormed the gate of the courtyard. All didn't quite go according to plan, though the result was the same. The defenders thought they had got Bogis and his team cornered and decided to force them out. They set fire to the chapel. It was a bad move. Amid all the smoke, no one could see what was happening. So Bogis and his mates slipped out and let the drawbridge down, allowing their comrades to swarm in. The defenders now retreated to the inner ward.

This next bastion was the one protected by Richard's famous ripple walls. And penetrating this was going to be the toughest stage of the whole campaign. The biggest of the big guns was needed. And word went back: bring up *Caballus*. *Caballus*, 'the Horse' was a siege engine which the French king's men were particularly proud of. It was a monstrous catapult. They wheeled it up and it began hurling massive rocks at close range against the walls. But the series of convex curves along its length did its job as Richard had intended and the heavy missiles bounced off at angles, unable to hit the masonry head-on.

Cue the miners again. Behind the shelter of a spur of rock jutting out from the walls, they had managed to start hacking out another tunnel. From the battlements above, Roger de Lacey spotted what was happening and ordered his own miners to dig a counter-tunnel, presumably so they could fight the enemies' tunnellers hand-to-hand below ground. But it was a risky tactic, as de Lacey soon discovered. Although the French king's miners were forced to stop their work before they had the chance to start a fire under the wall, all this burrowing in the foundations had done the job for them. The wall had been weakened, and with some more mighty barrages from *Caballus*, first a crack appeared, and then a broad section of the masonry toppled in another massive cloud of dust and grit. In the heat of the moment, de Lacey made a wrong call. He concentrated his men around the breach in the wall, expecting the enemy to pour through. He left the tunnel poorly guarded, and the French king's attackers rushed through it.

The sight that met them inside the inner ward was extraordinary. According to William the Breton, the defenders were so tightly crammed together and were so exhausted and demoralised that they couldn't even raise their arms to use their weapons. It was still possible at this point for de Lacey and his officers to retreat to the very last defensive refuge, the keep, the highest tower of all, within the inner ward. But it must have been clear that this would be futile. There was no chance of a relief force arriving from King John to rescue them in the brief time that supplies inside the keep would last. A few of the defenders did make a dash for the little postern gate on the north-western corner of the castle, but they were cut off before they could reach it.

There were just 140 defenders left within Château Gaillard. They all surrendered without much of a fight. Casualties in this last encounter within the inner ward amounted to only four wounded.

★★★

And so it was that the most unassailable castle in Europe, the brainchild of the finest military strategist of the day, failed at its first test, just five years after it was built. We could blame John. After all, if he hadn't given orders for a chapel to be built with windows on an outside wall, there would have been nowhere for Bogis's raiders to climb in. Arguably, that was what sealed the fate of Richard's 'fair daughter'. A Château Gaillard without the chapel windows, as Richard had designed it, might have held out until Philip's army melted away into the spring sunshine. We'll never know. But the real appeal of the theory is its irony. If it's correct, then it wasn't the evil character of King John – he of the 'Devil's Brood' – that lost him Gaillard and ultimately Normandy, but his devout religious faith, his insistence on somewhere for him and his men to say their daily prayers.

With the fall of Gaillard, the way was clear for King Philip Augustus of France to advance into Normandy. The French monarch soon took Rouen, its capital, and captured the rest of the region. The duchy of Normandy, united with the English crown since 1066, was lost. John, King of England, was no longer also Duke of Normandy. That title now belonged to the French king.

★ ★ ★

The loss of Normandy was one of those events – like the Battle of Hastings, Europeans' first sighting of America, the French Revolution – after which nothing would ever be quite the same again..

With Normandy no longer tied to England, the birth pangs of modern Englishness were first felt. When William, Duke of Normandy had conquered England in 1066, he regarded his new kingdom as a junior adjunct to his Norman heartland. And that attitude persisted among kings of England for the next 138 years. They were dukes of Normandy first. That tradition was dealt a lethal blow in 1204. Kings of England from now on would see England as their main power base. And gradually, over the centuries ahead, that perception spread down through the layers of English society, and the independent culture of an island nation took root.

That new outlook had an immediate, practical result. The French monarchy was now in control of territory only 22 miles away across the Straits of Dover. England was vulnerable to invasion. King John recognised that danger, and he put a significant part of his resources over the next decade into building fighting ships. The investment was to pay its first dividend just nine years after the fall of Gaillard, when – as we shall find out later on our journey – England would win its first great sea victory. The English naval tradition was born.

And 1204 was a hugely significant year in the story of Magna Carta too. For both John and the barons, the loss of Normandy was a violent push in the back that propelled them along the road to Runnymede. Both the king and many of his mightiest subjects now found themselves squeezed back into England and jostling for supremacy there. Most of the barons who recognised King John as their overlord had, until then, held estates both in England and in Normandy. The splitting of those lands and the hostility between John and Philip Augustus meant that each of those barons had to decide. Would he abandon his Norman holdings and hold on to his English lands? Or instead, would he let go of his English castles and territories and base himself in Normandy, so recognising the French king as overlord? Those who plumped for their English domains would be concentrating all their efforts on fortifying and safeguarding their remaining interests there. And of course the same applied to the king. Although John made some attempt to win back Normandy in the next few years, he too would be spending much more time in England than had his brother Richard or any other monarch before him. And what's more, with his power diminishing on the French side of the Channel, he would aggressively assert his authority in England. So, following 1204, the tug-of-war between the King of England and the English barons hotted up. That intensified struggle on English soil would ultimately lead the king's most powerful vassals to extract from him a charter limiting his rights and confirming their own, the Great Charter of Liberties, Magna Carta.

What most irked the barons during the years between Gaillard and Runnymede were the methods John employed to try to bring his mightiest subjects to heel. It was not the occasional brutality which drove some of them to rebellion – violence for political gain was a common tactic in the thirteenth century. It was more the unpredictability of John's actions that was unnerving. You never knew, as a baron, from one moment to the next, whether you were in the king's good books or whether he would suddenly turn ruinously against you. That was John's undoing.

The story of one baron's rise and bloody fall did more than all else to make his fellow magnates apprehensive for their own security. William de Briouze was a mighty man for a king to crush, a mini-king in his own right who held sway in the mountains and borderlands of South Wales. That's where we're going next.

8 THE MARCHES, SOUTH WALES

RULE BY VENDETTA

eauty in nature and violence in humans often seem to go hand in hand. The most tranquil or awe-inspiring stretches of landscape can turn out to have been the scene of bloodshed, suffering and brutality. Take the great national parks in the west of the USA; the Black Hills of Dakota, for instance. Today the Black Hills' tree-covered mountains and fiery sunsets are favourites with hikers and families of campers. But in the late nineteenth century, this was an unimaginably dangerous place, as the US army set about subduing the proud Sioux who had lived there for centuries. Each side slaughtered the other, and in the end, at Wounded Knee in 1890, the US cavalry massacred 300 old men, women and children.

Or, consider South Armagh, on the border of Northern Ireland and the Irish Republic. Its hedge-lined lanes and rolling sheep pastures are presided over by the peaceful dignity of hills which were immortalised in song, 'Where the Mountains of Mourne sweep down to the sea'. But during the Troubles in the second half of the twentieth century, South Armagh was where the most ruthless element of the Provisional IRA ruled almost unchallenged. The Provos of South Armagh killed 123 British soldiers and 42 policemen, while another 75 civilians met their deaths here in over 1,200 bombings and countless shootings.

There are lots of such places across the globe: The Khyber Pass in north-west India, Cuzco in Peru, Blood River in South Africa, the Falkland Islands in the South Atlantic – beautiful settings spattered through history with killing, havoc and terror.

So why have we often chosen to be at our most savage where nature is at its most glorious? The reason's simple. Places where warring tribes meet – and therefore shoot, stab and blow each other up – are frontier lands, usually remote and often mountainous. In other words, just the sort of spots where you don't find cities, and which – once the fighting has died down – sometimes even become treasures of natural heritage.

That's exactly what has happened in South Wales. Here today the mountain wilderness and sleepy valleys of the Brecon Beacons are protected as a national park and admired by those who love nature's uninterrupted grandeur. But during the reign of King John and throughout most of the Middle Ages, this place was part of the Welsh Marches, 'march' being an old word meaning border country. In this case, the Marches separated lands controlled by the English king from those where fiercely independent Welsh tribes ruled, or tried to.

England's medieval kings found Wales and its mountain lairs difficult to conquer and hold. Royal armies made frequent incursions and faced almost constant rebellion and guerrilla warfare from the Welsh, who had the advantage of knowing the *mynyddoedd* (mountains) and *cymoedd* (dales) like *gefn eu dwylo* (the backs of their hands). So for much of the time, the king had to make do with a policy of containment, i.e. just keep the enemy boxed up in the mountains. And he did this by establishing loyal barons in the Marches and by giving them free rein to do whatever it took to hold the Welsh at bay and if possible to drive them back towards the sea.

The marcher lords then were a law unto themselves. Their methods often amounted to unrestrained brutality. One of the most powerful of these baronial families of the march were the de Briouzes. They held the Brecon area and much of the surrounding lands as well. The family's head when John came to the throne was William de Briouze, the third of his family to hold that name, and it's his story that leads us to Magna Carta. A couple of examples of his methods will tell us a lot about life in the Welsh Marches, as well as about the character of de Briouze himself.

On Christmas Day in 1175, a number of tribal princes from the South Wales area arrived at the de Briouze base in Abergavenny Castle on the southern edge of the Brecon mountains. The Welsh leaders had come in peace. They had been invited by de Briouze to air their grievances with the aim of reaching an agreement following a period of protracted fighting. Some Welsh chiefs stayed away, distrusting de Briouze's motives. Among those who rode up to the castle on Christmas morning was one Seisyll ap Dyfnwal, Lord of Upper Gwent. He brought his elder son with him. Seisyll, his fellow princes and their bodyguards all laid down their weapons on arrival at the castle in a spirit of friendly negotiation. But once inside the fortified walls, they were set upon by de Briouze's men, who massacred the lot of them. De Briouze then mounted his horse and, with a troop of armed guards, rode to Seisyll's home at Llanover 5 miles away. There he murdered the Welshman's 7-year-old son, Cadwalladr, and took his wife prisoner. Her fate is not recorded.

This was no isolated episode. In 1197, de Briouze ordered another Welsh leader, Trahaearn Fychan, to be dragged by his feet behind a horse through the streets of Brecon before being hanged. His offence isn't known.

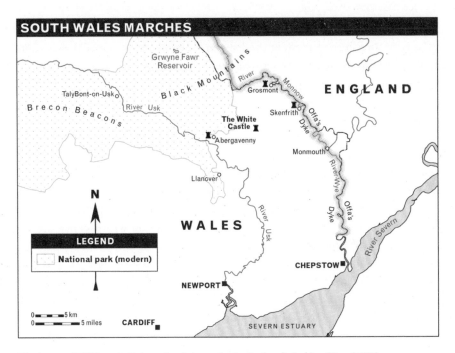

The heart of William de Briouze's mini-empire in the borderlands of South Wales.

But it's the ugly fate of de Briouze himself, a few years later, that brings us here to his South Wales heartlands. John was to hound him and his family to death. More than any other single factor, the king's treatment of William de Briouze, Lord of Brecon, Radnor and Abergavenny, is what made many of the other English barons fear for their own power and for their very lives, and turned them against John in the rebellion that led to Magna Carta.

★★★

Today, from the mound on the southern outskirts of Abergavenny, where the mournful grey ruins of de Briouze's castle still stand, you can look west up the valley of the River Usk to the mountains of the Brecon Beacons. There are two roads there. One flattish and filled with the noise and fumes of eighteen-wheeler container trucks heading for the port of Fishguard on the west coast of Wales. The other road on the opposite side of the valley is a half-forgotten route, occasionally touching the river bank or crawling through the middle of oversized villages, and that's the one we're taking.

Amid the scattered four-square stone cottages of Tal-y-Bont on Usk, there's a left turn. I swing the car into it, and soon start a steady climb. To the right, impenetrable woodland rises up the hidden hillside. To the left, there are glimpses of water, just visible through the prickly branches that scratch against the car as I try to avoid the odd tractor or camper van – kids waving in the side window – coming the other way.

As the trees thin out to the left, a lake is revealed stretching across the valley for a mile or more, and I pull off on a wider bit of the road and get out for a better look. There's a sudden shout in a rich Welsh accent, 'You can't be stopping there.' A young man in heavy boots and muddy yellow reflective jacket is clomping down the road towards me. 'They're cutting the trees, see,' he yells pointing over the road. His next words are drowned out by the sudden squeal of a motorised saw. Up above and opposite the lakeside, there's a clearing full of toppled trunks and heaps of branches. 'Dangerous,' he shouts over the din, and by raising his right arm then snapping it down in a mock crash he mimes the perils awaiting me if I lurk here.

So it's on to where I can park safely. The lake, according to the map, is man-made, a reservoir. But that doesn't matter, because what spreads before me is no less a classic view of tranquil nature, that could just as well be in the English Lake District, the state of Maine, or New Zealand's south island. There's no trace of humans to be seen. No dam wall, no jetty, no boat even, and across the other side of the water where a rounded mountain top – eroded smooth over billions of years – rises above a pine forest, there's no sign of a path or a house. On this side, there's a track leading down through knee-high grass to the water's edge. The surface glitters with needles of light. It's quiet here away from the tree fellers, the peace punctuated only by a sudden plop. Little circles ripple across the water, where a fish has dived. A pair of swans glide by, wings rounded, heads still.

The scene would be a cliché if you tried to paint it in oils or watercolours. But when you're part of it, watching it and feeling the breeze on your face, it gets inside you. If you walked this path every day of your life, you'd not get tired of it.

Further on, after I've explored a wide stream bubbling noisily over black pebbles, the terrain suddenly changes. The little road has weaved and climbed above the pine forest, struggling to throw off the last tree, and is now no more than a scratch on the landscape. It's open on both sides to moorland, flat boggy ground broken by tufts of wiry grass and humps of rock, that lure the eye slowly upwards to where the bare mountains rise even higher. A few thin sheep are busy grazing. The wind's picking up and it's a chill one. You wouldn't want to find yourself caught with a broken-down car up here late at night.

The mountains of the Welsh Marches, once you get beyond the gentle vistas of the lower valleys, are one of the remotest places in Britain. Apparently in 1211, King John's troops were pursuing the Welsh prince Llewelyn in the hills north of here. The men were stranded, without supplies, and were forced to kill and eat their horses. Not a hardship in terms of food quality, but a last desperate resort for a thirteenth-century knight whose steed was his most valued possession.

And there's been a more recent reminder of just how unforgiving these mountains can be. For the past few decades, the Brecon Beacons have been used as one of the main training grounds for Britain's toughest and fittest soldiers, the special forces of the SAS. In July 2013, three soldiers on an SAS selection test collapsed and died during hot weather on the mountain top a handful of miles west of where I'm standing now.

So the barrier formed by this beautiful wilderness was what made it so difficult for successive kings of England to conquer Wales, and what led them to install on the border semi-independent princelings with the freedom to be as ruthless as the job required.

✷ ✷ ✷

To be a marcher lord was to have power, and in the early years of his reign, John granted this privilege only to his most favoured and loyal barons. And that is exactly what William de Briouze became when John was crowned in 1199.

The first de Briouze had come over with William the Conqueror, but the family had remained minor aristocracy on the national scene. Small fish in a big pond. That changed under King John, who vested huge amounts of land in the third William de Briouze, including many castles and enough territory in the South Wales Marches to make him not only the most powerful baron in the area, but one of the greatest in the English realm too. In addition, the king granted him estates in Ireland, and arranged rich marriages for the many de Briouze children. It would probably be wrong to say there was a close friendship between the king and the now mighty baron. They were useful to each other. John wanted a ruthless lieutenant in southern Wales and elsewhere in his kingdom, and de Briouze needed royal patronage in order to fulfil his towering ambition. He repaid John's trust in him with a fierce loyalty, and was at the king's side throughout the bitter fighting in Normandy right up to when it was lost in 1204.

But by 1207, it was all starting to go wrong.

De Briouze suddenly found himself out of favour with the king. It's likely that John was beginning to regret that he hadd vested so much authority in one man, and to worry that the jumped-up magnate might be a threat to the crown. So he began to take back some of the lands he'd granted to him. He seized Glamorgan, the area of valleys immediately south of the Brecon Beacons, drove out de Briouze henchmen, and installed there instead one of the most trusted of his foreign mercenary soldiers, Falkes de Breauté.

Then, in 1208, John decided to break William de Briouze once and for all. Why? The most obvious reason can be found in a few words uttered by William's wife, Matilda. Words that took only seconds to utter, but whose echo could still be heard in the baronial tents at Runnymede seven years later.

John's favoured way of keeping a tight hold on any powerful subject whom he suspected might be treacherous was to demand he give up his children as hostages. With the lives of his treasured offspring at risk, no baron would dare betray the king. So John sent his messengers to de Briouze's base at Abergavenny Castle with instructions to bring his sons to the royal court. De Briouze's wife, Matilda, erupted in protective anger. She declared: 'I will not deliver up my sons to your lord, King John, because he basely murdered his nephew, Arthur, whom he ought to have kept in honourable custody.'

It was an outrageous accusation to utter in public, and all the more so because she had reliable inside knowledge. The one person – apart from John himself – who probably knew the truth was her husband, who had been there at Rouen with the king on the night of Arthur's death.

De Briouze quickly stepped in between his wife and the royal representatives to try and undo the harm. He chided his wife: 'You have spoken like a stupid woman against our lord, the king.' But he backed her up when he turned to the messengers and said: 'If I have offended him [the king] in any way, I am ready to make amends without the security of hostages according to the judgement of my fellow barons in his court, if he will fix a time and a place for my doing so.'

The king's men reported all this back to their master, who was beside himself with rage. He organised what amounted to a small army – 500 infantry and twenty-five mounted sergeants – commanded by the foreign mercenary Gerard d'Athée, and ordered them into the South Wales Marches. They were to take de Briouze, his wife and their children prisoner, and bring them before him. But de Briouze had been tipped off, and the mission failed to find him. With humourless irony, John ordered the ill-fated baron to foot the bill for the expedition sent against him.

The official justification put out by John for his vendetta against the de Briouze clan was that the baron had failed to pay his debts to the crown and had forcibly resisted the officers of the Exchequer when they tried to collect what was owed. But there is strong evidence that the true cause of John's vengefulness was in fact Matilda's outburst. When the baron tried to buy his way out of trouble, by offering the gigantic sum of 40,000 marks to recover the king's goodwill, John refused to negotiate any terms unless de Briouze first handed over his wife as prisoner.

By the autumn of 1208, de Briouze decided he had no alternative but to abandon his domains in the South Wales Marches. He fled with his wife and sons over the high mountain passes of the Brecon Beacons and on to the coast 60 miles away, where the family took ship for Ireland.

For eighteen months, John let them be. Then he raised a huge army – he called up all the feudal magnates of England and their men as well as several companies of Flemish mercenaries – and prepared to cross the Irish Sea to flush out de Briouze. Anticipating the attack, de Briouze slipped back to the mountains of South Wales, where there were still vassals loyal to him. He sent a message to John again seeking negotiations. The king turned him down flat. De Briouze, however, had made a grievous mistake. He had left his wife, Matilda and the children behind in Ireland. They managed to escape to Scotland. But they were spotted there and taken captive by a Scottish laird, who handed them over to royal agents.

At this point, with the guilty Matilda now in a royal jail, John agreed to meet de Briouze to discuss terms. The two men – each equally capable of the most merciless brutality – came face to face. The king's later version of events was that he had agreed a large payment from the baron in return for the freedom of his wife and children, and that de Briouze had then gone away to raise the money. But either this account is untrue or else de Briouze didn't trust the king to keep his word, because the baron fled to France 'in despair', it was said, and disguised as a beggar.

It was a humiliating end for a man who'd once held such untrammelled power. And 'end' it was. William de Briouze died in exile at Corbeil in France the following year, never to see his family again.

According to one chronicler:

> Matilda and her son William were imprisoned in Corfe Castle with a sheaf of oats and a flitch of bacon. After 11 days Matilda was found sitting upright between her son's knees and leaning against him, a dead woman. Her son too was dead, his cheeks gnawed by his mother in her anguish.

William de Briouze had never been popular with his fellow barons. He was too single-minded in his ambition for that. But his fate struck terror into the hearts of his peers. If the king could crush such a powerful nobleman, who had been a loyal servant of the crown, then surely no one was safe. To lose the king's 'goodwill' could spell ruin, ignominy and even death. The historian W.L. Warren has suggested that the one factor that can be singled out above all others as provoking the rebellion that led to Magna Carta was the fate of de Briouze and his family.

★★★

The Welsh Marches can also tell us about another thread in the story of Magna Carta – the rise of foreign mercenary captains who under John often replaced the barons in their traditional role as the king's lieutenants.

A few miles east of the Brecon Beacons is Offa's Dyke, the 177-mile-long earth rampart and ditch that had once separated Welsh tribes from the English. It was already 400 years old by John's time. Spanning the dyke is the Monnow Valley, a small relatively flat triangle of land that in the Middle Ages controlled the approaches to South Wales. The Normans built three castles here, Skenfrith, Grosmont and the White Castle, one at each corner of the valley. Known simply as the Three Castles, they were always kept together under the same stewardship to form a powerful block, difficult to penetrate from either side. It had been a mark of King John's trust in William de Briouze that he had given them to the baron in 1205. And it was a mark of how quickly that trust was reversed that he seized them back from de Briouze two years later.

But even more significant for our understanding of Magna Carta is what the king then decided to do with the Three Castles. He didn't grant them to another baron, to one of de Briouze's rivals, for instance. Instead, he put them in the hands of one of his most favoured mercenary soldiers, Gerard d'Athée. In other words, the key to the Marches of South Wales went not to some lord, powerful in his own right, but to a paid employee, whose life and livelihood depended entirely on the efficiency with which he executed the king's orders.

Today all three castles are open to the public. The best preserved of them is the White Castle, which is the most southerly of the three, close to Offa's Dyke. Where once marauders had to fight their way over earth ramparts there stands today a small wooden kiosk belonging to CADW, the Welsh Government's historic environment service. There's a chatty attendant, who'll explain that she has been doing this job for over twenty years and will also try to sell you a discounted Welsh rugby shirt.

The White Castle, so named because it used to have a white render covering its walls – rather impractical, you might think – has all the features which you want to find in a castle, and on a grand scale. It has a huge outer courtyard, with walls so high that your voice echoes from one end to the other. It has two sturdy, towering barbican gates where you can still see the slots for the portcullis. And it has a moat, deep, wide and still wet. But what's of most interest to us is the inner ward, like the one we saw at Château Gaillard, a high-walled fortress which in John's day – before the outer courtyard had been built – was the White Castle.

To appreciate its size and importance we need to climb the steep, narrow spiral stairway that leads to the top of one of its towers. The view from the top – all the way across to the Brecon Beacons – is sheer beauty to twenty-first-century eyes. To those of thirteenth-century soldiers, it would have been tactically useful. Attackers could be spotted miles away, giving time to raise drawbridges and prepare defences. And from up here, we can get an idea of the size of the castle in the early thirteenth century. The area enclosed by the curtain walls is big enough to hold the Wimbledon Centre Court complete with seating. The White Castle was a symbol of power as well as a military fact.

In a proclamation issued by King John in 1210, he describes how William de Briouze had mounted an assault to try and win back the Three Castles after they had been confiscated from him. We can't be sure of the accuracy of the king's account, but it does show the strategic importance of Skenfrith, Grosmont and the White Castle:

> After a short time when Gerard d'Athée [the mercenary commander], to whom we had granted the three castles, had requested the constables to come to receive their pay, which they did each month, William, realising that the constables were absent, attacked the castles with his sons and a crowd of his family and supporters; all three were besieged on the same day. When Gerard heard of these events he sent help to those areas as best he could and William was forced to flee from place to place and eventually fled to Ireland with his wife and sons and their families.

The use of mercenaries as the king's favoured fighting men was nothing new. We saw John's brother Richard the Lionheart relying on them more and more in times of war. But John's mercenary captains did a different job. He used them on home soil to control the country and its borders. What riled many of the barons was not only that John could crush such a powerful one of their number as William de Briouze, but that the king would then replace the nobility of the realm with common, paid foreigners, men like Gerard d'Athée. John required the royal proclamation, just quoted, to be witnessed by five earls and seven barons. That was really rubbing their noses in it. And six of those noble witnesses were among the leaders of the barons in the rebellion that led to Magna Carta.

Gerard himself died in 1213, two years before the Great Charter, but by then he had managed to get a pack of his relatives into political and strategic positions of power. The barons' rage was such that they got a special clause put into Magna Carta. Clause 50 reads:

> We [that is, King John] will remove completely from their offices the kins-men of Gerard de Athée, and in future they shall hold no offices in England. The people in question are Engelard de Cigogné, Peter, Guy, and Andrew de Chanceaux, Guy de Cigogné, Geoffrey de Martigny and his brothers, Philip Marc and his brothers, with Geoffrey his nephew, and all their followers.

The story of the Welsh Marches, the hunting down of William de Briouze and the rise of the foreign mercenaries tells us a lot about why the rebellious barons rose up against John. It was less because of his brutality. It was a brutal age. It was because, in the continual push and pull of power between the crown and the baronage, King John employed new – perhaps we might say 'unkingly' – strategies. He showed the barons he could destroy them at will. But more than that, he seemed to despise their noble right to high office. He sidelined them with his paid henchmen in a way that no king had done before him.

In our tale of kings and barons, it would be easy to overlook the other, non-baronial 99.9 per cent or more of the thirteenth-century population of England. The myth makers of Magna Carta were to claim that the document represented the birth of universal freedom of the citizen. So how did the common people fare under King John? And what did Magna Carta do, if anything, for them? To find out, we're going to a village in Nottinghamshire which is a unique anomaly. Its inhabitants – now in the twenty-first century – conduct their affairs as though they were still living in the days of King John.

'King John sealing the Magna Carta' by Ernest Normand, on display in London's Royal Exchange, represents the classic myth of 'bad' King John, the 'upright' barons and Magna Carta as the 'birth of democracy'.

The gatehouse of Ramsey Abbey in the fens of eastern England, turned into a fort by the bandit baron Geoffrey de Mandeville. From the top of this building, during the anarchy of the mid-twelfth century, de Mandeville's men could see an enemy approaching 10 miles away.

The ruins of Clarendon Palace, near Salisbury in Wiltshire. Here, the end wall of the great hall where in 1166 Henry II set out a reformed system of royal justice.

The port of Acre in northern Israel. In the twelfth century it was infamous for its street violence and sexual immorality. In 1191, it was also the scene of King Richard the Lion Heart's finest hour during the Third Crusade.

From the ramparts of old Angoulême, looking down on the modern city. In the thirteenth century, Angoulême controlled all surrounding roads. John's marriage here to Isabella in 1200 gave him a strategic advantage in the region, but also created enemies who years later would help destroy him.

Eleanor of Aquitaine's tomb at Fontevraud Abbey in France, alongside her second husband, King Henry II of England. Eleanor three times came out of retirement at Fontevraud to go to the aid of her son John. He in turn rescued his 80-year-old mother when she was besieged at Mirebeau. (© George H. Reader, reproduced by kind permission)

Château Gaillard was built by Richard the Lionheart to defend Normandy against the French king. When it fell in 1204, Richard's successor John lost Normandy, which had been tied to the English crown since 1066.

The view down from Château Gaillard's inner ward to the River Seine and the town of Les Andelys. In King John's day, the island was the mid-point of a bridge. The French forces stormed across it at the second attempt.

View of Château Gaillard from its southern tip. On the left are the remains of the chapel, added to the castle by King John. During the siege in 1204 the French 'special ops' team led by Bogis crawled up a waste gulley and entered the castle through one of the chapel's windows.

The mountainous borderlands of South Wales, known as the Marches. This beautiful area was the heart of territories controlled by William de Briouze, the baron who John first rewarded, then turned against and crushed.

The view from the White Castle towards the Brecon Beacon mountains. The White Castle was one of three forts that controlled the approach to the South Wales Marches. With marcher lord William de Briouze out of the way, John put his mercenary captains in charge here.

At the village of Laxton in Nottinghamshire, elected jurymen hammer in stakes to mark the boundary between two farmers' strips of land. The medieval open field system, still followed at Laxton today, was already 200 years old by the time King John came here. (Photo: Joy Allison, © Laxton History Group, reproduced by kind permission)

King John hunting, from a fourteenth-century illuminated manuscript. The monk who painted it had a sense of humour. The king's horse has a delighted smile on its face. The rabbits don't seem to know if they're coming or going. John, like most medieval monarchs, loved the chase, and one of the attractions of Laxton for him was that it was in good hunting country.

Steep Hill in the old city of Lincoln. In the Middle Ages this was the heart of the commercial quarter. Cities and towns like Lincoln gained a remarkable level of freedom, usually by buying a charter from the king. They sided with the barons in John's reign, and as a reward had their privileges confirmed in Magna Carta.

The Jew's House, Lincoln. This is the oldest small domestic building still occupied in Europe, pre-dating King John by at least fifty years. Jews in towns like Lincoln were outcasts and subject to persecution, but performed a valuable role as moneylenders to all from kings to candlemakers.

Warfare at sea, from a thirteenth-century illustration. King John spent part of his resources building a navy. In 1213, at the Battle of Damme, the French were beaten and England won its first sea victory.

The church at Bouvines in northern France. Its twenty-one stained-glass windows depict the 1214 battle which decided the fate of three empires.

The old Roman road leading east from Bouvines village. During the battle here in 1214, the opposing armies both straddled the ancient road. This would have been the view (without the power cables) for King Philip Augustus in the middle of the French front line.

Stained-glass window in Bouvines church showing King Philip Augustus of France knocked from his horse. The blue and yellow of the king's surcoat merges with his steed's 'caparison', the horse's coat in its rider's colours. The violence and confusion of battle are startlingly captured in the vigour of the design.

The memorial to Magna Carta on the side of Cooper's Hill overlooking the meadow at Runnymede. It was paid for by 9,000 American lawyers and erected in 1957. The exact site of the Great Charter's birth is probably a mile or more to the east of here.

The British Library – where two of the original 1215 Magna Cartas are kept – on London's Euston Road with the Victorian wizardry of St Pancras railway station popping up behind.

The better preserved of the two original copies of Magna Carta held in the British Library. The text was written in abbreviated Latin and was not divided up into clauses; that was done later by historians. The ink was a mix of soot and oak gall, a natural acid that etched the writing into the parchment.

The vast mudflats of the Wash on the east coast of England at low tide. It is easy to see how in 1216 King John's baggage train, on a foggy morning and without a local guide, could get lost in terrain like this. The heavily laden packhorses and carts soon sank and the men attempting a rescue were sucked down with them.

Worcester Cathedral. The mortal remains of King John – the man the Victorians thought so vile that he would even befoul hell – lie beneath the tomb in the foreground, in hallowed position before the altar steps.

The Court of the King's Bench in Westminster Hall around 1460. Beneath the five judges in their scarlet robes, the record-keepers are getting through the parchment. The accused in the middle – you can almost see his knees trembling – stands between the advocates, one in green, one in blue. In the foreground, a dissolute bunch of manacled prisoners await their turn. The bar that two of them are leaning on gave its name to barristers.

Ranger Jerome Bridges making a dramatic point about the tribulations suffered by the first settlers at Jamestown, Virginia.

The *Susan Constant*, an exact replica of one of the three vessels that arrived in the James River estuary in 1607 bringing the first Englishmen to make a permanent settlement in America.

The central hall of the US National Archives building, known as the Rotunda for the Charters of Freedom, in Washington DC. It houses the Declaration of Independence, the Constitution and the Bill of Rights. The reverential way in which they are displayed reflects the American tradition of trusting in the written word to protect their liberties. Magna Carta is regarded in the US as the bedrock of justice and freedom. (Photo courtesy of US National Archive)

Both the state flag and state seal of Virginia show the figure of Virtue stepping on the breast of Tyranny. Being alert to the threat of tyranny is a constant theme in American political life. Magna Carta is seen as the most ancient safeguard. (Library of Congress)

9 LAXTON, NOTTINGHAMSHIRE, ENGLAND

THE SERFS IN THE FIELDS

We are the common people.

Some of us are arriving on foot in stout boots and thick socks. Others on wheels. A clapped out Ford Fiesta, and a small blue van, with 'Jack Greene, Time Traveller. Living History For Schools & Museums' on its side. Jack himself has a Farmer Giles hat, owl glasses, combat jacket, and, separating the last two items, a full set of snow-white whiskers. A shiny blue Volvo draws up. Out of it steps a dog, a brown and cream cocker spaniel. It gives the rest of us a scornful look, and, with what I'd swear is a sigh, allows its owner, a woman in dark green Barbour and headscarf, to fix a lead round its neck. A small boy and girl dart about playing tag, apparently parentless until a large man in a red bobble hat and a bulky camera bouncing on his chest calls them to heel. We stamp our feet and tell each other how cold it is. We adjust our hiking sticks and clean the lenses of our binoculars. In total, there are fifteen of us. I'm guessing that we're none of us queens, earls, countesses or even knights – the odds are against it. We're the common people.

We're gathering in the car park of the Dovecote Inn in the village of Laxton in north Nottinghamshire, and we've come here to learn about our medieval forebears, not specifically our family ancestors, but the ordinary folk, who – like us today – made up all but a small slice of the population. We're doing this because, unlike those ancestors, we're well educated and want to know about our past, and because, unlike them, we have enough spare time and cash to be free from work for the day. And of course we can travel freely out of the place where we live, something that most of the common people of Laxton in the thirteenth century couldn't do. We're not slaves, however much we may complain about the boss on a Monday morning. Our pet dogs don't have to have their front claws pulled out. We can carry a bow and arrows (if the mood should take us). And if someone robs or cheats us we can get justice in a royal court. We're not forced to pay out huge, regular sums to the Pope or the local vicar. And if we accidentally run over a deer on a dark night driving home, we probably won't be punished by having one of our legs chopped off.

And here's another difference. If we fifteen modern-day common people, stamping our feet here today in the pub car park, happen to be a statistically typical cross-section of England's population in the twenty-first century, only three of us will actually have our homes in a village or out in the countryside. In the early thirteenth century, it would have been more like thirteen or fourteen out of every fifteen people who lived and worked in – and probably never in their lives stepped outside of – some little agricultural community like Laxton.

So why have we chosen Laxton to learn about country life for our ancestors in the time of King John? It's because the village is unique. Laxton is the only place in the whole of Europe where people still farm and govern their working lives much as folk did at the time of Magna Carta. I say 'much as' because of course, as you might guess, not everything is the same now in Laxton as it was 800 years ago. But enough of it is unchanged to make the village an extraordinary place, worthy of a visit by anyone with a curious mind, not just by someone like me who's investigating the story of the Great Charter of 1215. And Laxton, as it happens, has a special link with King John. He was Laxton's landlord, and he made it the administrative centre for Sherwood Forest (home, of course, to Robin Hood and his mythical band of outlaws), where he liked to hunt. And the villagers of Laxton knew at first hand what it was like to suffer the king's wrath.

✷✷✷

You could easily drive through Laxton, remark what a charming little spot it seems, and not notice anything special about it. Like most pretty English villages, it has its comfortable-looking pub, a patently old church, and plenty of houses built before the age of planning regulations. And the place is small enough that from almost every point in its little streets you can see fields – some cultivated, others where sheep are grazing – and beyond, atop long, gently rising hills, trees grouped in stands and coppices.

But if you stop the car near the church, get out and take a walk, you'll notice something odd about the buildings. Many of them seem to be farmhouses. By this, I don't mean that they used to be farmhouses which have been converted into five-bedroom residences for retirees from London or Birmingham and have names like Old Glebe Farm or Corn-thrasher House. No, these farmhouses have muddy farmyards alongside them with heaps of hay, cowpats and grimy battered tractors. Now, the occasional working farmhouse, complete with barn and other outbuildings, in the middle of an English village isn't unusual. But what you won't find elsewhere are farms in the kind of numbers there are in Laxton. There are no fewer than fourteen farms plus five smallholdings which have their central build-ing right here in the village. It's a medieval phenomenon. Most villages looked like this in the Middle Ages. It was only later, around the time of Elizabeth I, that it became usual for farmhouses to be built in more isolated spots.

The system by which people lived and farmed in villages like Laxton – and the system which Laxton's farmers still work by today – was already at least 300 or 400 years old by the time of Magna Carta. Medieval peasant farmers – while owing allegiance, and much else, to the local landowner – scraped a living from the soil alongside other peasants in the village. Together, they divided up the village's common farmland into strips, and then each farmer got a share of them, not all in one place, but scattered, one up the hill, one in the valley, one by the wood, and so on. That way, everyone had a fair proportion of the most fertile soil as well as of the more barren, rocky or badly drained land. And at those times of year when land could be used for grazing animals, they shared that too. And because their working lives were so interlocked, they had to have rules about what each could do, everything from the type of crops they sowed, when to plough and harvest, or who could put their pigs, cows, sheep and goats in which field. So they had their own court of law to settle disputes and to fine those who overstepped the mark and broke the rules.

It would be a mistake to see this as an idyllic democratic collective, as some sort of medieval kibbutz. In fact, each man worked his own land. But because so many decisions had to be taken in common, there had to be a degree of co-operation among local farmers in the thirteenth century which is unknown today – except here in Laxton, of course.

The system started to fall apart in Tudor times, when the landowners began to drive their tenant farmers off the common land so that they could enclose it with fences and hedges in order to absorb it into their own large farms. The last remaining medieval farmers had been driven off to the towns by the time Queen Victoria came to the throne in 1837, and all that was left were their ghosts. Ghosts that still haunt the landscape today. They're all over the midlands coun-tryside. Look alongside the M40 motorway as you speed through Oxfordshire or Warwickshire, and you'll see them: long lines of parallel humps and dips on the surface of the fields. They're the vestiges of the old strips of land, ridges and fur-rows, once ploughed, harrowed, sown and harvested by strip farmers, year after year, for thirty generations.

By pure fluke, the system has survived in one, and only one, English village: Laxton. During all those centuries when everywhere else was being enclosed, Laxton's land was split between several owners. They couldn't agree about anything, never mind about who should fence off which bit. So Laxton's tenant farmers kept their heads down, quietly got on with their seasonal rounds, and the result was that their anachronistic way of life continued below the radar of the developing industrial age. By the mid-twentieth century, the village and its surrounds were in the hands of a single landowner, Lord Manvers. He appreciated the historic value of the place, and began to worry that on his death, the place and its open fields might be sold off and end up no different from every other rural community in England. The threatened loss of this astonishing little piece of medieval England prompted him to make over the estate to the Ministry of Agriculture, to be held on behalf of the nation in perpetuity. Then in the 1980s, Laxton's heritage again came under threat. It got caught up in Margaret Thatcher's drive to sell off the family silver, and its open fields were put up for auction. But a benevolent buyer was found, and Laxton acquired its present-day landlord. Or rather, landlady. The queen. To be strictly accurate, Laxton was bought by the Crown Estates. And as result, its fields and its farmers are now protected species. For the moment anyway.

★ ★ ★

Our guide arrives in the Dovecote Inn car park. He's a stocky chap with the sort of ruddy face you get only by spending all day in all weathers outside. He introduces himself as Stuart Rose, and he touches his John Deere baseball cap in a mock salute. He explains that his family, along with the other nineteen farm families in the village, still sow, plough and harvest in strips, just as their ancestors did. Stuart's own personal ancestors, it turns out, weren't originally commoners at all. In the year 1500, one Humphrey Roos made a shrewd marriage, and thereby became lord of Laxton. His son and grandson each inherited the title and the lands, and lived blameless lives as country squires. Then the family's fortunes took a dive. The next master of Laxton, Peter Roos, ran up huge debts, his daughter committed bigamy with a servant, and following a costly court case the Rooses went bankrupt. Peter's descendants, though, stayed on in Laxton, scraping a living from a small farm. Over the years, the name Roos shifted its spelling and became Rose. And so Stuart Rose, our guide, might – if his ancestor had behaved himself – have been lord of Laxton today. Instead, he's a commoner, like the rest of us.

Our tour starts in the Visitor Centre, a brick barn at one end of the pub car park. The fifteen of us, plus the dog, crowd in and settle ourselves on benches around the edge of the little room. Our introduction to Laxton is going to be a video. Stuart sticks a couple of pound coins into a slot on the wall and the TV screen in the corner changes from black to hailstorm. The film was made over thirty-five years ago, so we have to make allowances for its primitive cine-technique (though, like much else in Laxton, age adds charm to the experience). Its story, however, is unchanged today.

At first we see a grainy picture of trees and hedges, and the soundtrack kicks in with a two-finger version of *All Among the Barley* on a chapel harmonium. Then a crackly voice explains that farming here is governed by a medieval court known as the Court Leet. It's a court of law, established by act of parliament.

The Laxton Court Leet still meets each autumn, just as it has — without interruption — for the past thousand years. These days the judicial session is presided over, in a corner of the Dovecote Inn and with due formality, by the queen's representative, who in our film is a local solicitor (balding, specs, pinstriped suit and antiquated vowels, 'Weel, nyow, lits stort, shell wi?').

The Bailiff — one, Edmund Rose, who turns out to be Stuart's uncle — then announces to the assembled masses of the saloon bar:

> Oyez! Oyez! Oyez! All manner of persons who owe suit and service to the Court Leet of the Queen's Most Excellent Majesty and the Crown Estate Commissioners on behalf of her Majesty now to be holden, or who have been summoned to appear at this time and place, draw near and give your attendance, every man answering to his name when called, and thereby saving his amercement. God save the Queen and the Lord of this Court Leet!

The amercement is a fine. If anyone who should draw near doesn't when called, he'll have to pay. Twopence was the traditional sum — a stout encouragement to turn up in days gone by, but hardly the main incentive these days.

Next, the film shows the court electing a jury of twelve farmers from the village, each of whom, with care and reverence, kisses the Bible. The twelve then put on their flat caps and climb into the back of a hay cart hitched to a tractor, parked outside the pub. And in this style they set off to tour the wheat field of Laxton. The men trudge through the mud, and we see them scratching heads and gesticulating, as the commentary explains that they're investigating whether anyone has, maliciously or accidentally, encroached on his neighbour's strip of land. The members of the jury then hammer sticks, the length of a man's leg, into the ground to mark the boundaries between each farmer's allotted strip. If anyone has ploughed where he wasn't supposed to, the jury reports him to the Court Leet, which has the legal power to levy a fine at a level the jury thinks appropriate. The film ends with an idyllic scene of hedges and fields played out by the chapel harmonium again.

✯ ✯ ✯

Stuart rounds us up and leads us off on our walking tour. The route takes us out of the village along a narrow trackway, to see for ourselves the strips of farmland that make Laxton so special. At first sight, the cultivated fields don't look much different from fields anywhere in the country.

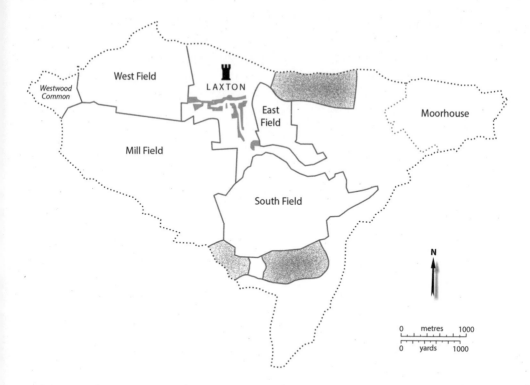

The four fields where Laxton's farmers still organise their seasonal rounds just as their ancestors did in King John's day.

Stuart explains: 'Each of us farmers has a share of the West Field here. Each man has his own strips.' He points with his gnarled walking stick. 'Look just there, you can see the posts that the jurymen have hammered into the ground to mark the boundaries, and running the length of the field is a small gap where no crops have been sown, to separate the two strips in front of us.'

The man with the camera round his neck asks why there's no sign of the old ridges and furrows.

'They were the result of horse-drawn ploughing,' explains Stuart. 'The old ploughshares always turned the earth over to the right, so if you ploughed up one way and back down the other, the soil got heaped up in the middle. And if you do that year after year, you eventually get a long mound of earth with troughs at the side. And that's very useful. You'll notice the old ridges and furrows nearly always run down hill, and that's because the furrows drain the water away. Today, I'm afraid, even here at Laxton, we don't use a horse and plough any more. We've got tractors and modern ploughs that can be reset to turn the earth either to left or right, and that's why the land stays flat.'

Running along the edge of the West Field is a lumpy, uncultivated grassy verge 20 or 30 feet wide. This, we learn, is called a 'syke', pronounced 'sick', an old word for land that's either too steep or too 'clarty' (that's thick and sticky, for the benefit of non-Laxtonians) to be cultivated. The ploughman was allowed to use it to turn his horse around at the end of each furrow. Or else a farmer, then as now, could keep livestock on it at those times of year when there weren't crops the animals could wander off and eat.

A lark is skittering high notes somewhere above us, but I can't see it against the dark grey clouds. Jack, the bewhiskered time traveller, touches my elbow and points up. 'There,' he says, 'See it?'

Stuart, who has overheard, explains, 'There are over eighty breeding pairs in this one field alone. The skylarks love the open fields because there aren't hedges to hide any predators.'

★ ★ ★

This, however, is only part of the story of medieval Laxton. We shouldn't imagine from Stuart's account that country life at the time of Magna Carta was some sort of happy valley of families working in well-regulated harmony to produce bountiful supplies of food. In every age, the life of those who work on the land has been hard. But in the early thirteenth century, in addition to the natural calamities of foul weather, failed harvests and murrain (the numerous unidentified diseases to which farm animals were prey), most folk in Laxton and in other villages across England were also subjected to the constant, severe, unpredictable and sometimes cruel demands of their masters.

The 90 per cent of ordinary English folk who lived in the countryside fell into three groups. The best-off were the freemen, tenant farmers who paid rent to the lord of the manor. Then came the villeins, also tenant farmers, but who had to work – unpaid – for up to three days a week for the lord. Then the lowest of the low were the cottars, who might have a little bit of land to help support the family, had to work – again unpaid – on the lord's land, but otherwise could earn a day's wage labouring for a villein or a freeman. You'll notice that it's free*men* not women. The law at this time hardly recognised the existence of this half of the population.

The big divide was between the freemen and the rest. The freemen had a degree of independence from the lord of the manor as well as certain legal rights. The villeins and the cottars had no such rights and were little better than agricultural slaves. The women were adjuncts of slaves. The term villein, incidentally, gave later generations the word 'villain', which tells us a lot about the low esteem in which they were held by the elite establishment of kings, barons, lawyers and bishops. In a place like Laxton there would have been very few freemen, a handful at most.

So, given that 90 per cent of the population lived in the countryside, and that most of them were villeins, cottars or women, you can see that the overwhelming proportion of our ancestors were unfree serfs. So what did that mean?

As well as working on the lord's own land for part of every week if you were a villein, a cottar, or one of their wives or children, you'd also have to help out on the lord's farm at busy times in the farming calendar, such as sowing and harvesting – all unpaid of course. Then, in addition, on those red-letter days that happen in every family you'd have to make a payment to the lord of the manor. So, for instance, you'd need to buy a licence from him when any of your daughters got married, or when you wanted to send your son to school, and even if you decided to sell one of your cows. When you died, the lord took your best beast, and your heir had to make another payment before he could take over the farm. If there were only a daughter to succeed, then the lord claimed the right to choose her husband for her, and he would normally offer the woman's hand to the highest bidder. And just in case all this was not enough, the lord had the right to 'tallage' you at will; in other words, he could tax you without excuse whenever the mood took him. It was economic, and to a degree social, servitude.

As an ordinary unfree farmer or labourer, you were the chattel of your lord, a possession he could use as he wished – with the generous exception of murdering you or beating you up so badly that you were disabled for life. You were not allowed to carry a weapon. Your lord could sell your land, and you and your family along with it, whenever he wished.

And the miseries of all those on the lowest perch of Laxton's hierarchy didn't end there. The church taxed you ruthlessly as well. All peasant farmers had to pay 'churchscot' to support the parson, and 'Romescot' to keep the Pope in the manner which was thought fitting. You had to give the parson hens at Christmas and eggs at Easter. When a villein died, his widow or heir not only had to pay the lord, but also the church to get him buried. But the most crippling burden was the tithe. As a peasant farmer, you were obliged to give one tenth of your produce to the church. That wasn't just the crops you harvested, but everything else as well: lambs and their wool, cheese, butter, fruit and honey.

✷ ✷ ✷

In addition to all this, the people of Laxton, like many countryside communities, had an extra burden to carry on their already hard-pressed shoulders. The evidence is still here today, and that's what Stuart shows us next. We climb a gentle slope past the old threshing barn. At the top of the hill, beyond the cricket field and its battered corrugated iron pavilion, the land looks as though some ancient giant baker has kneaded and thumped it like dough into banks, hillocks, humps and hollows. These strange formations are the remains of Laxton's once mighty castle, a building that would have needed continual – and expensive – repair and maintenance. And much of that work and cost ended up having to be borne by the villagers as well.

Laxton's first castle was built soon after the Norman Conquest in 1066. It was radically extended in the century before Magna Carta when the lord of Laxton was one Robert de Caux. He was appointed Hereditary Keeper of the Forests of Nottinghamshire and Derbyshire, a vast area of woodland later known as Sherwood Forest. De Caux's new role was an important part of the royal administration, and he rebuilt the castle in a much more opulent style. Today, when we climb to the top of the highest of the hillocks – the site of the motte, the word we encountered back at Mirebeau, that is the castle's most defensible fortress tower – we can see laid out below us the complex plan of banks and ditches which were the site of de Caux's palisade wall and moat. Here and there, hawthorn bushes sprout at crazy angles. One of the banks is now punctured with holes big enough to put your foot into. 'Badger setts,' explains Stuart. 'We're plagued with them here.'

Although the peasant farmers of Laxton in the early 1100s would not have had to bear the whole cost of extending the castle, it was inevitable that the de Caux family would turn to their tenants for at least part of the cash and labour needed.

And the castle's importance was not just military. It had to be equipped with kitchens, stables, bedchambers and halls because the king and his entourage might turn up here at any moment and expect to be fed, watered, wined and entertained for however long the monarch decided to stay. The big attraction of Laxton for John was the nearby forests, where he could indulge in his favourite pastime, hunting. In 1204, when he had just lost Normandy and his attention was concentrated back in England, he cemented his link with the place by taking Laxton's castle into his own hands. We get an intriguing glance into one of his visits from the records of the time. In 1213, two years before Magna Carta, he arrived here with Queen Isabella. According to the expense accounts, the King required 'six boarhounds and eight greyhounds', plus a 'veltrarius' – the man in charge of the dogs – and 'two tuns of wine'. This is around 500 imperial gallons (625 American gallons). It's tempting to imagine the royal couple threw one hell of a party during their stay, since there would have been enough wine for every courtier plus every man, woman and child in the village to knock back the equivalent of half a dozen bottles each. But a more likely explanation is that the royal butler was stocking up for the weeks ahead.

Living in a place like Laxton where the king could relax and enjoy himself did not imply any kind of royal favouritism. In 1207, the people of Laxton had to scrape together a fine of £100 'to have the King's peace and to spare their village from being burnt to the ground'. The records don't show what the folk of Laxton had done wrong to merit having all their homes put to the torch. But we may assume that at least part of the fine was met by another tax on the peasant farmers.

* * *

Today, from the top of the old castle hill, we can see cultivated fields for 20 or 30 miles to the north and east, broken only by the odd clump of trees. To the west, Laxton's sykes and strips spread before us like a counterpane. In John's day, Laxton and its little farms would have looked like a large clearing in Sherwood Forest. In many ways, life within the royal forests nearby could be even grimmer than it was for the farmers and labourers in the village itself. The forests had their own laws, mostly designed to stop anything which might in any way interfere with the king's pleasure in chasing and killing deer and wild boar. It was bad enough that the poorest forest dwellers couldn't supplement their meagre diet by killing any of the animals the king might wish to hunt and that their dogs, for instance, had to be 'lawed' – that is, have their front claws pulled out so they couldn't be used for poaching. But in addition, the commoners were also banned from cutting trees for firewood or for building material.

The royal officials who policed the forests and ran its courts weren't paid. They were expected to 'live off the land', which meant they were permitted to extort from the forest people in their area as much cash, corn and meat as bullying, threatening and physically abusing could deliver. It was an officially sanctioned reign of terror; even even the officially sanctioned methods used to enforce the forest laws themselves were little short of Stalinist. At Maidford in Northamptonshire, 80 miles south of Laxton, during the summer of 1209, the king's foresters patrolling the woods came across the severed head of a deer. To kill a royal beast was a dire offence that could be punished by having an arm or a leg chopped off. The royal officials summoned all the menfolk of Maidford to an extraordinary court of inquisition and demanded they name the culprit. Whether the villagers didn't know or wouldn't tell isn't recorded. It didn't matter to the royal foresters. Their vengeance was terrible. Everything the villagers of Maidford owned, all their crops and livestock, what little money they might have made from selling their produce, their cooking pots, even their ploughs and other farm tools, in short – as the royal records state – 'the whole of the aforesaid village of Maidford was seized into the king's hand.'

It has been estimated that by the end of John's reign, around one third of England was royal forest, including for example the whole county of Essex. John, like his brother and his father before him, was notorious for his woodland land-grabs. The barons regarded this as an abuse of royal power, and with Magna Carta, they tried to take back some of the forests seized into royal hands. Not through any charitable sympathy for the plight of the common people who lived there, but because they themselves were losing their own right to exploit and abuse these lowly folk.

***

The little village of Laxton, with its castle, was disproportionately important because it was the king's administrative centre for Sherwood Forest stretching 50 miles to the south and west. But at the same time it was typical of most small farming communities in the early thirteenth century with its peasant families working together on their strip farms in the open fields.

The fact that this system is still practised in the twenty-first century in this one village – though of course without the near-slavery, arbitrary fines and punishment by mutilation – is extraordinary. As Stuart leads us back along Laxton's main street past the rows of working farmhouses, I catch up with him and ask why he carries on farming in this way. It can't be a profitable way of life, surely?

'You're right,' he says, 'It's hard to make a living, what with having your land scattered, one bit maybe a mile or two from another. None of us in Laxton can get by just from farming. Take me for example. As well as working my farm, I'm a qualified agricultural engineer as well. And it only works for us because we get grants.' I give him a quizzical look. 'From the European Union,' he adds. 'It's 30 per cent of my income.' So why does he carry on? 'Well,' he replies, 'how could I not do it, when this is what my ancestors have done on this very same land for so many generations? I suppose it's in my blood.'

The tour is at an end, and Stuart invites us all to join him in the Dovecote Inn. Jack, the time traveller, says he'll buy him a pint, and the chap with the fancy camera says we'll all want that privilege. We laugh and troop into the bar, home of the Court Leet.

Now, beer was something that suffered no shortage here in Laxton back in the days of King John. The water supply was unreliable and often polluted, so everyone – children included – slaked their thirst with ale. And in between all that ploughing and sowing, and paying tithes and taxes, and avoiding the royal wrath, there were – it's a relief to discover – times when ale consumption was upped beyond the everyday quota. Merrymaking in Laxton was usually associated with Christian festivals or even ancient pagan rites: Christmas, May Day, Midsummer. The excuse was to call upon saints, or ancient gods, to deliver a rich harvest, and to thank them when they did. There would have been wrestling, cock-fighting, skating in winter and maybe even a game of competitive scrambling to see who could kick the head of a slaughtered goat (or *foteballe*, as it became known two centuries later).

So was there anything in Magna Carta that protected what *we* would call the 'human rights' of the peasant farmers and labourers of Laxton? Not a lot, I'm afraid. The Great Charter of 1215 decreed that royal justices should not fine a villein so heavily that he lose all his crops. An act of kindness on the part of the barons? No way. The barons were concerned that the king would strip the peasants bare before the lords themselves could milk them dry. And the handful of freemen in the village were on the winning side again. Magna Carta granted them the right not to be punished without a proper legal process. The villeins, cottars and women, with their near slave status, who made up the overwhelming proportion of the population, were given no such right. Their harsh lives – made no easier by Magna Carta – give the lie, perhaps more than anything else in thirteenth-century England, to the myth that the document laid down a universal right to freedom. It did achieve many things we can be proud of. But common people back then gained little from the Great Charter of 1215.

But if life in Laxton was typical of 90 per cent of English people back then, what about the 10 per cent whose homes weren't in the countryside, and who lived in towns or cities?

From the top of the old castle mound on the edge of Laxton, you can see on the horizon the towers of Lincoln Cathedral 20 miles away. Today, Lincoln is a modest place with some splendid old buildings. Back in the thirteenth century, it was England's third-wealthiest city, a thriving centre for trade. Its story is very different from that of Laxton.

10 LINCOLN, LINCOLNSHIRE, ENGLAND

THE SMELL OF MONEY

Steep Hill. It reads like a road traffic sign on a mountain pass in Wales or the Scottish Highlands. But it's not. It's neither a warning (though it ought to be), nor is this an isolated spot. Steep Hill here is the name of a narrow cobbled street that swerves and tumbles its way down through the middle of the ancient city of Lincoln. So Steep Hill – like London's Park Lane or New York's Broadway – is descriptive, although if the people of medieval Lincoln had wanted to be accurate, they'd have called it 'Precipitous Hill' or even 'Breakneck Hill'. I've no evidence that anyone has ever actually broken their neck skidding down Lincoln's Steep Hill, but it seems likely, especially if you imagine it sheeted in winter ice. Some of the ancient stone and half-timbered buildings that front on to it – mostly now shops, art galleries and cafés – start as two storeys at their upper end but are close to three storeys a few yards later.

This morning, Steep Hill is thronged with tourists, taking photos, buying souvenirs, searching out the best place for coffee and cake, or simply scaling the heights with dogged plodding steps to reach the top. Up there to the left, Lincoln Castle's walls, moss-grey and pock-marked, stand high above us, and to the right the triple towers of the city's magnificent cathedral rise behind a stone archway. On the corner is a pub – 'Curry and a drink only £6.75. You will be ready for a drink after the climb!' chalked on a board outside. As it happens, the pub is called *The Magna Carta*. Lincoln Castle is home to one of only four surviving copies of the 1215 Great Charter (at least thirteen were made at the time), though you'll be lucky to see it here because it's often – as now – away on loan to some institution in the United States.

Steep Hill and the old city of Lincoln exude the requisite quaintness and gentility that goes with such places. But Lincoln's ancient narrow streets have something more substantially historic about them. Several of their buildings date back to at least fifty years before King John sealed Magna Carta. They were what we might call middle-class homes, lived in by businesspeople. And that's what set city life in the thirteenth century apart from the rest of the country. Cities and towns were like oases in the middle of a feudal desert. On the one hand, in rural England, the common people – like those in Laxton – were almost slaves at the bottom of a hierarchical pyramid, with every man owing allegiance and obligations to the lord above him, right up to the king who sat at the apex. On the other hand, in cities like Lincoln, trade more than tradition ruled. Those who earned a living here did so by buying and selling, importing and exporting, by charging interest on loans, or simply by earning a wage in return for their skills or their strength. Towns and cities still had to pay taxes to the king; nevertheless they did very well for themselves under John, and they were beginning to govern their own affairs.

We should not, however, be fooled into thinking of medieval Lincoln as some sort of island of modernity. If we were transported by time machine back to Steep Hill in the early thirteenth century and were told to get on with our lives here, we'd be in for a few shocks. Four things would hit us among all the other alien encounters. The disease. The dogs. The fires. And the violence.

The disease, because there were no sewers. Bodily waste – both human and animal – as well as household rubbish, which, long before the over-packaging we suffer from today, consisted almost entirely of rotted food, often found its way into the gutters. Cholera, dysentery and probably E. coli were rife as well as other sicknesses which thirteenth-century Lincoln citizens couldn't name, never mind treat. The smell would perhaps be the first thing we would notice, not just from the putrefaction in the streets, but also from the stench of the leather tanneries and the animal slaughter yards.

Dogs, because among the terrors that medieval townsfolk had to brave when they went out at night were the feral domestic animals, abandoned by their owners and now scavenging the streets in packs.

Fires, because – at a time when many houses were built of wood, mud and straw, when fire brigades were unheard of, and centuries before the invention of smoke alarms, enclosed ovens and central heating – houses caught fire with devastating regularity. And in thirteenth-century Lincoln, as in other towns at that time, if a spark in your neighbour's home flew out from beneath a cooking pot into a bale of dry wool, before you knew it, yours and half the houses in your tight-packed little street would be burning, and there was not much anyone could do about it. A fire in 1141 badly damaged Lincoln's cathedral; scores of widespread fires were reported in London during this period. The one in 1212 was said have spread so fast that it outpaced a running man, and 3,000 Londoners perished.

The most constant peril, though, came from your fellow human beings. We in the twenty-first century have grown used to depressing statistics about the levels of violent crime in some of our gangland-dominated inner cities. But life in thirteenth-century Lincoln might have shocked even the most hardened of today's city cops. Already on our visit to Clarendon Palace we had cause to mention Lincoln's crime record. But it's worth spelling out in more detail. In 1202, one judicial session here dealt with 114 murders, 89 robberies (most with violence), 65 woundings and 49 rapes as well as numerous other more minor offences. And Lincoln's population was only around 7,000–8,000 at the time. Without a police force to track down the culprits, only two people were executed for these reported felonies. And it would be guesswork as to how many other crimes never came to light at all because of the victims' fear of reprisals.

For all its dangers, however, to live in Lincoln – or any other English city – was the dream of many in country villages like Laxton. If an unfree villein there or in any other rural community could slip away from the clutches of his lord, pass through Lincoln's city gates and survive here for a year and a day, a court would pronounce that henceforth he was a free man. These rustic escapees were often welcomed as a useful source of labour. And it was not unknown for them to achieve high office. A man named Richard the Villein, for instance, served for four years as a town bailiff in Lincoln, which meant he had responsibility for accounting to the Royal Exchequer for the taxes owed by the city to the king. Not bad for a country boy born a serf.

✯ ✯ ✯

So what was the source of Lincoln's wealth in the days of King John?

To find out, I stumble down Steep Hill, the soles of my shoes slapping on the cobbles, my knees working overtime to stop my body breaking into an ever-accelerating run. After a quarter of a mile, the hill starts to level out, adopting the name The Strait, and then on the flat becomes the High Street as it pulls clear of little old buildings, and begins to look as twenty-first-century standardised as any city in England – Waterstones, Debenhams, kids in coloured shorts listening to iPods and texting, young men with braided hair huddled on the pavement begging. There's a busker doing a Bob Marley tribute on guitar and mouth-organ. He's pretty good, and he's halfway through 'No woman, no cry' before I realise I'm standing on a small bridge. I recognise it as Lincoln's famous High Bridge.

High Bridge, which runs over the River Witham, is unusual because it has shops running right across it. They're mock-Tudor, Victorian probably. But there have been buildings here in some form ever since the bridge was built over 850 years ago – in other words, before King John came to the throne. To reach the riverside, I drop down a set of steps in a narrow alleyway alongside the half-timbered shops. I walk past a red and green narrowboat moored by the towpath, and a couple of hundred yards later, the Witham suddenly broadens out into a wide stretch of open water. This is Brayford Pool.

It's an extraordinary sight in the centre of a city 40 miles from the coast. Brayford Pool these days is a marina with lines of pleasure boats moored along its jetties. But up until the 1950s it was a working dock. It still has that feel about it, with its over-large piers, old warehouses – these days converted to offices – and its wharfs now prettified with trees. For over 800 years, the pool was abuzz with broad-hulled sailing barges loading and unloading their cargoes.

Lincoln in the Middle Ages was an inland port, with two routes to the sea. There was a canal dug out by the Romans to link the town to the Humber Estuary and on to the North Sea. But more important was the River Witham itself, meandering its way over to Boston, which after London was then England's most important seaport. Water routes were vital to the economy of medieval England. We have to remember that in the twelfth and thirteenth centuries the only half-decent long-distance roads were those paved by the Romans. Though hardly repaired since the legionaries left in the fifth century, these roads were still the main means of communication by land. Lincoln was the junction for two such ancient routes: the Fosse Way, a 250-mile-long track from the south-west, and Ermine Street, the main link from London to the north. So the city was the meeting point for important links by both land and water.

Where today fibreglass weekend motorboats and little sailing dinghies bob at Brayford Pool's moorings, in King John's day heavy barges would have been tied up, with bales of wool, rolls of fine cloth, and sacks of corn being loaded on board, ready to sail downriver to Boston and on to Scotland, Germany, Norway, the Baltic states and even to Iceland. It was said that the looms of Europe's finest clothmakers in Flanders would have stopped without supplies of Lincolnshire's wool, which was considered second to none in quality and quantity. In 1189, King Sverre of Norway praised the English 'who have come here bringing wheat and honey, flour and cloth'.

On their return voyages, the boats brought from northern Europe fish, oil, timber, furs for the noble families of England, and hunting hawks – particularly treasured by the king. They all found their way here to be unloaded at Brayford Pool, where they were packed on to carts and taken to Lincoln's famous fair in the streets around Steep Hill. There, local merchants would sell them on to traders who flocked to Lincoln on the old Roman roads from all around the east, north and midlands of England.

This vast enterprise meant jobs for the citizens of Lincoln in the days of King John, and it meant riches for some. And with wealth came aspiration. The most successful merchants turned up their noses at the stench, disease, fire and crime in and around Steep Hill. They wanted something more fragrant, elegant and safe for themselves and their families, so they built their houses outside the city walls to the south, and they've left behind there a remarkable testimony to their way of life.

✻ ✻ ✻

Ten minutes' walk south from Brayford Pool is an area of Lincoln known as Wigford. Today it's dominated by dark brick buildings, where the lurid letters KFC and Betfred stand out among the more modest signage of Cantonese restaurants, Polish supermarkets, Turkish cafés and 'Franks', which proclaims itself 'an Italian barbers'. It's not an area where you'd expect to find a unique specimen of twelfth-century architecture. But that's what Wigford can boast, though it's quite hard to spot. With its soot-stained stonework butting up to the pavement's edge, the building we've come to see could at first glance be mistaken for a Victorian chapel of some obscure denomination. Only a pair of wide-arched, iron-studded wooden doors, aged to the darkest brown, suggests something much older. And I'd bet that ninety-nine out of a hundred passers-by never notice the doors' stone framework in a pattern of finely carved dog tooth, and above that, a line of fantastical creatures and scrolling acanthus leaves.

As I step back to take a photo, the left door opens and out pops a chap in maroon sweater and matching tie, who with neat little circular motions starts to polish a small brass plate on the adjacent door that reads 'Lincoln Civic Trust'. Have I come to the right place? I ask. He nods, and introduces himself as one of the trustees. Giving the brass a last quick buff, he invites me inside to look around, first directing my attention to a larger slate plaque on the wall to the right:

> St Mary's Guildhall,
> the former home of the
> Great Guild of St Mary,
> the leading religious and
> social guild of the city,
> was built in the 12th century.

Guilds were a peculiarly urban phenomenon, and they're hard to define. Usually they were a cross between a professional standards association or even a trade union on the one hand and a church community group on the other. Sometimes, they were more like Rotary Clubs with religious affiliations, and this is closer to the status of Lincoln's Great Guild of St Mary. Its members were the most powerful men in Lincoln. This building is where they met, and it was built in Wigford just outside the old city walls to be handy for the wealthy citizens who had moved here to escape the dangers and smells of Steep Hill. The mayor's house, according to my host, used to be right next door, 'where the Cyclesport shop is now'.

At the top of a spiral stone staircase is a large rectangular room. This is the grand meeting hall. It's a ghostly place. Its roof, with oak beams rising to a peak in the middle, is much lower than it would have been in the early thirteenth century. But there are spectres all around the walls to remind us of its former glory. Decorated arches spray out like petrified fountains from the tops of a stone colonnade. There's a massive fireplace, its back packed with thin stones pilfered from a nearby ancient Roman ruin. The lower halves of two massive stone window frames remain, as do their intricately carved capitals.

Anyone who was anyone in Lincoln society had to be a member of the Guild of St Mary. And as in all such clubs down the ages, it was inevitable that the great and the good would have discussed more than just guild matters when they got together. Many of the Guild's brethren were merchants, so business deals would have been clinched over a goblet of wine during ceremonial dinners. And these men were the political movers and shakers of medieval Lincoln as well, so other kinds of deals – Who should represent the city's interests to the king? When should the borough court convene and who should preside? – in other words, matters of city governance, would have been thrashed out and settled within these illustrious walls too.

During the reigns of Richard the Lionheart and John, cities like Lincoln managed to win a significant degree of self-government. How they did it was simple. They used their wealth to buy it. And they found very willing sellers in the two kings, both of whom were desperate for cash to finance their military exploits. No fewer than 300 English boroughs had been granted charters by the time King John died in 1216. Lincoln paid 500 marks (remember, 4,000 dinner plates cost just 4 marks about this time) to King Richard for a charter which, among other provisions, placed the city beyond the control of the king's most diligent local official, the sheriff. And in 1200, a year after John came to the throne, the citizens of Lincoln bought another charter, this time for 300 marks, which allowed them to elect – from among their own number – their own city officials who would administer the king's law in Lincoln.

In Lincoln, in London and in other cities around the country, the burgesses, that is the moneyed middle-class businessmen, were organising themselves into associations, and swearing before God their support for and trust in each other. The burgesses of Lincoln seems to have been particularly independent-minded. In 1201 they instituted a local city tax to pay for purely local amenities, and they even declared that they could not be taxed by the king without their consent, though there's no evidence they made this precocious claim stick. They began to elect a chief officer who, acting with a council of twelve or twenty-four other citizens, would in theory represent the whole community. In other words, a mayor. In 1206, we see the first recorded mention of Lincoln's mayor, a man called (fittingly, as the first one) Adam, son of Reginald. Of course, we should not imagine that this burgeoning city government involved one-citizen-one-vote. Political decisions lay with Lincoln's wealthiest and most powerful – that is, with members of the exclusive club that met here in the hall of the Great Guild of St Mary.

But just as remarkable as the rise of city government is the development of a sort of democracy throughout the lower levels of urban society. Lincoln in King John's day had at least forty guilds, in addition to St Mary's. Most of them were trade associations, not unlike closed-shop trades unions. If you wanted to practise your trade, then you had to pay your dues to the guild. In addition, like a modern friendly society, guildsmen looked after their sick brethren, buried their dead and provided for their members' widows and orphaned children.

There were guilds for shoemakers, saddlers, leatherworkers and tanners. If you were in the catering business as a baker, cook, butcher or miller, you each had your own guild. In the construction industry, masons, carpenters and plumbers all had a guild. If you were in the thirteenth-century transport and distribution business, you needed to be a member of the guild of porters, carters, farriers or ostlers. Among the skilled makers of things, such as turners, coopers and potters, who each had their own guild, the most famous of all were the goldsmiths', though we shouldn't forget the guilds of the parchment-makers and of the soap-makers. More surprising is that preachers had their own guild, and so did leeches – i.e. doctors, so named because attaching the slimy little blood-suckers to a patient's body was thought to cure all ills. But most important of all the craftsmen in Lincoln – which became known as a producer of high-quality cloth, especially in scarlet and green – were the weavers, the dyers, the wool-combers, the shearmen, the tailors, the hosiers and the mercers (who sold the textile products of the others' labours), each of whom had their own guild with its own rules. All of these guilds established themselves as monopolies. Whether your skill was looking after horses or fashioning gold-leaf jewellery, if you weren't in the guild, you'd find it near impossible to work.

★ ★ ★

Although only 10 per cent of the population got to experience the opportunities and the dangers of city life, boroughs like Lincoln were disproportionately important. In the king's eyes, at least. This was not only because he could sell them charters and tax their wealth. Cities housed another vital source of cash for him. To investigate further we need to return to Steep Hill.

At the bottom on the left, where The Strait finishes and the steepest part of the hill begins its climb, stands a small house. It's constructed from honey-coloured stone, a surer protection against devastating fires than wood and straw, and a sign that the occupants were well-heeled. Something about the place looks odd, in a small-scale magnificent way. Its central doorway sits beneath a round stone arch, with intricate, interlocked carvings, and its two main upstairs windows are crowned with similar arches, supported on little columns with acanthus-leaved tops. It's the sort of decorative masonry that we nowadays are more used to on Norman parish churches, not on houses. And that's the mark of its rarity. It's known as The Jew's House.

Today it's a restaurant that still bears that name. And – strictly in the interests of research – I go in for a meal. The young woman who owns the business, once she taken my order and served me my pigeon breast salad, proudly tells me about the origins of the place. It dates back to the mid-twelfth century. This section of Steep Hill was the Jewish quarter of Lincoln in medieval times. Where I'm sitting is the oldest surviving small dwelling in Europe. Recently, she explains, a fire broke out at the back of the kitchen when a tumble dryer exploded in the middle of the night. But the old medieval stones did their job and stopped the flames from spreading. She and her partner, the chef, are permitted to own only the interior of the building, from the plasterwork inwards. The external structure, the historically important part, belongs to the city council.

The Jews in England during the Middle Ages, as throughout much of their history, were regarded as outcasts and suffered appalling oppression. Anti-Semitism was built into society in the twelfth and thirteenth centuries. Jews lived *in* cities like Lincoln, but were not *of* them. They were not able to become citizens, they could not join guilds, and so could not carry on a trade. The only outlet for their skills was in finance. The church banned Christians from practising usury, the charging of interest on loans. At the same time, the great institutions of the Church, as well as the Crown, the barons and in fact people at all levels in society needed from time to time to borrow money, and it was the Jews who provided that service. As a result, they found themselves in a peculiar, not to say ironic, position. They themselves and all they owned were regarded as the property of the king. This meant that he could tax them at will and could seize the property of any Jew on his death, a clever arrangement as far as the king was concerned, because it enabled him to share legitimately in the immense profits of a practice prohibited by the Church. Because of this bizarre relationship between Jewry and royalty, the king offered his special protection to the Jews. It was, after all, in his economic interests to do so.

Lincoln had one of the largest and richest Jewish communities in England. When in 1194 John's brother King Richard was held hostage on his way back

ugino utatuaui iui piututos uppuo —unn/
er scripta quaxoa littar que in thecautia uni

Jews being persecuted, from a thirteenth-century English manuscript. Periodic outbreaks of mass violence against the Jewish community are recorded throughout the Middle Ages, and anti-Semitism was a constant in town life.

from crusade, Jews across the country were called on to help pay the ransom, and the contribution from the community on Steep Hill was topped only by their co-religionists in London.

Lincoln was also home to the most famous Jewish financier in medieval England. For many years it was believed that Aaron of Lincoln, as he was known, lived in another old Norman house that still stands further up the hill on the opposite side of the street. It too has a striking, carved archway, and is now a specialist tea and coffee emporium. But the idea that this was Aaron's home is now discounted, though it was built during his lifetime and was likely to have been the home of one of his fellow worshippers and rival financiers.

We know little of Aaron the man. But we have a great deal of information about his business operations. Henry II himself borrowed from Aaron, and the king's debt was so huge that he had to order the sheriffs of nine separate counties to direct part of the taxes they collected into Aaron's coffers. This period was one of great ecclesiastical building, and no fewer than nine Cistercian abbeys owed Aaron a total of 6,400 marks. Bishop Chesney of Lincoln got himself into such a financial mess that he was obliged to pawn the cathedral ornaments to Aaron. And when, on the great financier's death in 1185, his assets passed to the king, a special department had to be set up in the Royal Exchequer to handle his affairs. The list of those who owed money to Aaron – and now to the king – was astonishing. It included the King of Scotland, five English earls, the towns of Winchester and Southampton, as well as numerous princes of the Church including the Archbishop of Canterbury. And we can only guess at the stories behind the myriad of much smaller debts, many of them owed by Lincoln folk. Saulf of Wigford, for instance, owed Aaron 50 shillings. James, brother-in-law of the first mayor, Adam, was in debt to the tune of two and a half marks. Outi, the priest at Lincoln's Eastgate church, owed 10s.

The resentment this sort of debt generated must have intensified old-fashioned xenophobia, which in turn was legitimised by the medieval Church with its long-held, illogical belief that the Jews (rather than the Romans) were responsible for Jesus's crucifixion. The result was a deep-seated and often violent anti-Semitism, which flared up with alarming regularity. One of the worst outbreaks came in 1190. King Richard's declaration of a crusade prompted a fanatical wave of hatred right across the country that amounted to 'We can do our bit at home against the enemies of Christ!' In Lincoln, as in many other cities, a mob gathered in the streets and worked itself up into a frenzy of Jew-hating. As the rioters advanced up The Strait, the Jewish inhabitants of Steep Hill grabbed what belongings they could, seized their children, and scrambled up the street to the gate of the castle and sought refuge in its great courtyard. There they were given royal protection until tempers outside cooled down.

The Jews of York, 70 miles north, were not so lucky. In a similar outrage in the same year, 150 of them met their deaths, either slaughtered by the mob, or so terrified of what would happen if they were caught that that they killed themselves and their families.

To their credit, royal officials in Lincoln set about tracking down the anti-Jewish rioters, and almost a hundred were fined for their part in the attempted attack. Among them were several city notables, including one 'Godwin the Rich'. Others were more lowly craftsmen, including four tanners, three weavers, a dyer, a porter, a mercer, a draper, a boatman, the son of a smith, and a moneyer (a skilled manufacturer of coinage) who, since there was no Royal Mint in Lincoln at this time, must have come from outside the city. Fines were set to fit the pocket of the miscreant. So Godwin had to pay £100, while the poorest offenders were made to stump up 6s 8d or one third of a pound. But despite these swingeing punishments, anti-Semitic violence in Lincoln and elsewhere continued, with more serious outbreaks in 1202 and again in 1220.

★ ★ ★

If evidence were needed that the barons and the churchmen who were to negotiate the terms of Magna Carta in 1215, saw it as far more than a rule book for the king, then the clauses dealing with the Jews provide that proof.

Clause 10 says:

> If anyone who has borrowed a sum of money from Jews dies before the
> debt has been repaid, his heir shall pay no interest on the debt for so long as
> he remains under age, irrespective of whom he holds his lands.

The clause then goes on to clip back the king's own profits:

> If such a debt falls into the hands of the Crown, it will take nothing except
> the principal sum specified in the bond.

In other words, the king cannot collect the interest. We may detect the hand of
the Archbishop of Canterbury here, aiming to enforce the ban on usury among
Christians. And the barons, of course, were hardly likely to object to a reduction
in their debts.

The next clause says:

> If a man dies owing money to the Jews, his wife is not obliged to pay off the
> debt from her inheritance, and the man's under-age children shall be prop-
> erly provided for before any debts are paid from their inheritance.

So whatever else Magna Carta may have been, it was also an early attempt to
regulate the financial markets. And it did so by introducing a bias in favour of the
buyers. The sellers of debt, the Jews, had no voice at Runnymede, of course. There
is no evidence, however, that these clauses had much practical effect, and they
were quickly forgotten. The loans business continued with violent ups and downs
until 1290. In that year, the Jews throughout England were rounded up and were
expelled from the country.

Clause 13, on the other hand, was more resilient. It states:

> The City of London shall enjoy all its ancient liberties and free customs, both
> by land and by water. We [i.e. the king] also will and grant that all other cities,
> boroughs, towns and ports shall enjoy all their liberties and free customs.

This is the free market in operation, a politico-economic market. The wealth
of London, Lincoln, Southampton, Norwich and all the other towns and cities
made them vital allies of the barons, who made sure they were not forgotten
in the Great Charter. And clause 13 is one of only three clauses which have
survived eight centuries and still have the force of law in England and Wales
to this day.

If Magna Carta can be said to be in any way a beacon of freedom, then there's a strong case for pointing to clause 13 as its basis. It's not the sort of freedom we would necessarily endorse of course, born of self-interest amid money, violence and evil smells. But then, perhaps that's where many good things are born.

★★★

At the top of Steep Hill this morning in the little square outside *The Magna Carta* pub, there's a fair in full swing. It's not like the fairs of old Lincoln where fine Flanders cloth and the fur of arctic squirrels were bartered, where the king's agent used to snap up a bargain pair of Norwegian hunting hawks, and where sacks of corn were piled high on four-wheeled carts. Today there's a farmers' market here, but – to give it its due – its stalls are packed with some relatively exotic twenty-first-century produce. There are ostrich burgers, goose eggs, truffles and something labelled 'Mutton', a wonderful old word, derived from the Norman French for sheep and all but killed off nowadays by the marketing departments of super-market chains who have persuaded us all to call it 'lamb' regardless of its age.

As I hand over £6 for two chops, what sounds like the peal of at least twenty bells suddenly crashes into my ears. The west front of Lincoln's cathedral stands in all its medieval glory less than 100 yards away. The building was described by the Victorian art connoisseur John Ruskin as 'the most precious piece of architecture in the British Isles'. In King John's day, it was not so magnificent. Earthquakes of any destructive power are rare in these islands, but one in 1185 almost completely destroyed Lincoln's cathedral. One chronicler wrote that it was 'split from top to bottom'. And if we had been here thirty years later, while John and the barons gathered at Runnymede, we would have seen the cathedral clad in wooden scaf-folding as the masons still laboured to rebuild the place.

The Church, as an institution, was itself rocked to its foundations during the reign of King John. A bitter six-year dispute between king and pope left the population of England out in the cold without many of the traditional consola-tions of their religion. The row also resulted in another clause in Magna Carta that still has the force of law.

To tell this chapter of the story, we're going to a small parish on the south coast of England, where King John prostrated himself before the Pope's representative, and won a cunning victory into the bargain.

11 TEMPLE EWELL, KENT, ENGLAND

A TRIUMPHANT HUMILIATION

King John is arrogant. He swaggers before his lowly subjects, and pulls his shimmering green cloak tight around his shoulders as though protecting his own godly presence from their dirt and infection. A peasant carrying a sheaf of corn lowers his anxious gaze in case the king should see him and strike him dead. Women in simple woven garments, brown and grey scarves wrapped round their heads, mumble to each other. They sneak a glance at the armour-clad knights arrayed alongside the king, faceless men, like robots in iron helmets where hair, nose and mouth should be, their eyes hidden inside two dark slits. As the king turns, a ruby embedded in his golden crown catches the sun for an instant.

A small boy in the crowd boos. Those around him laugh and start booing too. King John ignores them. The Mistress of Ceremonies adjusts her mob cap, raises her microphone and announces, 'King John, one of the great villains of English historical folklore … described as greedy, a poor administrator and a poor warrior.'

We're in the village of Temple Ewell, 3 miles outside Dover on the Kent coast, where the locals are holding a pageant to celebrate the millennium-and-a-half-long history of their little town. We've seen a monk, grey hair, knobbly knees and pudding belly, who – we were told – had ridden out from Canterbury to preach to the people here. Next came a mob of Vikings, who rushed on to the showground, their horned helmets bobbing, with much brandishing of swords and blood-curdling shouts. They did something you don't usually see in a polite Kent village, not these days anyway. They grabbed the women (mostly around the waist) and carried them off. The victims failed to look worried, and laughed a lot. The MC explained that in the ninth century, the unfortunate villagers were subject to fifty summers of Viking rape and pillage.

Next, a fearsome escort of knights appeared, each man in full steel body armour and a white cloth surcoat decorated with blood-red crosses to signify that they're from of the Holy Order of the Knights Templar. They were carrying heavy broadswords, and were led by a teenaged boy in mail, who kept pushing a piece of chewing gum into view with the end of his tongue.

But these are all supporting acts. Top of the bill is King John. What's being commemorated here is his arrival in Temple Ewell in 1213 for a ceremony which was to catapult the village into the history books. The *Temple Ewell News* summarises the background for us: 'King John, a true baddie of English history, had picked a fight with the Pope and lost, so like almost all bullies throughout history, he caved in and grovelled for forgiveness.' That 'grovelling' took place in Temple Ewell.

Our King-John-for-the-day grabs his cardboard crown with its glassy gems, just in time, before the wind can snatch it away. The village vicar, the Reverend Father Paul Christian (is this an example of what Stephen Fry calls 'nominative determinism', i.e. we do the job suggested by our name?), dressed in wide-brimmed hat and elbow-length black cape, then processes into the scene with his ecclesiastical retinue and mounts a low wooden platform. Today the Reverend Christian is Pandulf, the Pope's representative. He's about to accept John's surrender of his kingdom to Pope Innocent III, and to hear the king recognise the Pope as his overlord. In 1213, this event was to bring an end to a six-year Interdict, a period when England was cast out from the protection of God and the church, as a punishment for John's defiance of the Pope.

So at Temple Ewell, bad King John was humiliated, and Mother Church was victorious.

That's certainly what it looks like in the afternoon's sunshine on the King George V playing fields in Temple Ewell. But, as ever with the story of King John, that's far from the whole story. The truth is more complicated. It's a tale of power politics and devious manoeuvring that far from making John a loser, brought him vast treasure as well as a powerful ally who almost managed to kill Magna Carta stone dead as soon as it was born.

✯✯✯

The battle between king and pope that led to the Interdict on England had roots going back at least 150 years. Bishops and archbishops often owed loyalty to both crown and papacy, and they tended to have two jobs as well. Not only were they high-ranking officers of the Church, but they were frequently also employees of the king, managing his governmental administration. In addition, 25 per cent of the land was in the hands of the Church, which meant bishops and archbishops owed allegiance, and what's more, military service to the crown. That meant they had to keep a small army of knights and foot soldiers at the ready. Some powerful clergymen even chose to fulfil the military role in person. The Bishop of Winchester, Peter des Roches, for instance, might hear pleas in a dispute over royal lands one day, preside over mass at high altar the next, then swap surplice and mitre for plumed helmet and armour as he rode into battle. We were supposed to be comforted to learn that he limited his weaponry to a mace, or metal cudgel, rather than a sword, since churchmen were forbidden to shed blood, though how such a brutal instrument could be effective without piercing the victim's skin is a mystery the Church didn't reveal.

So kings of England had a strong interest in the appointment of high-ranking members of the Church. Monarchs needed bishops who were well-organised administrators and compliant providers of military support. The Pope, on the other hand, wanted spiritual leaders, and of course effective exponents of papal policy. It was rare that both the royal and papal first choices for an episcopal job were the same candidate. In practical terms, it was usually the king – who was on the spot – who got his own way, rather than the Pope who was miles away. Technically, the choice fell to neither of these rulers. Bishops and archbishops were chosen by the local chapter of monks. John's technique, like that of his father, was to show up suddenly at the cathedral and make sure the voters knew whom to elect. Out of fear or an acceptance of the inevitable, that's what they usually did.

Therefore, when in 1205 Pope Innocent III declined to accept John's candidate as the new Archbishop of Canterbury, and instead proposed a man favourable to himself, it was something of a shock. John would have none of it and he refused to let the Pope's nominee, Stephen Langton, enter the country. Innocent accused John of being insolent and impudent. John was furious, and he took out his anger on the monks of Canterbury, turfing them out of their cloisters and then expelling them from the country.

For the next three years, John and Innocent tried to outfox each other. The Pope sent an open letter to the barons of England, asking them to persuade John of the Pope's way of thinking. He pointed out that though they owed loyalty to their earthly ruler, they shouldn't at the same time offend their Heavenly King. Innocent was wasting his time. Even one of the religious chroniclers reported that, 'all the laity, most of the clergy, and many monks were on the king's side.' The reason was simple: it was established tradition that the king decided who should hold such important political posts as the Archbishop of Canterbury.

Pope Innocent III being advised by the Holy Spirit during an audience with a visiting abbot. When Innocent's six-year battle against John ended, he became the king's most powerful ally.

And John played to this sentiment. He sent letters around all the shire courts berating the Pope for 'the wrong and injury which is done to us.'

By March 1208, Innocent decided to ramp up the pressure. He placed England under an Interdict. In effect, he declared a general strike by the clergy, with emergency service only. No offices of the Church were to be performed except for baptism of infants and the confession of the dying.

John immediately retaliated with his own nuclear option. On the same day that the Interdict came into force, he sent out royal officials to seize the land and property of the clergy. It's a tribute to the efficiency of John's government that this was carried out with speed, right across the country. But the task distracted the royal administration from their routine work, so John hit upon an alternative ruse. He informed all priests, monks, bishops and archbishops that they could regain control of their land and buildings, on one condition: that they paid him for the privilege. It's debatable how much revenue this brought into the royal treasure chests. One theory is that the chief reward to the royal coffers came from seizure of the lands and wealth of the several bishops whose conscience or fear for their personal safety drove them to flee the country. But other calculations suggest that the Interdict relieved John of his financial worries for several years.

The success of this scheme also gave John another idea. Men in holy orders were supposed to be celibate. But their lodgings were often brightened up by the presence of 'housekeepers', 'hearth companions' or 'lady friends', whom everyone knew did rather more than cook, sit around the fireplace or offer advice on etiquette. One contemporary chronicler wrote that 'the houses and hovels of the parish clergy are full of bossy mistresses, creaking cradles, new born babes and squawking brats.' John gave orders that all such concubines be taken into custody, to be released only on payment of bail. Most priests coughed up, to the further enrichment of the king.

So the Interdict, far from shaming John into submission, had him rubbing his hands with glee.

Innocent's hope was that the Interdict would work by hitting the ordinary people of England so hard that they would rise up against their faithless ruler and bring him back to the fold. It didn't work out like that. For a start, the clergy weren't always clear about what they were and weren't allowed to do. Could babies be brought to church for the permitted baptism, or should the priest perform the ceremony at home? And often the men of God worked around the ban. Though the main church door was locked and bolted, pilgrims were often let in through a side entrance. People still got married, for instance, because in the thirteenth century the Church's blessing, though usual, was not considered essential, and men and women continued – as they had done before – to plight their troth in the church porch; they just couldn't go inside to hear mass afterwards. However, there was clearly less work for priests during the Interdict, and there are reports of some of them doing other jobs, or just having a jolly time in alehouses.

The Interdict, however, did hit the religious life of the country in two ways that affected the common folk in Laxton's fields and Lincoln's streets. When relatives died, you were not allowed to bury them in hallowed ground. Bodies were sometimes thrown into roadside ditches or even left in the open to rot. In addition, priests were not permitted to bless livestock or crops, nor to curse caterpillars and other pests. In the minds of the 90 per cent of the population who farmed, these acts of blessing and cursing were as essential as disease control is for today's agriculturalists, so the ban must have caused widespread anxiety. However, nowhere is it recorded that there was any civil unrest as a result of the Interdict.

Innocent needed a more powerful weapon, and in 1209 he excommunicated King John. Excommunication condemned the sinner to the flames of hell forever, and it was performed by the awful ceremony of bell, book and candle. The priest would sound a death toll by ringing a bell, close the Bible to symbolise the excommunicant's separation from the Church, and snuff out a candle then knock it to the ground to represent the sinner's soul being extinguished and cast out from the light of God. A terrible punishment. Or it was supposed to be. The trouble was that the clergy had used it rather too often, sometimes in frivolous cases, or to deal a blow to their political enemies, rather than to punish sinners. Its currency had been devalued. Innocent's sentence of excommunication against John hardly seems to have made the king falter in his steps. The main sufferers were a handful of bishops whose consciences told them not to associate with an excommunicate. They left the country and duly had their estates seized by the king.

And how did the barons of England react to John's excommunication? By 1209, they had the perfect excuse to initiate full-scale rebellion against him. In fact, Pope Innocent made it clear that they had an obligation to do so. And did they? They did not. Why? The reason was simple self-interest. The barons, like the king, had got used to appointing their own men to Church positions in their own territories. To challenge the king's right to do so would by implication deny their own privileges to do the same.

The Pope had one more shot in his locker. He could declare the king deposed. Towards the end of 1212, the rumour spread that this is what Innocent had done. It wasn't quite true – not yet anyway. Innocent knew that such a sentence would be meaningless unless it was backed up by armed force. But when the following year it became known that King Philip Augustus of France – John's old enemy – was preparing to invade England, and that he would be happy to do so flying the Pope's banner, John wisely decided it was time to do a deal.

It was now that the spotlight was turned on Temple Ewell, thanks to the presence here of those knights we saw with blood-red crosses on their chests during the village pageant. The village gets the first part of its name from the Knights Templar. They were a religious military order – a strange concept to the twenty-first century mind. It meant that a Knight Templar was part monk, part soldier. So, for example, like a monk he was supposed to be celibate; in fact, all contact with women, even members of his own family, was forbidden. At the same time, his military duties put him in the front line of battle. The Order was formed in the early twelfth century to protect pilgrims in the Holy Land from bandits and marauding Muslims, and to fight alongside crusading armies – such as that led by Richard the Lionheart at Acre. Their full title was The Poor Fellow-Soldiers of Christ and of the Temple of Solomon. Their emblem was of two knights riding on a single horse, to emphasise the order's poverty. That rule was soon forgotten. Within a few decades, they had amassed so much wealth that one historian has classed them as the world's first multinational corporation. They established bases throughout Europe. In 1163 they decided they needed a place close to Dover, where crusaders and pilgrims boarded ship for France en route to the Holy Land. They chose Ewell, 3 miles from the port, and built a substantial church here as well as a preceptory or living quarters. It was the Templars' prestigious presence in Temple Ewell that made it the choice for King John's meeting with the papal legate, Pandulf.

★★★

Back in the sunshine of twenty-first-century Temple Ewell, the moment has arrived for the re-enactment of the fateful face-to-face encounter between John and the Pope's man. The village king, whose previous cockiness has now been replaced by slumped shoulders and a hangdog expression, approaches the wooden platform where the Reverend Paul Christian (i.e. the Legate Pandulf) awaits, attended by his churchwarden (i.e. an assistant papal emissary) wielding a ceremonial staff. John kneels and lowers his head to the ground.

'On the fifteenth of May 1213,' announces the Mistress of Ceremonies, 'the king submits to the Pope, and does so in the most abject, grovelling terms.' It's a credit to the village king that he manages to bring off the grovelling with more dignity than we've a right to expect from a man whose bottom is now fractionally higher than his head. Pandulf gives a sign to the escort of Templar Knights, and they help John back to a more elegant posture. The papal legate turns out to have lightning reactions, and as the king removes his cardboard crown, Pandulf's hand shoots up and grabs his own wide-brimmed headgear before the wind can whip it off too. There's then a dangerous moment when the holy representative could do with three hands, one for his hat, one for his Bible and one to receive the crown. But he manages. Fortunately, his assistant is holding the microphone.

'John of England,' asks Pandulf, 'do you swear to become liegeman of His Holiness the Pope?'

There's a squeal from a small child in the watching crowd as John replies, 'I do swear.'

'Then by the power given to me by His Holiness the Pope,' declares Pandulf, 'I forgive your sins and accept your kingdom into the Pope's hands.'

The two men shake on it, and the bare-headed king retreats to the sidelines, all grovelling done. I half expect a round of applause. But there's only background chatter among the spectators. Perhaps we're not sure who has won, which is as it should be.

★ ★ ★

We don't know the exact form of words used in this unique ceremony back in 1213, but the village pageant's rendering probably captures the gist of it. Nor for that matter can we be sure precisely where the formalities took place. The choice of location for today's event, the King George V playing fields, we can be sure wasn't it, but only a pedant would be worried by that. There are various theories – that it was in the chapel of the Templar Master's house in Temple Ewell (a building that has now disappeared from the landscape without trace) or else in another little church on the hill overlooking Dover harbour 3 miles to the south. But it's likely that neither of these places would have been big enough to hold all the retainers from both sides who needed to witness the oath-swearing by a king before God. The more obvious spot is the much larger church in the village itself. The Templars had knocked down the old wooden place of worship when they'd arrived in the village fifty years earlier, and had replaced it with a longer-lasting stone building. It was very close to where John had been staying in the Templar Master's house during the two-day negotiation that preceded the surrender. It's now the parish church of Saints Peter and Paul.

Temple Ewell sits in a steep-sided, narrow valley, and we have to climb up a winding lane to reach its church. It's hardly visible from the iron gate at the road-side. The view is blocked by two massive, gloomy yew trees, reckoned to be around 1,000 years old. So they would already have presided over the churchyard for two centuries by the time John passed between them. The church itself would have looked as stern and severe then as it does now. Its stone walls are packed with brittle lumps of black, shiny flint, sharp-edged enough to cut your finger.

Inside, the nave is austere, with plastered walls and those terracotta floor tiles that look like they belong in a Victorian scullery. But I can never resist the chance to put myself in the footprints of history, or in this case, the knee-prints. There's no one else about, so I get down low and touch the cold stone of the altar steps with my forehead – just for a few seconds – in the place where John would have prostrated himself before Pandulf. I can report no flash of sudden insight.

In the absence of Templar Knights to help me to my feet, I give a groan and straighten my back, then nod in the direction of the altar, before heading back to the doorway on the north side. Its round arch in milky brown limestone and its simple decorations are as neat and satisfying as they must have been on the day the masons crafted them in the 1160s. To the right, set back against the wall, there's a 5-foot-high block of stone. Carved along its length is a Templar cross. It's all that's left here now of that mighty order. A century after its knights oversaw John's submission in Temple Ewell, the French king – who was heavily in debt to the Templars – persuaded the then pope to dissolve the Order. Under torture, many of its knights confessed to heresy, idol worship, obscene rituals, financial corruption and homosexuality.

★★★

In return for making his submission to the Pope, John was admitted back into the Church. His excommunication was lifted and he was no longer condemned to hell's flames for all eternity. The end to the Interdict had to wait a little longer while John paid back some of the money he had seized from the Church. But the thaw in relations between king and pope was instant. Innocent positively gushed now in his praise for his erstwhile enemy. He wrote to John, 'You now hold your kingdom by a more exalted and surer title than before, for the kingdom is become a royal priesthood.'

John's timing in agreeing the deal at Temple Ewell was spot on. If he had delayed by even a week, he might have been lost. Some of the barons who later led the Magna Carta revolt had begun to proclaim their right to sever their allegiance to the sinful king. There was even talk of a plot to murder John. In addition, just a few days before the king prostrated himself at Pandulf's feet, Stephen Langton, the Pope's nominee for archbishop, had been dispatched from Rome with a letter from Innocent in his satchel declaring John deposed and calling on Philip Augustus of France to take over the crown of England. While the ceremony was taking place in Temple Ewell, Langton, ignorant of the latest turn of events, was somewhere on the road between Rome and the Channel ports. A papal emissary managed to intercept him with an order from the Pope that the letter of deposition should be chopped up into small bits or burned. That's how tight it was.

Meanwhile, King Philip Augustus was pushing ahead with his plans to invade England, now without the Pope's blessing. What happened next was remarkable.

It was the medieval equivalent of the Battle of Trafalgar. What's more, the little village of Temple Ewell was again to play a key role in developments, something which history seems to have all but forgotten.

On the evening of 25 May 1213, ten days after John's submission to Pandulf, the king held a conference with his advisors in the Templar Master's house. On the agenda was what action to take in the light of Philip Augustus's build-up of an invasion force a few miles away across the English Channel. Temple Ewell was the scene of a second momentous event in under two weeks. Since the loss of Normandy, nine years earlier, John had steadily built up a fleet of fighting ships. At the conference on the night of 25 May, he took the decision to order his fleet across the Channel to intercept the French king's forces before they could put to sea.

Two days later, 500 small ships with 700 knights and an unknown number of mercenaries set sail for the port of Damme in present-day Belgium. Sadly, a visit to present-day Damme can tell us nothing about the ensuing battle – centuries of coastal reclamation have now put it 9 miles inland from the modern port of Zeebrugge. The chroniclers, however, have left us a detailed account. In the face of offshore winds, the English fleet manoeuvred into the estuary under cover of darkness without raising the alarm. At first light, the scene that greeted the men on board the English ships must have caused them to gape. A huge number of small French vessels – by one account 1,700 of them – lay at anchor. The English commanders acted swiftly and dispatched spies in small boats. They reported back that there appeared to be no soldiers on board the French ships, that the vessels were loaded with stores, and that the only guards were a handful of sailors. Orders were given for an immediate attack, and within hours many of the French ships were set ablaze, while others were cut loose and towed away.

The English knights and their mercenaries must have been flushed with success because they now put ashore confident of taking on the French army, which was rushing in to try and save the situation. But good sense triumphed. The English commander, the Earl of Salisbury, realised he was outnumbered and withdrew his forces to the safety of his ships.

The attack on the enemy's fleet, however, had done the trick. Philip Augustus abandoned his planned invasion, and he even set fire to his remaining warships in the harbour at Damme, worried that he couldn't now protect them from being hijacked by the English. 'Never,' wrote one chronicler, 'had so much treasure come into England since the days of King Arthur.'

John, the so-called grovelling loser, had done something which you might just think would earn him a place, alongside his brother, in the panoply of English national heroes. Having laid the foundation of England's navy, he had presided over the first great English sea victory. John had also turned the tables on the French king who had defeated him at Château Gaillard. And he now had a staunch ally in Pope Innocent III, who was unswerving in his support for the English king, which in turn meant those restless barons who were stirring up revolt could no longer claim God on their side.

King John was riding high.

For the moment anyway. Runnymede and Magna Carta were less than two years away. So what went wrong? For the answer, we need to cross over the Channel ourselves to the coast of northern France, then head 60 miles inland to the village of Bouvines just outside the city of Lille. Two great armies faced each other at Bouvines in July 1214, and the ensuing battle was a catastrophe for John.

12 BOUVINES, NORTHERN FRANCE

A BATTLE FOR THREE EMPIRES

I nearly didn't make it to Bouvines.

I'd seen on the internet that hundreds of men were going to dress up in armour, helmets and mail, and wield all manner of medieval weaponry from axes to crossbows in a re-enactment of the battle that took place just outside the village in 1214. Women were invited too, so long as they donned smocks *à la mode du treizième siècle* and brought along plenty of cooking pots and flagons for the pre- and post-match refreshments. Very thirteenth century. It was all going to happen on 27 July, the battle's 800th anniversary.

Perfect, I thought.

But whenever I went online to check out the arrangements, I got confused. There seemed to be no mention of start time, parking, or any of the usual hows, wheres or whens you get in the 'Visit Information' page of websites. It might be my inadequate French. So on the re-enactors' internet forum, I tracked down the organiser, who revealed to me – in more or less plain English – the puzzling truth. The re-enactment would not be held at Bouvines at all, but at a place called Argy, which, it turns out, is 300 miles south. Apparently the re-enactors hadn't been able to reach an agreement with the upstanding burghers of Bouvines which would permit what the organiser called 'a good historical level' to the re-enactment. So they had decided to take their show elsewhere, though it was not immediately clear how a 'good historical level' could be achieved somewhere five hours' drive from where the fighting had actually taken place. But that wasn't all. My contact added something else. Come the day when he and his fellow combatants would rush at each other, rattling their swords on their shields and uttering foul and terrifying cries, no spectators would be allowed! 'This is not our policy,' he explained. The event would be staged purely for the amusement of the participants.

For a day or so, I considered buying some fancy dress, paying the €15 registration fee, turning up at Argy on 27 July, then feigning immediate, though not life-threatening injury, so I could spectate (illicitly) from the sidelines. But that would hardly be in keeping with a book about places where important things in history actually happened. Argy is not Bouvines.

Further research indicated that the big day in Bouvines itself would be marked by speeches from various elected officials. Now, I've never met the Mayor of Bouvines, and he or she may well be an inspiring orator, but this did not seem to me like the stuff of living history. However, all was not lost. I discovered that on the weekend three weeks ahead of the anniversary, the village would be staging its own dramatic presentation of the great battle. With *son et lumière*. And fireworks too. Now that sounded more like it.

It would indeed have been unthinkable that the event should go uncelebrated in Bouvines itself. The name 'Bouvines' may be unheard of on the English side of the Channel other than among a few medieval historians. But in France, la Bataille de Bouvines is held in the sort of reverence that Trafalgar is by the British. (Do we – all nations? – get amnesia when it comes to battles we lost?) Bouvines marked the first great step in the establishment of the territory we know today as France. Of course, one nation's gain is another's shrinking frontiers. Thus Bouvines would bring the ruination of English power on the continent of Europe. And for King John, Bouvines was to have devastating consequences back in England as well. It led to a rebellion among his barons, to an encounter in the meadow at Runnymede, and to Magna Carta.

✳ ✳ ✳

The catastrophic collapse of King John's overseas power was to come little more than a year after his great naval triumph at Damme. But his humiliation in France was not as unexpected as might be thought at first glance. It was a disaster waiting to happen.

At first all went well. With the victory at Damme, John had thwarted a French invasion of England. If he could now strike back quick and hard, there was a chance not only of crushing once and for all his old enemy, King Philip Augustus of France, but also of retaking Normandy – lost ten years earlier following the fall of Château Gaillard. John did not waste the opportunity. He mounted a strategic counter-attack that was bold and ambitious. He organised an assault on three fronts.

First, he ordered his trusted general – and half-brother – William Longsword, Earl of Salisbury, to mobilise an army of several thousand, then ship them across the Dover Straits so they could come at the French king from the north-west.

At the same time, John cemented an alliance with his nephew, Otto of Brunswick, claimant to the title of Holy Roman Emperor. The plan was for Otto to sweep in on Philip Augustus from the north-east with a troop of vassals and allies that included three dukes, eleven counts and nine seigneurs, all with their own assorted mini-armies.

John himself landed at La Rochelle in the Bay of Biscay, and advanced into Poitou to the south-west of Paris. His immediate objective was to undermine the French king's military support in the region. And during the spring and early summer of 1214, in a rapid series of sieges and skirmishes, castles and fortified towns fell into John's hands one after another. Finally, he brought to heel Hugh de Lusignan – the same Hugh whose child bride John had snatched at Angoulême fourteen years earlier – who was forced to put his knights and soldiers at John's service. Philip Augustus recognised the very real threat that John might now advance towards Paris, and he dispatched an army led by his son Louis to stop the English king.

It was then that John's plans went awry.

Prince Louis intercepted him just outside the city of Angers, near the small town of La Roche aux Moines. There was every reason to think John would triumph. But it was not to be. At the last minute, Hugh de Lusignan – who needed little excuse to stab his old rival in the back – deserted, followed by the rest of the Poitevin nobles. The religious chroniclers could call it the curse of the devil's brood on the man who had married a 'child witch'. The simple fact was that Louis's forces now outnumbered John's, and the English king was forced to retreat, back to La Rochelle, where he was boxed in.

John needed reinforcements, and he sent word to England demanding that the barons fulfil their feudal obligations and support their king either with money or men. But he waited in vain. No help came. The barons pulled the rug from under their monarch's feet.

The trouble had in fact started even before John had departed for France six months earlier. In order to employ mercenary soldiers for the forthcoming campaign, he had demanded 'scutage' from his barons, that is, payment in lieu of the military service which by feudal custom they owed to the king. Some had paid up. But a significant group of powerful magnates from the north and east of England had refused point blank, claiming – on very doubtful legal grounds – that they were under no obligation to support the king on ventures outside England, Normandy or Brittany. It was the first open act of defiance in what was to become the Magna Carta rebellion.

However, despite his defeat in Poitou, despite the desertion of the Poitevin nobles, despite being abandoned by the barons of England, and despite his own personal humiliation, John's war against the French king was far from lost. His hopes now rested with William Longsword and Otto, who by now had joined forces north of Paris. On paper, the odds favoured John's allies, who outnumbered the army mustered by King Philip Augustus.

And so it was that on Sunday 27 July – beneath a baking hot sun – the two armies clashed in the fields just outside Bouvines, 140 miles north of Paris, close to the present-day border with Belgium.

✱ ✱ ✱

Bouvines these days is an inconsequential village. At least, that's how it looks to an outsider. You drive south-east from the city of Lille for twenty minutes, dodging on and off motorway links, with no mention of it on the road signs, until suddenly you're on a narrow country lane, and if your mind were to wander for a moment, you'd be into Bouvines and out the other side before you knew it. The houses on each side of the narrow main road with their long dark brick facades and their forbidding, drab front doors hardly warrant a glance. There's no sign of shops, or a village square. The one daub of colour in the place comes at Bouvines' only bar, called L'Allumette, 'The Matchstick', which bristles with those gaudy, over-large illuminated signs that advertise *Tabac, Loto, Presse* and a local beer. Even that's shut. This, despite the fact that there are plenty of visitors in Bouvines today – all potential customers. But today's Sunday. Sunday's a day off.

This is the outsider's-eye-view. But it misses something special about Bouvines. Set back off the main road where you can easily miss it is the church of St Pierre. It's built of pure white stone, with an 80-foot-high steeple-topped tower, its steady magnificence an alien among Bouvines' squat grey houses. And inside, hidden from the hurrying traveller, is a treasure. Or should I say twenty-one treasures? More of these later.

For now though, I park the car and join the scores of folk all heading up the main street, families with kids on dad's shoulders, couples hand-holding regardless of age, and bands of teenagers barging about and tweeting. I'm not sure where we're going. The *son et lumière* doesn't start for another six hours. At first, I think the big attraction is a mobile *Friterie* (*'Cornet de frites', 'Sandwich Mexicanos + frites', 'Burger + frites'*) where scores of us are queuing. But then I see that the real action is a little further on, where three women in white mob caps and floor-length robes, like shepherdesses in a nativity play, seem to be guarding a line of *WC-Locs* (Portaloos to the English). Behind them, a couple of dozen tents are dotted about in a field enclosed by barbed wire fencing. It's a medieval fair.

I pay my €2 entrance fee, get my hand stamped to prove it, then discover that the field is truly medieval, in the sense that it seems to predate health and safety regulations. The straggling grass has not been mown, and hidden beneath it are potholes, patches of squelchy mud and unpleasant proof that cows recently inhabited the place. Beneath the open canopy of each tent, various allegedly medieval activities are taking place. Two men in white smocks are hammering at a blackened sword blade which they keep pushing into a bed of feebly glowing charcoal. A woman in regulation ankle-length robe is fashioning medieval jewellery, while others are selling Bière Bouvines 1214. A mountainous man in a full set of black whiskers with matching black cloak and hood looks at me blankly when I ask, '*Qu'est ce que c'est?*'

– then replies, '*Ah … je suis raconteur* – I am storyteller,' then adds with a shrug and a smile, 'but I 'ave no audience.' Next to him is a tent stacked with open boxes containing what look like different grades of small half-burnt logs. The vendor, who with pointy cap and cross-gartered leggings resembles an over-grown elf, spots my puzzlement, leaps up from his stool and cries, '*saucissons, saucissons!*' grabs one from the nearest box and produces a knife with which he cuts off a piece of sausage meat and offers it to me. Too polite to refuse, I pop it in my mouth. It's spicy and chewy. And with a '*très bien, merci,*' I retreat.

✳ ✳ ✳

It's time to explore the fields immediately to the east of the village, which is where most of the fighting took place 800 years ago. The land here is flat with occasional slight rises, and the wheat field by the road where I'm walking stretches away for maybe a mile, uninterrupted by trees or hedges. The battle in 1214 was not the only time that blood has been spilt in the mud here. This is Flanders:

> We are the Dead. Short days ago
> We lived, felt dawn, saw sunset glow,
> Loved and were loved, and now we lie
> In Flanders fields.

(by poet and soldier John McCrae)

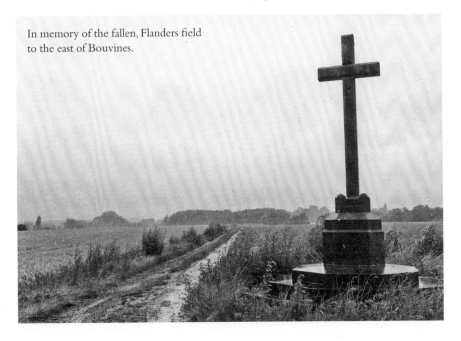

In memory of the fallen, Flanders field to the east of Bouvines.

In 1914, exactly seven centuries after the original Battle of Bouvines, the English and the French – now allies – were defeated and, in what became known as the Great Retreat, were pursued over these fields by the German army. Today, on a low hill, a bleak stone cross stands in memory of those who died in that long and most terrible campaign.

By comparison, in July 1214, the fighting here was over in the blink of an eye. It lasted no more than three hours, and was for much of that time a vast disorderly scrimmage.

At first, the French were caught on the hop. Philip Augustus was manoeuvring his army across a small bridge over the River Marcq just south of Bouvines. We don't know today the exact site of that crossing. The road from Lille does cross a small bridge which drivers would only notice from a set of iron railings on each side, and it's likely that Philip Augustus's bridge was here or somewhere close by. The river is little more than a stream nowadays, but may have carried much more water 800 years ago. All we know is that it posed a real barrier for a medieval army. Philip's infantry and baggage train had already crossed over, and his knights and mounted sergeants were just preparing to follow them. The French king watched the operation as he picnicked in the sunshine, convinced that his enemies would not want to insult God by fighting on a Sunday. But they did. Otto ordered his men in to make a rearguard attack on the French forces waiting to the east of the bridge.

It could all have been finished there and then with the French king trounced. But Philip Augustus took a crucial and prompt decision. He ordered his foot soldiers to turn around and cross back over the bridge as fast as possible. Meanwhile, his horsemen held off Otto's troops just long enough for the French army to come together in line of battle across these fields to the east of the village. Otto was left with no choice but to form up his own troops, face to face with the enemy. Now neither side appeared to have the upper hand.

The two confronting armies both straddled the ancient Roman road that linked Bouvines with the nearby town of Tournai. This ancient trackway has long since been replaced by a metalled road half a mile further south. But the old road still exists as a cart track, and as you walk along it today, you can appreciate that much of the surrounding area is low-lying and would often have been muddy and treacherous underfoot. The previous winter of 1213–14 had been especially wet. The marshy ground was to give a key advantage to horse-mounted troops.

We shouldn't picture the two hostile lines as unbroken phalanxes of uniform fighters. Both armies were made up of scores of different little groups. Here, a minor baron with a dozen knights and twenty-odd sergeants. There, foot troops and a small force of horsemen loyal to a bishop or an abbot. Then opposite there might be a militia of crossbow men from some distant town. And scattered

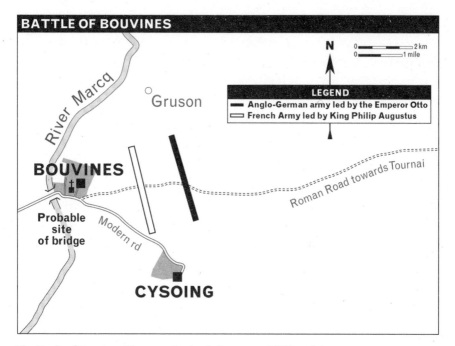

The Battle of Bouvines. The opposing battle lines were 2,000 yards long.

among both sides would be mercenaries, which could mean anything from gangs of 'routiers' – thugs and criminals – to groups of landless younger sons from aristocratic families.

And it would be a mistake, too, to imagine that the two opposing commanders – one a king, one who called himself emperor – spent the battle on some remote redoubt from where, safeguarding their own dignities and skins, they could order men to their deaths. King Philip Augustus positioned himself in the centre of the front line. He was clearly identifiable both by his own men and by the enemy, astride his charger beneath the oriflamme – the battle standard of the kings of France – fluttering alongside his personal ensign of golden lilies on a blue background. In the opposing line, Otto was equally visible, his silken imperial dragon flying from a pole topped by a carved eagle with golden wings, mounted on a gold-encrusted chariot. It's difficult to estimate numbers. The Anglo-German forces commanded by Otto probably amounted to around 9–10,000, including 1,500 mounted troops of knights and sergeants. Philip Augustus had fewer men, around 7,500, but he had just as many cavalry, and this was the key factor.

Within minutes, the two armies clashed. Axes, swords, pikes and arrowheads flashed in the sunshine as a hundred deathly struggles were waged down a line 2,000 yards long. On Otto's side, Count Renaud of Boulogne did manage a sudden cavalry assault from behind a screen of routiers. In the centre, Otto's horsemen broke French lines. But this was a rare organised tactical manoeuvre amid the furious and confused melee.

In the middle of the battle line, a force of German infantry armed with spears, iron hooks and long curved knives made a rush to snatch King Philip Augustus. He was struck in the neck by a pike. He might have been killed, but the weapon's point lodged in the padded collar of his vestment. Then, as he strove to free himself, he was pulled from his saddle by a couple of imperial foot soldiers. While one of his knights threw himself on top of the king to protect him, another, Galon de Montingny, signalled for help by raising and lowering the *Oriflamme*. The assailants were fought off while the king got back on his horse and rejoined the fray.

Over the next two hours, it became more and more clear that Otto's German and Flemish foot soldiers, slowed by the sucking mud, were no match for the French horses and their highly experienced armoured knights.

Otto too was in the thick of it. We're told that he wielded his battleaxe with courage, despite being hit several times in close combat. A French knight grabbed at the bridle of his steed, while another attempted to stab the emperor. The blow bounced off Otto's armour. His horse reared, and a second lunge with the knife pierced its eye. In agony, the animal bolted with Otto still in the saddle, but it didn't get far. The dying beast collapsed beneath him. As Otto plunged to the ground, the famed French warrior William des Barres rode in and would have captured the emperor if his personal bodyguard of Saxon knights hadn't reached him first. Otto was badly shaken, and when his retainers managed to get him back on a fresh mount, the Holy Roman Emperor turned tail and fled the fighting. He spurred the horse without stopping until he reached Valenciennes, 22 miles away.

It was a fatal blow. The resolve of the Anglo-German forces was broken by the very public desertion of their commander-in-chief. And although William Longsword, Earl of Salisbury – in effect deputy leader of the Anglo-German alliance – battled on, when he was clubbed from his mount and taken prisoner, the battle was over.

During the three hours of fighting, an estimated 1,000 men on each side were killed. One hundred and thirty knights, five noblemen and untold numbers of foot soldiers who had fought with Otto were taken prisoner by the French and led off in triumph to Paris.

★ ★ ★

It is with some excitement then that I take my seat at 9 p.m. along with 1,500 fellow spectators in front of a sawdust arena and an extra-wide cinema screen. We're ready for the staged presentation of the battle with full *son et lumière*.

Horses, it soon transpires, are going to be the star turn. As we wait for it to get dark enough for the *lumière*, we're entertained by acts that wouldn't disgrace the Calgary Stampede. Horses race across in front of us while their riders variously hang upside down with legs pointing at the sky, swing around till they end up riding backwards, and stand bolt upright on their horse's back, a challenge to gravity and common sense. Whether any of these techniques was ever useful in a pitched battle is debatable, but we all cheer anyway.

The show starts. A bunch of peasants, many of them children, are seen laughing and having a good time while they work in the fields. Suddenly, the mood changes. Half a dozen soldiers in mail, swords drawn, march in from the right. The peasants cry out in alarm, '*Les soldats! Les soldats!*' then throw down their hoes and rakes, and run for safety.

Several scenes follow in which bright-robed personnel representing the noble leaders of the two warring factions hold conferences to decide the best tactics. There's a good deal of operatic laughter, 'Ha … haa … haaaaa!' to signify each side believing the other will be a risible pushover. And there's also a set of puzzling dances, before the appearance of two dozen women gliding over the sawdust in ghostly white robes. They're oracles, foretelling that the Count of Flanders, who is chosen to join Otto's side, will enter Paris to the applause of the mob. Those of us who know the result of the battle suspect irony to come.

Next to me in row eleven, a little girl, approximately 2 years old, is getting restless on her father's lap, and starts pointing over to our right and crying 'Shove-ho, shove-ho' (*Chevaux, chevaux?*), from where a strong aroma of horse dung indicates the animals that interest her more than what's going on in the arena. I sense that many in the audience are getting similarly impatient for the main event.

We don't have to wait long. There's a quick jousting tournament – cue more rodeo tricks – and then comes the battle itself. With shouts of '*Aux armes!*' and '*Alors!*' and 'Aaghhh!' the Emperor Otto's men in yellow, and the French king's troops in a royal blue, set to in an untidy line across the back of the arena. As the battle proceeds in this fashion for the next fifteen minutes, one man, on the French side, increasingly stands out. He looks like a cross between a sumo wrestler and Mike Tyson, with hair halfway down his back. This, believe me, does not make him look girlie. While all the other soldiers swing their swords, inserting a little hesitation at the final moment to make sure the blow lands harmlessly on their opponent's shield, this giant seems to think he really is back in 1214 with a mission to maim and kill anyone dressed in the enemy's yellow colours. He picks them up bodily, lifts them above his head and slams them on the ground, then jumps on them. He grabs two imperial soldiers by the hair and smashes their heads together. And when a rather poncy-looking knight rides his white horse a little too close to him, the big man appears to rugby-tackle the beast, which topples over, sliding its rider uncomfortably to earth where he receives a full-throttle kick.

Meanwhile, at the front of the stage, the rest of the horsemen have arrived and begun their own slashing, clubbing and lancing. They may not need to stand on their steeds' backs nor stick their legs up in the air, but it's clear that these men – especially now they're wearing full-head helmets and armour – need to be skilled equestrians, just as they would have 800 years ago in the muddy fields a few hundred yards from here.

The unhorsing of Philip Augustus is performed with daring and apparent authenticity. An enemy lance wedges in his costume and he's knocked from the saddle. As the imperial foot soldiers rush in to finish him off, the royal bodyguard do their stuff and rescue him. He remounts and fights on, as one would expect of a French monarch at a French spectacle representing a French triumph.

By now, the bodies are mounting up at the back of the arena, and not all of them are sumo-Tyson's victims. Another important-looking horseman enters left. This is the Emperor Otto. He goes through a similar routine to Philip Augustus, his horse cleverly faking death by lying still on the ground. Then, true to history, Otto – on a different mount – looks around at the devastation, and with his head drooping, gallops off, deserting his loyal followers.

Suddenly the stage is in darkness. We hear wailing, and a few moments later the lights come up to reveal a dozen women hugging the corpses of their fallen menfolk. The yellow-clad prisoners are marched in, hands bound, and are thrown in a heap at the front of the arena. This is another favourite bit for sumo-Tyson. Geneva Convention rules do not apply. Not only does he do a good deal of bashing in the face and hearty kicking in the kidneys, he also seizes the Count of Flanders by the hair, drags him for 10 feet to where there's a muddy puddle, and shoves his face into the mire, holding it there for about fifteen seconds. Then he lifts up the blighted count to show the audience, and does it again. We – to our credit – now start to murmur in shock, and some of us even boo, though I think sumo-Tyson isn't the sort of fellow you'd want to find out that you'd booed him. Fortunately, the French king now intervenes to show the prisoners mercy, and the giant struts off, shaking his long locks in satisfaction.

The evening ends with the triumphal entry of Philip Augustus into Paris, and with the oracle's prediction come true: the Count of Flanders is indeed greet by the Parisians, though not applauded as victor but in chains as the murky-faced loser to be mocked. Suddenly, there's a mighty bang, a whoosh and the sky lights up with fireworks. '*Vive la France!*' we cry, and then go home.

★★★

I, however, come back the next day. I've yet to see the great attraction that casual visitors to Bouvines might miss. It's inside the towering white church of St Pierre: a striking and unusual set of stained-glass windows. There are twenty-one of them, each 25 feet high by 10 feet wide. They tell the story of the battle, and were designed in the late nineteenth century by the renowned artist Pierre Fritel. After being put on public exhibition at the *Exposition Universelle* in Paris, they were installed in the church at Bouvines, work which took seventeen years, from 1889 to 1906, to complete. In subsequent decades, they became faded and dirty, but in 1994 they were restored to their original magnificence.

The light that pours through these windows into the nave and chancel on three sides turns the church interior into a cascade of blues, reds, yellows and greens. But the most remarkable thing is that – unlike the still, calm reverence that church stained glass usually portrays – the windows here almost leap down at you as the characters in them thrust, stab, fall, struggle, twist, shout and cry out. If the word 'piety' sums up the pictures on a normal church window, at Bouvines it's 'action'. A fallen soldier tries in vain to kick away a toppling horse. An infantryman grapples with a knight's lance. A mailed warrior has one hand round his wounded enemy's throat while the other is bringing down a dagger. Horses rear and plunge in agony. We see the Emperor Otto cowering as he flees the field pursued by William des Barres. And everywhere there are faces, distorted in death as in life. Even when the picture is of quieter moments, a conference between leaders, say, horses are restless, pawing the ground, and watching soldiers brandish their spears. When the king kneels in prayer, the bodies of his attendants are alert, or torn by weariness, or crouched like leopards ready to pounce.

Most wonderful of all is the window that shows the unhorsing of King Philip Augustus in the midst of a cluttered struggle. King and horse almost merge into one as they hit the ground together shrouded in the blue and gold of the royal colours. His faithful servant raises the oriflamme to summon help, and knights tread heedless over their dead comrades to fight off those who would kill their monarch.

In the final window, we see the French king's triumphal entry into Paris, the streets full of people surging and waving to applaud him.

This is the real spectacle of today's Bouvines. The artist has captured the desperation, the heroism and above all the confusion of combat. The stained-glass windows in the church of St Pierre, Bouvines, are a work of expressionist art and a reliving of history. This unpromising little village has something which Paris itself might envy.

★★★

Even allowing for the understandably patriotic representation in the parish church, it's no exaggeration to say that the battle at Bouvines was an astonishing victory with far-reaching consequences. It decided the fate of three great powers.

First, Otto's claim to the Holy Roman Empire was left trampled in the muddy fields to the east of the village. He was overthrown, and his tattered imperial insignia were carried in triumph to Paris.

Then there was the victor himself, Philip Augustus. When he had ascended the throne thirty-four years earlier, his domains had amounted to little more than the hinterland of Paris. At the same time, his great rival – John's father, Henry II – had ruled a solid swathe of French soil from Normandy in the north down to Gascony and the Pyrenees in the south, and from Brittany in the west to the Auvergne 600 miles to the east. But Philip's constant battering of the Angevin kings – first Henry, then Richard, then John – had paid off. With his victory at Bouvines, Philip Augustus saw the French territories of his English rival now reduced to just Gascony in the far south. Philip Augustus's predecessors had been known as Kings of the Franks. His title was King of France. When news of his victory reached the university students in Paris, we are told that they celebrated with seven nights of 'feasting, leaping, dancing and singing'.

And finally, there was King John. Stripped of his lands in France, he was humili-ated on both sides of the Channel. We could say that he was unlucky to have been born at a time when he had to face such a militarily talented, intelligent and well-organised enemy as Philip Augustus. What is certain is that John's struggle to hang on to his French possessions placed a massive burden on England's wealthiest landowners, the king's chief vassals. John's demands in the Bouvines campaign had driven them to defy him and to refuse him vital support at a critical moment.

John lingered on at La Rochelle for two months after his allies' defeat at Bouvines. Then he set sail and a week later the royal galley put into Dartmouth in south-west England. He faced his barons, as the historian Michael Wood has said, 'as a sitting duck'.

And yet, even then, it was not a foregone conclusion that John would become the king who conceded what over the centuries would be regarded as a charter against tyranny. One of the greatest surprises in the story of Magna Carta was soon to become apparent. The opposition to the king in England was shaky. It was far from united. To discover the truth, we'll go now to the most famous of all the places associated with Magna Carta, Runnymede, the meadow on the banks of the Thames where the Great Charter was born. We'll take a closer look at the array of aristocrats who came there and lined up against each other. And we'll discover that the group who were really responsible for getting Magna Carta agreed weren't in fact the barons who opposed John. And they weren't the king's party either.

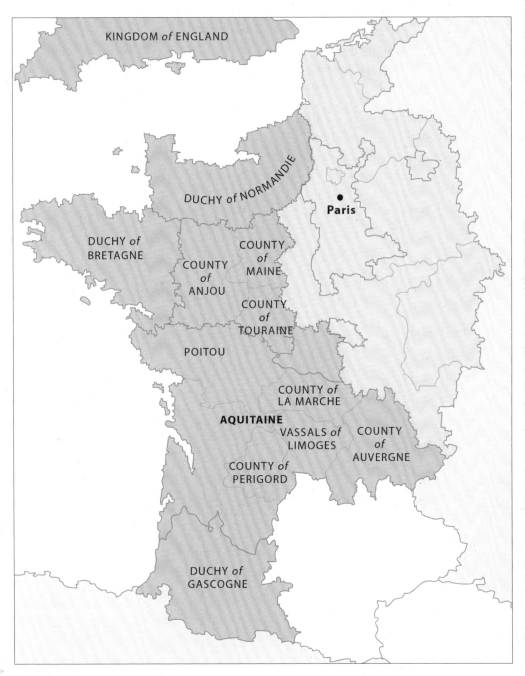

Continental lands held by the kings of England in the mid-twelfth century. By 1214, following his allies' defeat at Bouvines, King John retained only Gascony in the far south.

  The precise spot at Runnymede where the great event happened isn't easy to find. We might expect there to be a museum explaining the history of the struggle for liberty, or maybe a memorial funded by a grateful English nation, or at least there will be a few road signs. Well, no. There is a monument. But, as ever with the story of Magna Carta, it's not what we might expect.

13 RUNNYMEDE, SURREY, ENGLAND

THE LINE-UP

I 'm standing in the car park of the Runnymede-on-Thames Hotel and Spa. To my left, kitchen staff in starched white jackets and chequered trousers are bustling about dumping what I guess are bags of waste food in the rubbish bins. It's a noisy spot because a few yards to my right is Junction 13 of the M25 London orbital motorway where it links with the Egham bypass. And from somewhere behind me I can make out the whining drone of a train on the London to Reading line. We're also only 2 miles south-west of the world's third busiest airport, Heathrow. I can see an American Airlines jet climbing high above the hotel roof.

You may wonder why – having come to Runnymede, where King John met the barons – we haven't gone straight to the official Magna Carta memorial, which stands a mile and a quarter to the west of here. The reason is that I'm searching for the exact location where the Great Charter was born.

Yes, it was at Runnymede, but Runnymede isn't a specific spot. It covers an area of several square miles along the River Thames halfway between Windsor and Staines, plenty of room in fact for the site of the birth of Magna Carta to be the subject of as many errors and falsifications as anything else associated with the Great Charter.

There's a persistent myth, given worldwide credence by Jerome K. Jerome in his 1889 best-selling novel *Three Men in a Boat*, that the great event happened on an island in the Thames, across from the meadow at Runnymede. Jerome treats us first to rousing images of 'slippery' King John and his 'French' mercenaries facing the 'grim ranks of the barons' men' before they all step ashore 'on the bank of the little island that from this day will bear the name of Magna Carta Island … a great shout cleaves the air and the great cornerstone in England's temple of liberty has, now we know, been firmly laid.' There's even a stone in the grounds of a cottage on the island that marks the spot where the Great Charter was 'signed'. *Three Men in a Boat* is one of the funniest books ever written. But, historically speaking, it's rubbish – charming and humorous rubbish, but rubbish nonetheless. Even so is still popularly believed today. Just to be clear:

nothing – not the thinnest sliver of evidence – supports the idea that John and the barons assembled on any island.

And prepare to be shocked. There are doubts too about the positioning of the official memorial itself. According to the Ordnance Survey map for south-west London, it's in a field towards the bottom of a gentle slope. And that's the problem. It's shown on the side of a hill, not a steep hill, but a hill nevertheless, running parallel with the river. It's called Cooper's Hill. However, that doesn't fit with contemporary accounts. Magna Carta itself ends with the words, 'Given in the meadow that is called Runnymede between Windsor and Staines, 15 June'. The name 'Runnymede' is Anglo-Saxon, and doesn't mean, as we might imagine, 'runny', i.e. a 'wet', meadow, but derives from the word 'runieg' meaning meeting-place. Since as far back as at least the ninth century, the meadow at Runnymede had been somewhere where kings gathered to consult their vassals, and where enemies could meet to negotiate in safety. Security was guaranteed because it was bounded by the River Thames to the north, by a stream to the west, and by marshy ground to the east and the south. It was almost an island, not a real island, but more like a reverse oasis, of dryness surrounded by water. It was accessible only by the causeway road from Windsor in one direction and from Staines in the other. This was important because King John and the barons had a deep distrust for each other. And the last place either would have chosen for their meeting was one where attack was possible from nearby high ground. Finding the exact spot today that fits that definition is no easy task. Over a period of 800 years, marshland has been drained so houses and roads could be built, and small streams can disappear at the same time. But what doesn't tend to rise up out of the earth unexpectedly over just a few centuries is a 3-mile-long hill. In 1215, it would have been exactly where it is now. So the conclusion seems clear: Magna Carta cannot have been born where the official memorial is shown on the map, on the side of Cooper's Hill; nor can the big event even have taken place in front of the memorial where the stretch of meadow is exposed to attack from that hill.

So, where did it take place?

What we're looking for is a section of flat land alongside the Thames, which is not overlooked by sloping ground to the south. And the OS map shows that the only place that meets that specification is right here, where they've built the Runnymede-on-Thames Hotel and Spa. In fact, given that the two opposing camps would have occupied several hundred square yards of meadow, the betting must be that much of the site where the Great Charter was born lies somewhere under the hundred thousand tons of concrete and tarmac that make up the several roundabouts, bridges, underpasses and slip roads by the M25 motorway nearby to my right.

Truth can be ugly.

★ ★ ★

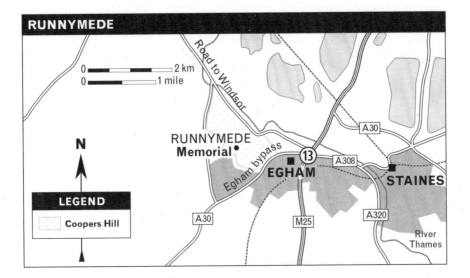

'Runnymede' denotes a large area of meadowland halfway between Windsor and Staines. John would have wanted to be well away from Cooper's Hill from where he would be vulnerable to attack.

I have to concede though that a pretty field and, according to the map, a bosky hillside makes a more romantic spot for an altar to freedom and justice than does a deafening, polluting stretch of brutal urban desert. So next stop, the official memorial. To find it, I have to travel west along the A308 towards Windsor, along what would have been the old causeway road in the thirteenth century. The map indicates a turn-off to the left. Sure enough, there's a small silver plaque on a pole which – beneath the oak twig insignia of the National Trust – announces in inch-and-a-half high lettering:

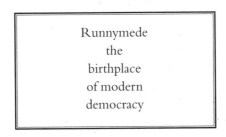

Runnymede
the
birthplace
of modern
democracy

At the entrance to a little car park, two slightly larger plaques warn:

> Gates close 7 pm

and urge:

> Please take your litter home

The immediate attraction here is a single-storey brick building with a plastic banner fixed to its wall announcing 'Magna Carta Tea Room. Tea-Coffee-Breakfast-Lunches-Cream Teas. Open All Year.'

Inside, it's a pleasant enough little provider of refreshments, whose homely, old-fashioned atmosphere is reinforced by a visitors' book on the counter next to a help-yourself basket of crisp packets and a topless tea-pot with knives and forks poking out of it. Recent entries include one from a Mr and Mrs Clerides of Tasmania, Australia ('Great!'), another from a Bill and Sarah of Nebraska ('Fantastic. Very welcoming.'), and one by somebody illegible from Egham, 2 miles up the road ('Must get recipe for carrot cake.')

This morning there are few customers: two matronly women comparing gardening tips, a family whose kids are competing to see who can make most noise with a drinking straw, and a chap with a coffee reading the *Daily Mail*. Apart from beverages and sandwiches, the Magna Carta Tea Room also sells souvenirs, notably Magna Carta Tea Room Biscuits and Magna Carta Tea Room Jam. But just when I'm thinking the place only promotes itself, I spot a black cardboard tube with the words 'Magna Carta 1215' in gold letters on it. I ask a young waitress with an unsteady bouffant hairdo what it is.

'Just a bit of paper, I think,' she replies. Oh how the mighty are fallen.

I shell out £4.99, and discover I'm now the owner of a facsimile of the Great Charter of Liberties, in the original Latin, complete with a facsimile royal seal on the bottom, plus – in full colour – the coats of arms of the more prominent barons around the outer margin. And on a separate sheet, an English translation.

✶ ✶ ✶

Leaving behind the Magna Carta Tea Room and what it might say about the place of the Great Charter in twenty-first-century Britain, I strike out across the meadow in search of the official memorial. This unprepossessing riverside field has had a surprisingly spicy and at times dramatic history. For 150 years up to the late nineteenth century it was a racecourse, which for some reason was a particular favourite with pickpockets. They used to come out here by the trainload from London to practise their profession. Then, during the Second World War, a US Airforce B-17 bomber crash landed on this bit of grass, just missing the river. Luckily, the whole crew managed to scramble out unhurt. There's no relic of these dramas here now.

I guess I'm on the right track for the memorial because a little fingerpost by the car park had pointed this way. But there's nothing in sight to aim for. The only clue is a trail of muddy grass, trampled down alongside the hedge. Apart from a mum, dad and two kids playing football over to the left, there's no one to ask.

There are in fact three monuments at Runnymede. There's the Air Forces memorial to those killed in the Second World War, sited on the far side of Cooper's Hill. There's a memorial to US President John. F. Kennedy which is hidden away in the woods to my right. Then, a few hundred yards further along, over a field gate, the Magna Carta memorial eventually comes into view. A broad stone slab pathway diminishes up the hill to what from this distance looks like a small stone bandstand or the kind of domed war memorial found in many English towns. It stands about 15 feet high. It has eight simple columns supporting the roof, and in the middle is a bolt of granite 5 feet tall. There's a five-pointed star and a short inscription in blue letters on the side that faces down over the meadow towards the river.

This monument is a striking lesson in the significance of Magna Carta today. Take the wording of the inscription. It says:

> To commemorate
> Magna Carta
> symbol of freedom
> under law

It does not say 'Magna Carta, the earliest constitution', or 'Magna Carta, which gave us freedom and justice', nor even does it echo the National Trust sign we saw when we turned off the main road, and claim 'Magna Carta, mother of modern democracy'.

The key word is 'symbol'. So, to those who composed these words, Magna Carta has the same function as a national flag, which after all is no more than a piece of cloth, which we make to represent loyalty to country. So it seems the folk who erected this memorial didn't regard the Great Charter as a statute or a constitution. The monument's founders – unlike Ernest Normand and the Historian William Stubbs – weren't going to get involved in any myth-making.

So, who were they, the ones who decided to put up this colonnaded monument with its nine words written large? They were people who were careful not to put anything in writing that could be thrown back at them later as a lie or an error. They were lawyers. Nine thousand of them in fact, who all made a donation to pay for the memorial. But they were not judges from the Old Bailey, nor QCs from Middle Temple, nor solicitors from small country towns across Great Britain. They were Americans. Every last one of those 9,000 lawyers who wanted to be associated with the place where was born the earliest symbol of freedom under law was a member of the American Bar Association. And until they decided to erect this memorial in 1957, there was nothing here to mark the place.

But what does this mean? That the Brits don't love freedom under the law? Surely not. Maybe we're just a modest nation, happy to be admired by others,

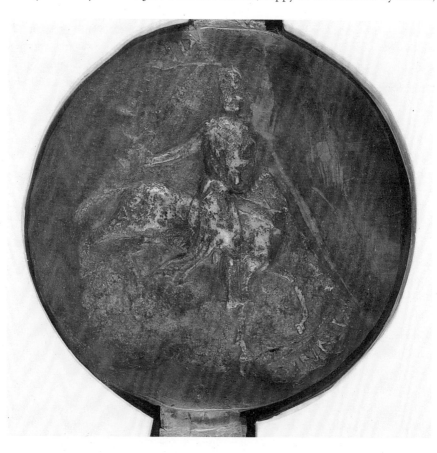

A wax impression of King John's seal, similar to the ones which would have been appended to each of the copies of Magna Carta. It is around 6 inches in diameter and we can make out the faint image of the king on horseback.

but don't wish to blow our own trumpet. The story on the other side of the Atlantic, however, is clearly very different. On the pavement around the edge of the columned dome are more inscriptions, announcing that representatives of the American Bar Association 'returned to this place to renew its pledge of adherence to the principles of Magna Carta.' One of these slabs is dated 1971, another 1985, and a third says 2000. Maybe Americans are keener on symbols than we are? After all, many if not most homes in the USA have the national flag flying in their front yards, whereas you could travel hundreds of miles in the UK before you spied a Union Jack fluttering over the daffodils and roses. That doesn't mean we're an unpatriotic nation. We just do things differently. Or maybe the idea that freedom and law have ancient roots is somehow something that the modern American state needs more than Britain does. We shall be crossing the Atlantic later to investigate.

Before leaving, a few yards from the monument at the foot of a small oak tree I spot a black polished marble plaque set in the earth. Its inscription reads:

> *Quercus robur*
> Planted by
> P.V. Narasimha Rao
> Prime Minister of the Republic Of India
> As a tribute to the historic Magna Carta, a source of inspiration throughout the World and as an affirmation of the values of Freedom, Democracy and the Rule of Law which the people of India cherish and have enshrined in their constitution.
> March 16th 1994.

And all we Brits can manage to do is to bury the true birthplace of Magna Carta under an eight-lane highway, and to open a tea room.

I cringe back through the gate to the water meadow and the ghosts of John and the barons.

★ ★ ★

The events that brought King John to travel down that causeway from Windsor and meet his enemies face to face at Runnymede moved quickly following the defeat at Bouvines. The crisis, which had come to a head with the northern barons' repeated refusal to supply the king with military aid, hit rock bottom with the utter failure of his overseas venture. In the words of the historian Geoffrey

Hindley, it 'shattered … his credibility at home'.

One of the most remarkable things about Magna Carta is that we have so little information about what exactly happened between Bouvines and Runnymede. The chroniclers' accounts are patchy. The facts we can piece together are as follows.

A group of barons from the east of the country began discussing whether John's demands for scutage could be curbed by getting him to agree to the ancient customs of England. They talked a lot about the good laws of Edward the Confessor. The dissidents were wrestling with the age-old problem: what can be done – short of rebellion – to curb the unacceptable actions of a king?

Over the next few months, the two sides circled each other like wild beasts, sizing up the other's strengths and weaknesses. At Christmas 1214, the dissident barons demanded that John confirm the laws of King Edward the Confessor and a charter of Henry I, neither of which, as it happened, had anything to say about scutage. John played for time and said he would look into the idea. In the following weeks, a more general campaign was launched among the country's magnates for some sort of new charter which would define and limit the king's authority. But the extreme opponents of the king wanted a more violent solution. They began to organise themselves for rebellion.

At this point, John pulled off a coup. He took a vow to go to the Holy Land on crusade. This brought Pope Innocent III, who had become John's enthusiastic supporter following the king's submission to the papal legate Pandulf at Temple Ewell, right into the middle of the conflict between John and his mightiest subjects. The Pope ordered the barons to renounce any idea of armed resistance, to show John the respect due to a monarch, and, what's more, to pay him the outstanding scutage still due from the Bouvines campaign.

The dissidents ignored the papal instruction, and on 3 May 1215 they formally renounced their allegiance to the king. In other words, they were resorting to the old-fashioned feudal solution to the question of what to do about an unsatisfactory monarch. They were now in open revolt. John proposed that his disagreement with the magnates be settled by arbitration, to be carried out by men appointed by the Pope. For obvious reasons, the barons refused. Within a week, hostilities broke out across the south Midlands and on the Welsh borders. Then came the turning point. London fell to the barons. In the words of the historian J.C. Holt: 'If Bouvines brought on a political crisis … the baronial seizure of London led directly to Runnymede.'

John needed to do a deal to buy time. It was now that he moved his base to Windsor a handful of miles north of Runnymede. The rebel leaders installed themselves at Staines to the south of the meadow, and the Archbishop of Canterbury, Stephen Langton, began to shuttle between them in an attempt to broker an agreement.

On 10 June, King John and his entourage rode down the causeway from Windsor and set up the royal camp on the meadow here at Runnymede. We can picture the scene, smoke swirling up from cooking fires, horses in corrals, carts heavily laden with food, furniture and whatever else the royal party needed, and probably fairly simple shelters. It's unlikely there was the sort of red-and-gold high-canopied throne or the grand pavilion envisaged by Ernest Normand in the painting of his that we saw in London's Royal Exchange. The barons moved on to the meadow slightly later, via the same causeway, from the opposite direction. They were in position by 15 June.

★★★

It might be imagined that the Great Charter must have been provoked by some desperately brutal act on the part of King John, some spectacularly cruel, exploitative or aggressive deed that prompted the barons of England to say, in effect, 'Enough is enough. This is the last straw.' According to the – admittedly thin – information we have, that was not the case. There was almost certainly a major row about the barons' failure to support the king during the Bouvines campaign. But the antecedents of Magna Carta lay as much in the lives and attitudes of individual barons as in any great events of state.

So let's take a closer look at the powerful men who assembled in the meadow here at Runnymede in mid June 1215. Who were they? And what were their motives?

For a start, the barons were not – as the myth makers would have us believe – a single-minded force made up of the aristocratic magnates of England united against the king. The true story is much more complex than that. It's a tale of personal, and sometimes sordid, hatreds on both sides.

England in 1215 was home to approximately 170 earls and other lords of high rank. Of those, fewer than forty had declared themselves in rebellion against the king. Most of these had a personal grudge against him. For instance, William Mowbray felt he had been tricked when John had made him promise to pay for royal justice, then delivered a verdict against him. Mowbray, who was said to be as small as a dwarf, made up for his lack of stature with frequent outpourings of vitriolic anger, directed against the king.

But the undoubted leaders of the rebellion against John were Robert Fitzwalter, lord of Dunmow in Essex, and Eustace de Vesci, lord of Alnwick Castle in Northumberland. At first, they tried to rally support for a rebellion by putting out stories that John was a sexual predator who had targeted the wives and daughters of England's most exalted noblemen. Now, such tales were not entirely improbable given what we know of John, but Fitzwalter and de Vesci's accusations were confused and without any evidence to back them up. It seems the two would-be chief rebels were no intellectual giants. In the words of one historian, it's 'hard to believe they were anything more than baronial rough-necks'.

Fitzwalter, in any other walk of life than the powerful lord of vast tracts of south-eastern England, would have been dismissed as a blustering, malevolent clown. Some years before the meeting at Runnymede, during one of the many conflicts with the French crown, he had surrendered without a fight to King Philip Augustus. The French king said afterwards that men such as Fitzwalter were 'like torches, to be used then thrown in the cesspool'.

The most telling episode began a few years later. One night the royal court arrived at Marlborough. Fitzwalter and his family were part of the retinue. His son-in-law decided the lodgings allotted to him were beneath his rank, got into an unseemly brawl with a young servant, drew his sword and killed the lad. John was outraged and threatened to hang the man for murder.

Fitzwalter went berserk and shouted at the king, 'You would hang my son-in-law? By God's body you will not! You will see 200 laced helms in your land before you hang him!' By 'laced helms' he meant the crested helmets worn in battle by members of the nobility. In other words, he was threatening John with an uprising by 200 of his fellow barons. It's unlikely the king would have gone through with his threat to hang a member of the baronial class, but he did summon the man to trial. Fitzwalter turned up in court with 500 knights. There was a further face-off with John before Fitzwalter fled across the Channel with the yobbish son-in-law and the rest of his family.

Lovers of irony will appreciate the idea that a man who seeks to pervert the established judicial process with the threat of extreme violence should appear in Normand's painting at the Royal Exchange as the ramrod-backed, look-'em-in-the-eye champion of justice.

Another popular notion we need to abandon is that ranged against the forty rebel barons on the riverside grass here at Runnymede was a royal party made up of just a few servants and loyal courtiers. In fact, there were almost as many barons supporting the king that day as there were against him. They were men who had stayed loyal to John throughout the tense time leading up to Runnymede. What's more, the foremost among them were more powerful, more influential and a good deal wiser than the Fitzwalters of this world.

In the lead on the king's side at Runnymede was William Marshall, Earl of Pembroke. Marshall – as much as was possible in the late twelfth century – was a self-made man. From being a comparative nobody he'd risen to the very top of the baronial ladder, controlling territories along the Welsh border as well vast tracts of Ireland. His birth in a noble family had been only a limited career launch pad, because as a younger son he had started out with no land and no money. He was virtually a servant, though his biographer does tell us that as a boy, sixty years before Magna Carta, he once played conkers with King Stephen. He grew up to be one of the country's leading exponents of an entirely different sort of game. The tournament.

The word 'tournament' today may conjure images of picturesque ceremonial jousting with knights, in a spirit of good-humoured sportsmanship, trying to knock each other off their steeds with blunted lances. A sort of twelfth-century rugby match with horses and metal protective clothing. In fact, the tournament in William Marshall's day had more in common with Roman gladiatorial contests than with the rough-and-tumble of young men who shake hands with each other when the final whistle blows. The only difference between a tournament and a real battle was that the tournament was put on for entertainment. It was sometimes even fought out between mini-armies over several square miles. The losing participants could expect to face death, maiming (which, given the state of twelfth-century medical science, often amounted to the same thing) or utter humiliation. The winners were allowed to seize the valuable armour and horses of the vanquished and, what's more, to hold them hostage until their family paid out crippling ransoms.

William Marshall turned out to be rather good at it. He claimed on his death-bed that he had beaten 500 knights on the tournament field. He was also the only man ever to have unhorsed Richard the Lionheart. This was during a real battle, in the days when the young Richard was in open rebellion against his father Henry II. Chivalrously – and sensibly – William didn't take the future monarch's life, but just killed his horse instead. William had already been rewarded for his prowess with the gift of various lands and titles, but the big leap forward in his career came in 1189 at the age of 43, when Richard, by now on the throne, gave him the hand in marriage of the 17-year-old heiress Isabel de Clare, who brought him her father's vast estates.

Relations between King John and William Marshall were tetchy to say the least. At first John gave him more land and titles. But then, in 1204, following a mix-up in a diplomatic mission that Marshal undertook to Paris, John accused him of treason and called on his fellow barons to stand in judgement on him. William turned to them and said: 'Let this be a warning to you. What the king is planning to do to me, he will do to every one of you when he gets the upper hand.' John had to back down, and he nurtured resentment against Marshall for years afterwards.

So it may seem paradoxical to us that this is the man who was at the king's right hand, leading the loyalist barons here on the meadow at Runnymede in 1215. The reason is simple. For Marshall, pillar of chivalry and defender of feudal custom, an oath of allegiance to the monarch trumped any personal grievance. The formal principle of loyalty came first.

Both Robert Fitzwalter on one side and William Marshall on the other were extreme examples of how the barons reacted during the years of tension that led to Magna Carta. Forced to choose between the vengeful thuggery of one and the unswerving my-king-right-or-wrong principles of the other, many barons simply stayed clear. And they weren't a small group of floating voters either. In fact, this group of waverers consisted of many more powerful men than those in the other two opposing groups put together. In total, more than a hundred great families, around 50 per cent of England's great barons, held back when the rebels first came out into the open.

And here's another irony. Those who were really responsible for the birth of Magna Carta were not the rebel barons. Nor even the sage William Marshall and the loyalist magnates. The fact that there is a Great Charter at all is mainly due to the members of this third, neutralist middle party who had dithered and dathered, and most of whom weren't even present here at Runnymede on the great day in June 1215. What happened was that John, on the one side, and the militant rebel barons on the other, both had to back off from their more extreme positions, because both lots were concerned that they might otherwise offend the powerful group of neutrals and drive them into the opposing camp.

Magna Carta was not a revolutionary document born of a nationwide uprising against a tyrant. Its terms were more of a common sense, middle-of-the-road compromise.

★ ★ ★

It's time to look at those terms, and at the document itself. Or I should say 'documents.' There were at least thirteen and possibly more of them issued from the royal scriveners at Runnymede, of which four have survived. Two of those ended up in the British Library in London's Euston Road, and that's our next stop.

14 THE BRITISH LIBRARY, LONDON

THE DEAL

You may think a library is a library is a library. It's not. The Inuit have forty kinds of snow. We have libraries. My first was in the little East Midlands town where I grew up. It was a pair of rooms converted from an old shop and smelled of floor polish. Its battered brown shelves held no more than a couple of thousand books, and there was nowhere to sit. In the 1970s it was replaced by a new, slightly larger library with glass and PVC walls, aluminium shelf stacks, and an 'Information Centre' in one corner. Then there was my university's law library, whose echoing acoustics ensured that a single cough could simultaneously shatter the concentration of a thousand students. So when I switched subjects to history I was happy to find myself cocooned by books in what looked like a gentleman's club.

The British Library on London's Euston Road doesn't resemble any of these. For a start, there's its gargantuan size. It's home to 150 million books and other documents, a figure which is growing at the rate of 3 million a year. And just in case you can't imagine that, it means an extra 6 miles of shelving every twelve months. As well as quantity, it also has world-class quality, Magna Carta being among its many treasures. And that's why we've come here.

From the outside, the British Library, with its windowless walls of dark red brick, could be the lair of some introspective monster. 'Books,' it seems to say, 'are for the mind, not the world outside.' Above its flat rooftop, I can see the Disneyesque neo-Gothic spires of St Pancras Station, in frivolous contrast to the British Library's deeply serious demeanour.

But inside, there's a surprise. It's as though I've accidentally wandered into a giant modern hotel, the sort that caters for business people in Dallas or Detroit. I'm in a huge atrium foyer rising over my head to a glass ceiling through which the sun pours down to be reflected off marble floors. Ahead to the right are what look like the hotel reception and concierge desks. There's a shop to the left. Ahead, a wide flight of steps alongside two escalators rises to a mezzanine level. There are some of those little indoor trees, so beloved of hotel architects, as well as overly fancy hanging lights. I mount the up-escalator, and at the top come upon a large cafeteria, every table occupied by earnest people having impromptu meetings, or stroking their iPads, or laughing and chatting too loud into their smartphones. And looking down on us are six levels of interior balconies from which presumably, guests reach their suites. Or they would do if it were a hotel, instead of a library.

It's only when I go up close to the lowest of these balconies that I see there are no doors with room numbers and key-card slots. Instead there's a glass wall that extends all the way up to the top of the atrium. And behind the glass, there are endless shelves packed with millions of books. Not paperback novels, but the sort of volumes you sometimes see in the corner of a snug bar in a country hotel, with titles like *A Gentleman's Compendium of Hedgehogs and Other Creatures of the Field, Volume 28*, all leather bound in faded gold and green, and then when you try to take one out, you find they're just book-spines glued together for decoration. I'm sure the ones I'm looking at now in the British Library aren't fakes. But I do wonder how, if I requested one, the librarian could get at it in its glass prison.

I wander up another flight of stairs and push open a door beneath a sign announcing 'Humanities, Floor 1'. The sudden silence makes me realise how noisy the foyer-cafeteria-atrium was. Inside here, there are hundreds of studious souls working at long ranks of desks, surrounded by a couple of miles' worth of books, real ones, the sort people read. I whisper to the young woman in black-framed glasses at the entrance counter, 'Could you tell me where to find Magna Carta, please?' Without replying, she flits round from her eyrie and leads me out again through the door, then directs me back down the stairs to the Sir John Ritblat Gallery.

Inside the aforementioned gallery it's dark. Like a cinema auditorium when the film's showing. The flickering of light is caused by my fellow visitors moving past the dimly illuminated display cases. These, it turns out, contain the pick of the nation's bibliographical treasures. Here, a first folio of Shakespeare's plays. There, a manuscript in Leonardo da Vinci's own hand describing with illustrations how to construct a 'snail staircase'. Then, England's oldest document, a parchment issued in the year 679 in the name of King Hiothhere of Kent. And, nearby, a bit of paper with a few lines scribbled on it in pencil by George Harrison giving directions to Brian Epstein's house in Sussex. Has the curator gone mad? Or is an out-of-control marketing department responsible? I search for Mick Jagger's Tesco shopping list or the Sex Pistols' apple pie recipe. In vain. But I do stumble on a small doorway beneath a sign reading 'Magna Carta'. It's between a pictorial account of the Buddha's life and a drawing of two Indian Flapshell Turtles.

★★★

So here I am at last, face to face with the central subject of this book. The most famous document in English history, regarded for 800 years right across the democratic world, by civil rights campaigners, constitutional lawyers and by those who've struggled against oppression, as the very foundation of the principles of freedom under the law and constitutional government. The trump card to beat tyranny. Magna Carta. The Great Charter of Liberties.

I'm afraid there's no way to break this news gently. It's a let-down.

In the tiny darkened room inside a glass cabinet is what looks like a grubby piece of paper, about the size of the front page of the *Sun* newspaper turned on its side, with tiny brown wiggly lines across it. No wax seal even.

That's it. Magna Carta.

I suppose that since I bought for £4.99 in the Magna Carta Tea Room at Runnymede that so-called copy of Magna Carta, with all those brightly coloured, baronial coats of arms around the outer margin and with a picture of the king's large round dark red seal at the bottom, I've imagined the Great Charter as a physically impressive document. Perhaps a little faded and maybe dog-eared from all that veneration, but nonetheless presenting a certain majesty of design and lettering as would befit the hallowed role centuries have bestowed upon it. But it's like discovering, after years of archaeological excavation, that the lost temple of the Mayan civilisation was a shed. According to a small information plaque on the Charter's display cabinet, it's thought to have been discovered in a tailor's shop, which is entirely believable, since it could easily have been mistaken for an order in a foreign language for a couple of suits.

There is in fact no single 1215 Magna Carta. During the days following the Runnymede agreement, the Great Charter was written out at least thirteen times, and maybe as many as forty-one, and these documents were then distributed around the country. Only four of them have survived. As well as the two at the British Library, there's one in Lincoln and one in Salisbury. The word 'survived', though, is not 100 per cent accurate. The second of the British Library's two Magna Cartas is in another display case alongside the first. It looks as though a full pot of coffee has been spilt all over it, completely obliterating all the writing. According to the information plaque, the brown-grey colour-wash that covers it is a burn mark. It was rescued from a fire in 1731.

But I soon start to feel guilty about these disparaging thoughts. A video screen in the corner of the small gallery suddenly comes alive (a boy of about 10 is kneeling in front of a small console and has pressed the right button) and the curator, Dr Claire Breay, appears. She puts me right, and explains the extraordinary process that went into making Magna Carta as I see it before me now.

In our own age, when pen-written documents have largely given way to electronic digits, it's hard to imagine communications technology as it was in 1215.

Producing each copy of Magna Carta was a laborious business. The parchment was manufactured from sheepskin. It first had to be soaked in a bath of lime. It was then stretched on a frame and once dry was scraped with a crescent-shaped knife until it was smooth enough to be written on. Because one little piece of parchment was such a valuable item, Dr Breay explains, the small writing on Magna Carta is in an abbreviated form of Latin in order to save space. The ink itself had special qualities. The key to its production lay in the stings of thousands of wasps. These insects lay their eggs in the bark of oak trees. The tree then reacts to the stings by producing nut-like blisters, called oak galls, whose sap is acidic. The ink makers used to gather tiny quantities of this sap and mix it with soot. The acid in the ink meant that, when applied with a quill pen, it would bite into the surface of the parchment, rather like an etching. The chancery clerks who did the actual writing – they were known as scriveners – would have had to sharpen their pen-nibs every few lines. Each copy of Magna Carta would have taken one scrivener a full working day to write out.

Most of us now take for granted the process which at the tap of a button or two transforms our thoughts into words on a screen and then instantly transmit them to the other side of the globe, a process so effortless that, as a species, we waste trillions of words every day. So there's something admirable about the ingenuity and thoughtfulness of medieval writing, where each written word was a handcrafted gem.

Humbled, I look again at the British Library's Magna Carta, with its oak gall script in abbreviated Latin, still translatable just as it was on the day it was written 800 years ago, and I give it respect.

The writing on the document is continuous, without breaks between paragraphs – again to save space on the valuable parchment. The traditional division of the text into sixty-three separate clauses is a device of later historians to help analyse the Charter's significance.

At the far end of Magna Carta's little gallery is an interactive screen that allows us to zoom in on an image of the text, discover that it's unintelligible to a lay person and then turn to the translation into modern English alongside it.

★★★

The first thing that strikes the general reader scanning Magna Carta is that it's peppered with feudal jargon, even in its modern English translation. Words like 'amercement', 'trithings', 'halberget', 'sevedges', 'socage', and 'darrein present-ment' pop up. Mumbo jumbo to most of us, though we might have an inkling that 'mort d'ancestor' has something to do with the death of a parent. It's risky, however, to make guesses, because some of the other terms that crop up time and again, such as 'aid', 'fee' and 'relief' are what linguists call 'false friends' and have little to do with help, payments to accountants, or emotional reassurance. This is not to say that the Charter is entirely unreadable. It isn't. You don't have to be a medieval specialist to understand clause 33, for instance:

All fish-weirs shall be removed from the Thames, the Medway.

But if what you're looking for is some resounding statement of political principle, such as, 'The king must always act in the best interests of his subjects', or 'All political power ultimately resides with the people', you'll be disappointed. Even its full name, *Magna Carta Libertatum*, The Great Charter of Liberties, is misleading in the twenty-first century. It was not the Great Charter of *Liberty*, meaning 'freedom' in the sense of that most cherished of prizes for which freedom fighters and freedom lovers have fought and died over the centuries. 'Liberties' in 1215 were something more mundane. The word meant specific acts which were permitted to individuals or groups. So for instance, the peasant farmers in a certain village might be allowed by their lord to graze their sheep on one of his meadow. That was a 'liberty'. Or, the lord himself might have been granted by the king the 'liberty' to build a castle on his land. Liberty in the thirteenth century had little to do with that resounding word 'freedom!' in the sense of freedom from slavery, or freedom from oppression.

Magna Carta is full of very specific detail. The reason is clear. It was a practical solution to a political crisis, a clash between the king and the most privileged echelons of thirteenth-century society. It's not surprising then that, in the main, it protected the interests of those highest rankers. For example, clause 21 states:

Earls and barons shall be fined only by their equals, and in proportion to the gravity of their offence.

Magna Carta tells us about the nitty-gritty of what irked the barons. For instance, they didn't want low-life foreigners muscling in on their traditional rights. The barons believed they had the exclusive privilege of acting as the king's advisors, generals and tenants-in-chief. John should not be entrusting lands and castles to foreign mercenary soldiers but to his customary lieutenants, the barons. And, as we discovered on our visit to South Wales, Magna Carta specifically names the foreign upstarts whom King John put in charge there following the crushing of William de Briouze and states that they must now be turfed out.

The Great Charter also makes it clear that the barons' quarrel isn't just with John. The picture that emerges from the clauses is not of an evil misfit monarch suddenly breaking with a more beneficent era in which his father Henry and his brother Richard ruled. Roughly a third of the clauses aim to block loopholes in feudal custom that kings Henry, Richard and John had all successfully exploited to the benefit of the crown. There are, for instance, clauses that aim to stop the king's interference in the decision about whom a baron's widow can marry or about the guardianship of an underage heir. In other clauses, John promises to restore to the barons any lands, castles or rights that he, his father or his brother had seized without justification.

So from one point of view, Magna Carta is just the latest round in the king-versus-barons tug-of-war, the Charter being the barons' attempt to win back some of the power they'd lost during the reigns of Henry II, Richard I and John.

★★★

But clearly there must be more to Magna Carta than this. It can't be just a charter for aristocrats, blocking the king from undermining their power. If it were, how could it possibly have become such a potent symbol of justice and freedom over the centuries? This brings us to by far the most influential and time-honoured clause in Magna Carta.

Clause 39 has been quoted, reinterpreted, at times misunderstood, more than the sixty-two other clauses in the Great Charter put together. It's both at the heart of the myths about Magna Carta, and at the same time has become its most concrete abiding strength, the inspiration to generations of freedom fighters. How, you may ask, can it be both?

Here's what clause 39 says:

No free man shall be seized or imprisoned, or stripped of his rights or possessions, or outlawed or exiled, or deprived of his standing in any other way, nor will we [i.e. the king] proceed with force against him, or send others to do so, except by the lawful judgement of his equals or by the law of the land.

In the words of one historian, this clause has 'echoed down the corridors of history'. It appears to state a fundamental legal principle: that ordinary citizens shall not suffer arbitrary punishment; that they have a right to a fair trial; and what's more, to trial by jury.

Resounding stuff. But is this what the authors of Magna Carta intended? The answer is a mixture of 'up to a point' and 'not at all'.

The first thing to notice about clause 39 is that it says 'no free man'. As we discovered back in the fields at the village of Laxton, 'free men' made up a very limited section of the population. Once we've stripped out all women, and all those villeins and other serfs, we're left with 12 to 15 per cent of the population.

So the clause has a very limited application. It's not a statement of universal civil liberty. The barons inserted clause 39 and made it apply to 'free men' as a favour to their knights and their retainers – the mainstays of baronial military power. They couldn't be forgotten in the Great Charter.

What did 'except by the lawful judgement of his equals' mean? On the face of it, this looks like Magna Carta is enshrining the right to trial by jury. In fact it was doing nothing of the kind. In the complex arrangement of feudal relationships and feudal law that had applied in England for at least 150 years before the Great Charter, legal cases had sometimes involved oath-taking by twelve men who were the social equals of the party involved. For a knight, that would be twelve knights, for a baron twelve barons. But they were more like witnesses than verdict-givers. In certain circumstances, an accused could be acquitted if these witnesses swore to his innocence. In the feudal system, there were few consistent rules about how or when these twelve men should get involved. Often, they were only called in when there was an argument about which kind of court should try a case. Clause 39 has nothing to do with trial by jury.

It's easy to see how later generations could mistakenly see the clause as the foundation-stone of universal freedom under the law, and we shouldn't entirely dismiss this interpretation as ridiculous. The clause may in 1215 have applied only to a privileged few, and it may not have had anything to say about trial by jury, but it was undoubtedly a step in the right direction. Let's not forget its final words – that the king cannot punish a free man 'except … by the law of the land'.

Clause 39 may not have laid the foundations of the temple of justice, but it was – if you like – an architect's model of what came to be built at a later date. And that has been enough – particularly given Magna Carta's great age – to make clause 39 the most important paragraph in English legal history. Exactly how over the centuries it achieved this star status we shall discover further on our journey.

Closely linked to clause 39, and almost as important, is the next one. Clause 40 states:

> To no one will we [the King] sell, to no one will we deny or delay, right or justice.

These fifteen words are particularly fascinating to the historian. They show the barons in something of a muddle in their attitude towards the king. With Magna Carta, they of course wanted to clip the king's wings. But at the same time, they seem to recognise that the strengthening of royal power that had begun with Henry II and continued under his two sons, Richard and John, wasn't all bad. Clause 40 says that royal justice is such a good thing that it should be available to all without any delays. Of course, Henry II had realised that impartial justice was an attractive product in the marketplace, and had started the system of charging a fee to those who wished to take advantage of it. Now, in Magna Carta, the barons were saying, 'Yes, we like royal justice. We just don't want to pay for it.'

However, leaving this thirteenth-century background to one side, clause 40 is genuinely valuable. It establishes a right to prompt justice.

And while we're looking at clauses which would come to have a long and fruitful life, there is one more that it would be easy to overlook. At first glance clause 12 seems like just another piece of feudal exotica, but it was to find a new role 3,000 miles away and more than five centuries later. Here's its wording:

> No scutage or aid [an 'aid' was a theoretically voluntary gifts of money to the king to assist him with unusual expenses; however, it was traditional to pay up and not argue] may be levied in our kingdom without its general consent, unless it is for the ransom of our person, to make our eldest son a knight, and to marry our eldest daughter. For these purposes only a reasonable aid may be levied.

You may recognise the word 'scutage' from what we discovered at Bouvines. This clause was inserted, of course, to satisfy those barons who, in the build-up to the Battle of Bouvines, had refused John's call for scutage, the payment of cash to the king in lieu of military service. However, 558 years later, Magna Carta – and specifically this clause – was cited by the American colonists in their fight against British rule. They used it to justify their revolutionary call to arms: 'No taxation without representation!'

★★★

Magna Carta was a rag-bag of solutions to thirteenth-century problems. Later generations, in regarding it as a beacon of justice and freedom, have had to be highly selective in the clauses they've chosen to revere.

Many, like the ones that deal with darrein presentment, trithings, halberget and other feudalia, soon became irrelevant. Conversely, Some clauses seem to be well ahead of their time. Number 35 for instance, demands:

> There shall be standard measures of wine, ale, and corn … throughout the kingdom

This would have required a bureaucracy of weights and measures far beyond the capabilities of thirteenth-century government. However, you can't help but admire its ambition.

Other clauses were inserted by the barons as pay-offs to their political allies. The citizens of London, whose support had been so vital in tipping the balance against John, had their ancient customs confirmed in Magna Carta. This privilege was extended too to Lincoln and other towns in England. It's unlikely that John would have had any argument with that. As we saw at Lincoln, he'd granted many of those liberties in the first place in return for cash payments and other support, and like the barons he wanted the towns on his side. Nevertheless, this clause was an important written statement about the status of towns, which was to be cherished by their citizens over the centuries.

The only other party – apart from the aristocracy – to get its self-interest recorded on the Charter's parchment was the Church. The man who brokered the deal between the rebels and the royal party was Archbishop Stephen Langton, and he made sure he got his own finger in the pie straight away. The Charter states at the outset that:

The English Church shall be free, and shall have its rights undiminished, and its liberties unimpaired.

In other words, no more arguments about who had the right to appoint the Archbishop of Canterbury.

By far the longest clause in Magna Carta is number 61, but it had a very short life indeed. The barons had a problem, and it wasn't a new one. The feudal system had always recognised it. What do you do when a king fails to follow the rules? The feudal answer was that you formally renounce your allegiance to him and go into open rebellion. Not very subtle. The barons at Runnymede produced pretty much the same answer, except with more formality.

Clause 61 said the barons should elect twenty-five of their number, who in turn would nominate four of their leaders. If the king or any of his officials were to break any of the terms of the Charter, these four would come to the king and give him forty days to set it right. If he failed to do so, then all the king's subjects throughout the kingdom – the Charter says 'the community of the whole land' – were supposed to get together and strip the king of his castles and other property till he was considered to have made amends. After that, says the Charter, everything goes back to normal, and the king's subjects are supposed to obey him again as though nothing had happened.

You can almost hear John, when he first saw this clause, smiling to his advisors and saying with a cynical shake of the head, 'I don't think so.'

The most fanciful of the myth-makers have claimed that Magna Carta's council of twenty-five barons somehow represented the birth of parliamentary democracy. We can recall that the entry sign at Runnymede suggested this was the Great Charter's legacy. But the barons at Runnymede represented no more than a quarter of the country's aristocracy – in other words a quarter of less than 1 per cent of the people, never mind the whole kingdom. In fact the baronial council was dead in the water as soon as it was born. Even contemporaries recognised it as an impractical fantasy, and when Magna Carta was reissued after John's death, just two years later, the clause was quietly dropped from the text. The best that can be said about it is that it spotlighted a conundrum that would take many centuries to resolve – how do you force a king to comply with the law?

✹✹✹

So if Magna Carta had nothing to say about democracy, did it make any mention of the common people and their rights? What about the 85 per cent or more of the population below the level of free men in the social hierarchy? Villeins, those unfree serfs we met at Laxton, make one appearance. Clause 29 says that they should not be 'amerced' (have to pay a monetary fine) except in proportion to the offence they have committed. So, no heavy fines for minor misdemeanours, and even when they are amerced, the villeins shouldn't be deprived of their ploughs, carts or other means of livelihood. But before leaping to the conclusion that here is proof that the rebel barons had the interests of the most vulnerable in society at heart, we need to pause. Present-day historians point out that the ultimate foundation of aristocratic wealth lay in hundreds of poor peasant farmers working on the vast baronial estates. The barons were deeply concerned that their property was being ruined by the constant amercements (fines) of their villeins by royal officials. With clause 29, the barons made it clear they didn't want the king to exploit their property (i.e. the near-enslaved men, women and children on their estates) and wreck their wealth; they wanted to do that themselves.

But you'll notice that this clause has nothing to say about the legal process by which to establish the guilt or innocence of a villein. The hallowed clause 39 still does not apply. So if you, as a lowly serf, are wrongly accused of some, by thirteenth-century standards dire, crime, you can still be imprisoned or exiled or have your leg chopped off purely on the say-so of a bent royal official, with no trial, just as easily after Magna Carta as before.

And while we're talking about how little Magna Carta had to offer the downtrodden of society, we had better get to clause 54. What an embarrassment that is. Nobody likes to mention it these days. But in the interests of historical truth, I think you should know about it. Clause 54 reads:

No one shall be arrested or imprisoned on the appeal of a woman for the death of any person except her husband.

In other words, Magna Carta lays down that if a woman's father or sister or her best friend are stabbed to death before her eyes, she has no recourse herself to the law. She has to get a man to see to it for her. It could be suggested that if Islamic fundamentalists wanted to do what we've been doing for the past 800 years, that is pick the bits of Magna Carta that we like and ignore the rest, they could cite Magna Carta in support of sharia law on the role (or rather lack of role) of women in society. The Great Charter's long history would make a great subject for the study of selective memory.

***

So what is the real significance of this delicate little piece of parchment, no bigger than a table napkin, lying in the British Library beneath a soft protective light in a security-strength glass cabinet with humidity and temperature closely controlled? What is it in reality, rather than in later myth? Magna Carta recognises the logical conclusion to what had been happening in England for the previous fifty years. If you are going to introduce a legal system which is attractive to the citizenry because it delivers fair and just decisions – which is what Henry II had done, partly with the less than high-minded motive of raising cash for the crown – then sooner or later, the king too has to be subject to it. Otherwise there can be no guarantee of justice. That's what Magna Carta implicitly recognises.

The Great Charter is not a constitution. It's not democracy in the making. It's not a beacon of freedom and justice for all. The document was never intended to be any of those things.

Magna Carta's greatest accomplishment is to put down in writing, not a principle, but examples of how a medieval king is subject to the law. And let's be clear. That is no mean achievement. It's one that sometimes gets forgotten among all the other froth that has often surrounded this little patch of parchment. The very fact that it stated that the king was not above the law meant that Magna Carta could become a treasured symbol for later generations when they felt themselves unjustly oppressed – not only by kings, but by presidents, dictators and, in fact, by any form government which human beings have devised.

***

It's highly doubtful that either John or the barons, on that June day in 1215, saw Magna Carta as anything more than a short-term stalling tactic while they each gathered their forces for the fight they expected to come. The rebel barons renewed their oaths of allegiance to the king before both sides departed from Runnymede, leaving the Charter for the scriveners to deal with. After being written out, the copies were all checked word by word for accuracy by representatives of both barons and king before the royal seal was pressed into hot wax and attached to the bottom by means of a twisted cord or a ribbon. Each copy was then carried on horseback by a king's messenger, under escort, to one of the principal cathedrals or cities of England, where it was read out, perhaps with an Anglo-Norman French translation.

And that was it.

Within three months, Magna Carta was a dead letter. Despite promises on both sides, its fine words were ignored by both king and rebels, and they resorted instead to old-fashioned solutions to their differences, the sword and the crossbow. Full-scale civil war broke out.

The Great Charter itself might then have been relegated to a footnote in the history books, forgotten by all but a few specialist medieval scholars, if it hadn't been for one unfortunate little happening. The king ate a bad bit of fish, or some other equally noxious food that upset his stomach. It killed him. But it put new life into Magna Carta.

John's luck ran out as he journeyed along the stretch of the east coast of England known as the Wash. And that's where we're heading next.

15 THE WASH, LINCOLNSHIRE, ENGLAND

AGONY IN THE WASTELAND

If I were asked to nominate the most mournful, desolate place in England, I wouldn't choose the North York moors on a mist-filled December day, or Dartmoor at night, or some nameless urban wasteland where couch grass and thistles push their way round the smoke-scarred rubble of half-demolished warehouses. Instead I'd go for the marshlands of the Wash.

On the North York moors, even as I pulled my jacket tighter for warmth, peering at the path ahead, I'd still likely stumble on some little patch of purple heather close to a rippling stream. And on Dartmoor, I'd know that it would soon be daylight. And even faced with a rusty wire fence around some man-made ugliness of smashed asbestos, jagged concrete and twisted metal, I couldn't help thinking the place was ripe for redevelopment – there'd be some hope. But the mile upon mile upon mile of miserable flatness that borders the huge east coast bay known as the Wash, looks beyond redemption.

It's where disaster befell King John sixteen months after the sealing of Magna Carta at Runnymede.

★ ★ ★

The events leading up to John's arrival on 11 October 1216 at the port of Lynn, now King's Lynn, on the Wash tell us a great deal about the significance – or insignificance – that contemporaries attached to Magna Carta.

The Great Charter, as we've seen, was designed on both sides – king and barons – as a stalling tactic to avoid outright civil war. In this, it utterly failed. Both parties indulged in double dealing.

At first, it seemed the king intended to implement the Charter. The machinery of royal administration was cranked into action and began the distribution of the document to cathedrals around the country. But it was soon clear that

John had no intention of submitting royal authority to a committee of lesser mortals, and he sent off a highly biased account of what had taken place at Runnymede to Pope Innocent III. John of course had promised to go on crusade, and Innocent, trusting in this avowal, backed the King to the hilt. He launched a ferocious attack against the barons and against Magna Carta. He 'utterly rejected' the Charter, which he condemned as 'shameful, degrading, illegal and unjust'. It had been 'extorted from a great prince who has taken the Cross'. The Pope declared that he would excommunicate anyone who tried to implement the terms of the document, a threat which he later carried out against thirty named barons. Within three months of the assembly at Runnymede, Pope Innocent III also declared Magna Carta 'null and void of all validity for ever'. John had played a clever hand. With the judgement of Christ's representative on earth so delivered, he could present himself as having no alternative but to reject the Great Charter.

The rebellious barons too were just as manipulative and duplicitous. Some of the die-hard rebels had even drifted away from Runnymede before the Charter was sealed. They felt John was being slippery and should have been crushed once and for all. So, as an excuse for keeping their army of knights battle-ready, they organised tournaments (for which the prize was to be a bear, provided by an anonymous lady sympathetic to their cause – though what exactly the winner was supposed do with the animal is not recorded). Some of the king's enemies fortified their castles, attacked royal manors and even assaulted royal officials who were trying to implement the Charter. The barons, in return for John's agreement to Magna Carta, had promised to keep the peace, and had pledged to guarantee this by giving the king securities, such as sending their children to him as hostages or paying over to him the equivalent of bail money. To a man, the barons reneged on this guarantee. The historian A.L. Poole has suggested that the barons' demand for a charter had been a subterfuge all along and that what they really wanted was to rid themselves of John.

Civil war was inevitable. By the autumn of 1215, widespread fighting had broken out. In the early days, John's fortunes rose dramatically. He was master of the south and the west, so he turned his attention to the north. He even crossed into Scotland to punish King Alexander II, who had sided with the barons, and his mercenaries butchered the inhabitants of Berwick on the border. Other towns in northern England then begged for mercy and paid John huge sums to avoid a similar fate. Within three months, only London held out against him.

But John's triumphs were short-lived. The barons had appealed for help to King Philip Augustus of France, and they offered the crown of England to his son, Louis – the same Louis who had blocked John in Poitou at the time of the Battle of Bouvines. In May 1216 Louis landed with an army at Thanet on the south-east coast, and within two weeks he had joined forces with the barons in London. From then on, the battle lines became confused. Though John lost control of many of his castles, a fair proportion of the barons, though opposed to him, weren't enthusiastic for the alternative – a foreign claimant to the throne.

It was at this point that the king arrived at Lynn. Sited at the south-east corner of the great bay known as the Wash, it was one of the most important ports in East Anglia with a thriving trade in food provisioning. It had prospered by buying commercial privileges from the king, so the citizens here welcomed John, and laid on a feast for him. It was not to be a happy celebration. Within a few hours, the king became violently ill. Blame has been laid variously on a dish of lampreys – a variety of eel found in local rivers – or possibly some over-ripe peaches, or else on some under-fermented cider. The chroniclers, ever quick to attribute some fresh vice to John, claimed he had just gorged himself and so made himself ill. But he soon developed full-blown dysentery, and you don't get dysentery from overeating. The guilty parties were the sloppy kitchen staff of Lynn. The fish, the fruit or the cider must have been contaminated with faeces. Dysentery is still a dangerous sickness in underdeveloped parts of the world, and in the England of the early thirteenth century it could suddenly turn fatal.

Exactly what happened next and where has been the subject of detailed debate among historians.

What is certain is this. The king was heading for northern England, and on 11 October, he rode – in increasing discomfort – along the coast of the Wash the 13 or so miles from Lynn to the town of Wisbech. Before he set off, he hadd given orders for his baggage train – the more slow-moving and cumbersome collection of carts, wagons, pack animals and horsemen – to take a short cut so it could meet up with him at the end of the day. Whether his illness distorted his judgement in this decision we'll never know. The baggage included not just his bedding, a portable lavatory, a mobile chapel and his other personal effects, but also more importantly the crown jewels and a wealth of other treasure. A short cut meant crossing the treacherous sandy marshland which bordered the Wash. Those in charge of the baggage, with a long journey ahead of them and anxious not to keep a short-tempered king waiting at the other end, started early, too early, it turned out, because the tide hadn't fully gone out. They may not have had a local guide, and they probably tried to follow one of the causeway tracks that crossed the desolate strand. It was a disastrous mistake.

Historians have argued about where exactly the accident happened. Part of the problem is that the coast in 1216 was nowhere near where it is today. Vast areas of land have been drained, reclaimed and have silted up over the past 800 years. So all the likely spots are now between 5 and 10 miles inland. The favoured site is far from any sandy marshland, and is thought to be somewhere near the small town of Sutton Bridge. Today an old, iron-girdered railway swing bridge there spans the River Nene, a wide canal big enough to take 3,000-ton cargo ships. Other historians have plumped for an area 3 miles further south, among trees and hedgerows near the mysteriously-named village of Foul Anchor. Neither of these places today – one semi-industrial, the other rural-idyllic – can give the remotest idea of the dangerous conditions facing the baggage train that October morning as it tried to cross the marshes.

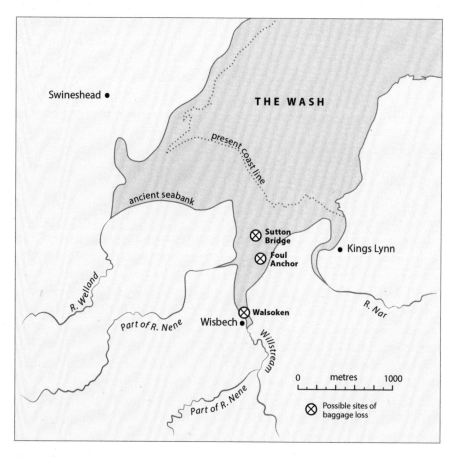

No one knows exactly where the crown jewels and other priceless treasures were sucked into the sandy mud of the Wash. The spot has long since disappeared as land was reclaimed from the sea.

But we can still get some feel for what it would have been like back then. There's a spot 8 miles north-west of Sutton Bridge where coastal conditions remain not too different from the way they were in 1216. And that's where I'm heading now. After passing the last house in the hamlet of Holbeach Saint Matthew, the road becomes a cart-track, and soon there are no more fields of yellow oilseed rape or sugar beet with green tops. Eventually, the track itself peters out completely, so I leave the car on a stony patch of ground by a gloomy concrete pillbox where seventy years ago volunteer soldiers of the Home Guard watched for a German invasion that never came. These days there's a long earth bank, 8–10 feet high, designed to keep the sea at bay when there's an extra-high tide or when a gale from the north-east is driving the waves on to the land. Catastrophic floods have happened here. The worst in living memory, in 1953, killed over 300 people along this coast, and the seawater wrecked homes a mile inland.

Today it's cold, windy and drizzling.

I climb the grassy sea bank, imagining that from its top I'll see waves lapping on to a sandy beach. But the only sea I can make out is a thin grey strip beneath a massive grey sky on a low horizon that seems many miles away. Between me and it is a salt marsh, oozing brown-black mud that encloses pools of murky seawater in snaking channels that seem to lead nowhere. Here and there the mud is caked, cracked and half-dry, where tufts of wiry marsh grass struggle and wave in the bitter wind.

There's what could be a path meandering ahead of me. It's hard to tell. It's just a winding stretch of marsh that's a bit drier and stonier than the rest and where no mud-spattered grass blades are visible. The causeway that the king's baggage train followed must have been no more recognisable nor safe than this. So I climb down from the earth wall, and for fifteen minutes, follow this line of half-compacted dirt and scattered stones until I discern a flat mass of dark grey sand several hundred yards before me. I eventually make out that hundreds of yards still further ahead it finally merges into the North Sea. This is as far as I dare go. The tide's coming in.

Before I saw this place for myself, I was puzzled as to how the king's baggage train could get lost and perish on a flat beach. Surely, I'd thought, you could see the land to your left and the sea to your right. How could you lose your way? But it's the vastness of this flat, dreary landscape that's the problem. And you can't just walk wherever you want. You have to stick to the indistinct tracks. You can't trust anywhere else not to squelch under your feet and then suck you down. And there are no landmarks. One stony stretch of mud, one murky stream, one patch of spiky grass is much the same as any other. And of course the tidal waters here race in over the flats at frightening speed, and then suddenly the marsh, which a moment before looked sodden but passable, can become an inescapable trap.

Add to all this that in October, the month when John's baggage train tried to cross here, an impenetrable morning fog often swirls in off the sea, and we can understand how strangers, unused to the place, could soon find themselves in trouble.

The chroniclers vary in their account of how serious the accident was for John.

Ralph, the Abbot of Coggeshall wrote that the king 'lost his chapel with his relics, and some of his packhorses with many household effects, and many members of his household were submerged in the waters of the sea, and sucked into the quicksand there.'

Roger of Wendover said:

> He lost by an unexpected accident all the wagons, carts and packhorses, with the treasures, precious vessels and all the other things which he cherished with special care; for the ground was opened in the midst of the waves and bottomless whirlpools engulfed everything together with men and horses, so that not a single foot soldier got away to bear tidings of the disaster to the king.

Matthew Paris, who can always be relied on to have a dig at John, embroidered the accident further:

> He lost there irretrievably the carts and packhorses bearing his booty and loot, and all his treasure and household effects. For the ground opened in the midst of the waves, and the sand which is called quick sucked in everything – horses and men, weapons, tents, victuals and all the things which the king valued too highly in the world – apart from his life.

Now, we can aim off for the way the chroniclers beefed-up their accounts with 'the ground opening up in the midst of the waves' and the 'bottomless whirlpools'. But it's easy to see how men, carthorses and wagons could wander from the causeway and find themselves sinking and sucked into the sandy mud with no firm ground where they could be dragged out to safety.

As for the extent of John's losses, we have surviving records to help us assess what got swallowed by the mud. We know that between the time of Runnymede and March 1216, the king gathered in from various monasteries, where they had been held for safekeeping, a huge quantity of jewels, ornamental plate and regalia. According to a detailed inventory that survives, this included dozens of gold and silver goblets, flagons, basins, candelabra, phylacteries – in Christian medieval times, these were boxes containing holy relics – pendants, jewel-encrusted belts, all the coronation regalia, as well as the remarkable treasures his grandmother had worn as Empress of Germany: her crown, purple robes, a gold wand surmounted with a golden dove, and what's called 'the sword of Tristan'.

So were all these items lost in the quicksands of the Wash? We can get a firm clue by comparing this list with the inventory of regalia on show four years later at the full coronation of John's son, Henry III. Almost none of John's treasures are there. Does that necessarily mean they' went down with the baggage train? Alternative explanations have been put forward. That John had sold all his valuables to fund his war with the barons. Or that the treasures were stolen from him on his deathbed. But there are holes in these theories. The king was not so desperate that he would have sold the crown and orb and other symbols of his royal power, and thieves would have had a tough job getting past the troop of royal bodyguards to cart off all that booty. In any event, if either of these explanations were true, you would expect some mention of these uniquely valuable items to turn up later in some baronial, municipal or church records. The most distinctive of these treasures were the items from the fabulous regalia of the Empress Matilda, and they were never heard of again.

So somewhere, maybe under the foundations of the wharf where today they're loading plastic containers on to the Dutch vessel *Ronja*, or perhaps buried beneath a field near Foul Anchor, there still lies a store of unimaginable wealth. Many searches have been organised over the years. Not a trace has been found.

✯ ✯ ✯

As I walk back along the stone track across the marshland, I notice that the grey-brown water in the muddy channels has risen several inches. A pair of oystercatchers give a desperate shriek as they swoop overhead, and I spot a small flock of Canada geese grazing over to the north-east. The salt marshes of the Wash may get my nomination as the most desolate place in England, but that doesn't mean they don't have their own peculiar attraction, especially when you know what a tragic drama was enacted here.

The news of the loss of his baggage train reached John on the evening of the same day at Swineshead Abbey, 10 miles west-north-west of where I'm walking. He was utterly exhausted by the symptoms of severe dysentery, and apparently when he heard the account of how his jewels, his coronation regalia and his grandmother's prized riches had been lost, his fever shot up. For John, now desperately ill, the news must have been seen as an omen. His earthly life was slipping from his grasp.

The king could now barely sit on a horse. But he struggled as far as Sleaford, where he rested for two days, and was then carried – probably on a stretcher atop a cart – to Newark Castle. There the Abbot of Croxton, who was renowned for his medical skills, attended him. But John was too far gone. He dictated his will to his secretary. It opened with the words:

> Being overtaken by a grievous sickness, and so, incapable of making a detailed disposition of my possessions, I commit the ordering and execution of my will to the fidelity and discretion of my faithful men, whose names are written below.

Those names include three bishops, the loyal William Marshall who had stuck with him to the end, plus Savary de Mauléon and Falkes de Breauté, two of the mercenaries so resented by the rebellious barons. He authorised these executors to do whatever they thought appropriate to make 'satisfaction to God and the Holy Church for the wrongs I have done them'. Then, on the night of 18 October, nine days after the loss of his treasure in the Wash, as a furious wind howled round the rooftops of Newark, the abbot heard the King's confession and performed the last rites.

By the next morning, King John was dead. The abbot removed his intestines, and oversaw the embalming of the king's body, which was then carried in a funeral cortège of armed mercenary soldiers for interment – according to his wishes – at Worcester Cathedral. We shall follow him there for our next stop.

★ ★ ★

By now, Magna Carta itself was as good as dead. The Pope had denounced it and condemned to eternal damnation anyone who implemented it. The king had rejected it. But perhaps the most telling blow had come from the barons who were credited with extracting the king's agreement to it. They had discarded the idea of curbing the king's power by force of law, and instead had resorted to an old-style solution: if you don't like the king, rebel against him and put another one in his place. They had invited a foreign prince to be their new ruler.

So that should have been the end of Magna Carta.

And so it might have been except for the timing of one event: John's death. His son and heir Henry was only 9 years old. 'A pretty little knight', it was said. In wartime haste and with little of the traditional ceremonial of a full coronation (which was to take place in more peaceful times, four years later) the boy was declared king by the Bishop of Winchester. A simple gold circlet belonging to his mother had to do for a crown. William Marshall, now in his seventies, became regent.

The barons' hostilities had been, as much as anything, a personal vendetta against a king they loathed. But it had taken the cack-handed cooks of Lynn to achieve what the barons could not. Now John was dead, the new infant monarch offered the possibility of a fresh start. But while the civil war rumbled on and with only a boy on the throne, Regent Marshall needed to be conciliatory. So, on 11 November, before an assembly of royalist magnates, he reissued Magna Carta in the 9-year-old king's name, as a blueprint of how relations between the new monarch and his subjects would be. Some clauses were omitted or modified: most significantly, the oversight committee of twenty-five barons was dropped. But otherwise, the spirit of the document remained. It was a clever move. The barons' opposition faded away, and the French pretender Louis made peace. He accepted a payment in lieu of the English crown and sailed away back to his father.

So the irony is that Magna Carta, an attack on the power of kings, was brought back in 1216 as a royalist manifesto.

If John had lived on a few more years until his son could succeed him as an adult, the transition would not have been such a vulnerable moment for the crown. There would almost certainly have been no need to reissue the Great Charter, which might therefore have been killed off for ever. As it was, Magna Carta sprang from its deathbed and found itself a new life.

And if John hadn't swallowed that mouthful of dirty food one evening at Lynn, I like to think that the course of history might have been different.

16 WORCESTER CATHEDRAL, ENGLAND

THE MAN LAID BARE

I always think the sign of a truly fine cathedral is if, on entering, you trip over a step or the edge of a stone plinth. Not because they're dangerously positioned, but because your eyes are inexorably drawn upwards by mighty columns that rise to a glorious vaulted roof. It's as though your body wants to be about 40 feet higher than it actually is, and your mind forgets to look out for your feet.

I know the explanation that religious folk give for this phenomenon. But for me, it's a tribute to human art and engineering. At Worcester Cathedral, two lines of elegant columns point skyward, and then urge our neck muscles to stretch to their utmost as we follow the criss-cross ceiling of stone ribs dwindling into the distance. What I do concede is that the faith of those who were inspired to plan and build such an architectural masterpiece must have been extraordinary.

Although much of the structure we can admire in Worcester Cathedral today was completed in the centuries after King John's death, the present-day impressive dimensions of the building – 67 feet high, and 425 feet long – were the same in October 1216 on the day that the armed escort of John's mercenary troops arrived here, bearing his body. Their journey from Newark where the king had died would not have been a stately progress. Civil war still raged. Baronial armies were on the move. There was need for haste. As the burial party entered the west door, the impact on the eyes and the minds of the military escort would have been even greater than on ours today. That's partly because religious faith was universal and unquestioned, and also because buildings of such massive magnificence had the power to stun by their very rarity.

This morning, as I eventually let my gaze descend from on high, it's my ears that take over. I'm suddenly aware of a hubbub of rapid, excited chattering as if from hundreds of children. And that's what it is. They're all ages, from about 5 to 15, in the middle of the nave, and seem to be bunched into classes, though the mixed swathes of blue, orange and green suggest uniforms from lots of different schools. Their teachers are shouting to make themselves heard.

Standing at the back near the door are two men, retirement age, both in but-toned blazers, sober ties, cavalry twill slacks, polished brown shoes. Each has a green sash slung from one shoulder, so I know they're official. I go and ask where I can find King John's tomb. The taller one offers to show me, and quick-marches off on a side route, moving temporary barriers, stepping over red velvet ropes, to skirt the mob of kids. 'It's a special school visits day,' he explains over his shoulder as I trot to keep up with him. 'And we've got a couple of pilgrimages thrown in, as well as the usual guided tours. Mind that step. We'll go round the back.'

I'd imagined that John, not being the most popular monarch in ecclesiastical circles, would have been banished to the crypt down some gloomy stairs, or at best relegated to the far side of the furthest side chapel. But suddenly, we find ourselves right in front of the high altar. And there in the very middle of the chancel at the foot of the sacred steps, in the most honoured position that any mortal could have in any cathedral, stands the marbled resting place of the man of whom the Victorian historian J.R. Green said, 'Hell itself was defiled by the fouler presence of King John.'

When I express surprise, my guide says, 'Well, he was a king, and kings got their authority from God.'

On the other side of John's 5-foot-high tomb, a woman who's in charge of some 10-year-olds turns to us and snaps, 'Would you keep your voices down. Please!' The guide adjusts his sash, gives me a covert *blimey-who-does-she-think-she-is* look, then says, 'I'll leave you to it,' and is off.

I go and read a small notice nearby. It sums up King John for us:

His tyranny led to the barons enforcing his signature of Magna Carta in 1215. His repudiation of the Charter provoked a civil war which was still in progress when he died at Newark.

No mention of the Pope declaring it null and void, nor of the rebellious barons ignoring the Charter and taking up arms, never mind the technical detail that he didn't sign it, but sealed it. The myth lives on.

The woman who doesn't like loud voices leads her brood away and is replaced by another, more smiley teacher – white jacket, shoulder bag and specs – with a dozen and a half of what look like 7-year-olds, in blue sweaters and ties with grey shorts or skirts. I ask her if she'd mind my sitting in on her chat. She beams and says, 'No, of course, please do.'

The children are sitting on oak benches 10 feet from the King John monu-ment. There's a space at the end of the second row next to the teaching assistant, so that's where I perch. The teacher points to the stone figure lying on its back on top of the tomb, feet towards the altar, and asks, 'Do we know what sort of person this is?'

A dozen hands shoot up. She chooses a girl in the front row whose answer I can't hear, but the teacher repeats it for the benefit of the rest of us. 'Yes, it's a king. How do we know?'

This time she picks a boy in the second row, who again speaks in a coy whisper.

'Right, Jonathan, he's wearing a crown. And where do you think he's king of?'

'…' Unintelligible front-row girl.

'No, Louise, towns don't have kings and queens. What can we see on the side?' She points to a red shield.

'…'

'Yes, lions. That's right, three lions. And where today do we see three lions? The boys ought to know this.'

'…'

'That's it, Joseph, on an England football shirt. So he's King of England.'

All these children, without exception, are on the edge of their seats, attentive to every word their teacher says and so eager with their raised hands that it makes you feel proud to be a human being.

'Do you notice that his feet aren't crossed?' continues the teacher. 'That means he wasn't killed in battle. And they're resting on a lion, which shows he was important. Less important people had a dog at their feet. So, what's this king's name?'

'…'

'No, he wasn't King Charles. Do you remember Robin Hood? Who was the king in Robin Hood? Annabelle?'

'…'

'Yes, good. It's a statue of King John. A lot of people have called him a tyrant because he took lots of money from his subjects. Who knows what a tyrant is?'

'…'

'Ooh, well done, Joanna. Yes, a wicked king. But John probably wasn't as bad as all that. He was quite a religious man. He liked to worship in this cathedral. People are often not all bad or all good, are they? And that's the same with kings. I think we could say that King John wasn't a nice man, but he wasn't an especially wicked one either.'

Time for their next stop on the tour. I thank the teacher for letting me listen, and she turns with a smile and says, 'Did I do all right about King John?'

'Oh yes, brilliant,' I say, wondering who she thinks I am. I'm about to add that she did a lot better than the cathedral's own small notice, but she and her class are off before I can get the words out.

★★★

The top of King John's sarcophagus is shoulder high, so to see the face and the whole figure properly I'll have to raise myself up a few inches on the base of its plinth. I'm nervous about doing this. I can imagine the guide saying that if everyone did it, the stone would wear away. But I decide to risk it, and if I get caught, I'll just have to apologise and step down.

No one seems to mind, so I'm free to have a good look.

The stone effigy of John has been carved to show his left hand gripping the hilt of a sword. Its blade is unsheathed, which is highly unusual because there was a convention in the thirteenth century that swords – whether real in the grip of a warrior or stone on a tomb effigy – should not be battle-ready within God's house. Historians have debated why it was that John's sword here at Worcester broke the rule. One theory is that once the Interdict had ended and the king had pledged allegiance to the Pope at Temple Ewell he became in effect a soldier of Christ, and so the unsheathed weapon here on his tomb showed he was ready to defend the Church. This brings us to an irony in the way King John has been regarded down the centuries. He wasn't always seen as a wicked failure. In Tudor times he was resurrected (literally) as a model king, whose six-year opposition to the Pope was seen as a precursor of Henry VIII's own battle with Rome during the Reformation. So in 1529, John's remains were dug up – carefully – in order that the original lower tomb could be raised up to its present height as better befitted the last resting place of a Tudor hero who had fought *against* papal tyranny. Once the new sarcophagus was in place with John's bones inside it, the original stone effigy I'm looking at now was put back in place.

His right, non-sword-holding hand is gripping what looks like a small tube, perhaps a phylactery, the container for a finger bone or some other small relic of his favourite saint. The surface of his figure from his crown to the lion at his feet is a shiny dark brown. The marble from which it's made was brought from Purbeck in Dorset, 140 miles to the south. Originally it would have been painted in bright colours and encrusted with gold, silver and precious jewels – emeralds from north Africa, amethysts from Germany, and opals and garnets from eastern Europe. You can still see the pitted holes in the cuffs of his sleeve and in the collar of his gown where they would have been embedded. There's no record of who stole these jewels or when.

The tomb was opened up again, this time by curious historians, in 1797. The king's skeleton was intact. On one side of him lay a sword, the bones of his left arm lay across his breast, and the bones of his feet were erect. His teeth apparently were in perfect condition. His remains had been draped in a robe made of damask, which showed little sign of decay, and its original crimson colour could still just be made out. It was calculated that John was 5 feet 7 inches tall, which would have made him about average in the thirteenth century. His skull was covered by a monk's cowl. This led his detractors at the time to suggest that John had been slippery to the last, and had requested the cowl to help him sneak past St Peter at the gates of heaven in the guise of a holy man. A less fanciful explanation is that the head was covered in this way during the tomb-raising exercise in 1529.

The marble features of John here on his tomb are the closest we can get to an accurate picture of his face. It was sculpted around 1231, fifteen years after his death, and there's a reasonable chance that the craftsman responsible had himself seen John several times – assuming, that is, that he was a local man. The king liked hunting around Worcester and seems to have formed a special attachment to the memory of St Wulfstan, the eleventh-century bishop here. Wulfstan was declared a saint in 1203, and this apparently made the king feel close to him. Typically of John, however, his relations with the place were inconsistent. He spent two or three Christmases in Worcester and gave money to help repair the cathedral after a fire. But he also fined the monks for supporting the Pope during the Interdict, and hit the townspeople in the pocket for siding with the rebellious barons. One way or another though, the king was seen a good deal around Worcester.

The marble of the royal face itself has been slightly damaged. At some stage in the past eight centuries, someone has knocked the end off his nose and chipped the front of his lips, most likely a zealous seventeenth-century parliamentarian opposed to all things kingly. But despite that, we can get a clear impression of what John might have looked like. He had high cheek bones, a small downturned mouth, a high forehead and relatively flat – rather than sunken – eye sockets. The ends of his moustache were carefully groomed into little downward curls. His short beard was tucked under his chin. And what's most noticeable – something that's appeared in every painting of him ever since – is his neat, wavy, long hair reaching down to his shoulders.

Can we read anything about his character in this face? John's detractors might say it shows him as vain, mean-spirited and suspicious. His supporters could claim he looks to be fastidious about his appearance, proud – as a king should be – with the expression of someone who makes cool judgements about those around him. But all this is probably just about as accurate as the Victorians thinking they could tell whether someone was a criminal by feeling the bumps on their head.

✫ ✫ ✫

If there's one thing our account of John's life has shown, it is that he was full of contradictions. Ignore one set of his qualities and you can easily convict him of being a tyrannous demon; ignore the other side and he gets off as a strong ruler who was a victim of circumstance.

The only near contemporary image we have of King John's features, on his tomb in Worcester Cathedral.

So, first the case for the prosecution:

1. He was maliciously disloyal. He took up arms against his own father, Henry II, and then later, when his brother Richard the Lionheart became king, against him too.
2. He was violent, hot-tempered and vindictive. He is said to have murdered Prince Arthur, his nephew, with his own hands in a drunken rage. And when Matilda de Briouze accused him publicly of that murder, he starved her and her son to death in prison.
3. He was suspicious to the point of paranoia. He regarded those who should have been his right-hand men – i.e. the mighty barons of his realm – as potential enemies. Instead he relied on foreign, low-born mercenary soldiers, who were without land or title and so were in his power.
4. He was grasping and greedy. He ignored traditional feudal obligations and demanded ever heavier taxes from the great families of England to support his military adventures. And he used and abused the machinery of royal government as a means of taxing, fining and milking his subjects dry.

5. He was cowardly. He caved in to the French king as soon as he came to the throne, which earned him the nickname 'Softsword', and he lost Normandy, which had been associated with the crown of England since the Norman Conquest. He failed to win it back.

6. He was irreligious. He persecuted the Church, stole its lands and treasures, and was excommunicated as a result.

7. In short, he abused his power to set up a regime of extortion and terror. He was a tyrant. And Magna Carta, however narrow and local in its detail, struck a blow against such despotism.

The counterargument for the defence runs like this:

1. Yes, he rebelled against his father, but he did so in alliance with his brother Richard and urged on by his mother, Queen Eleanor. There was nothing unusual about armed conflict between members of the Angevin royal family.

2. He certainly had a violent temper. In this respect he was little different from his brother and his father. His murder of Arthur – never proved – would be a dreadful crime in another age. But such acts were not unknown among the ruling classes in the thirteenth century. Remember Robert Fitzwalter's son-in-law slaying a servant in a fit of rage, and it was John on that occasion who tried to bring the culprit to justice. What's more, even the Pope defended John, being quoted as saying, 'Arthur was no innocent victim. He was a traitor … and could rightly be condemned without judgement to die even the most shameful of deaths.'

3. It's true that John didn't trust many of the barons. But can you blame him? The worst of them were no better than self-serving thugs who would stab a king in the back if they thought it would bring them an earldom. And so he had to rely on mercenaries because they were loyal paid employees.

4. Because they could not be trusted, he needed the barons to meet their obligations in cash rather than with a few knights who would pack their bags and go home once their allotted days of military service were up. And this was at a time when warfare was getting more expensive. As for the idea that he abused the machinery of royal government, the truth is that he was an energetic administrator and turned the judicial system created by his father into a powerful tool, which brought a fairer system of justice to many of his subjects. Of course the barons didn't like that because it deprived them of the tools of power as well cash from fines which would otherwise have flowed into their own coffers.

5. There's no doubt that John was not an outstanding military leader like his brother Richard. But he wasn't without his successes, for instance in his decisive

action at Mirebeau to rescue his mother. he also built a navy that won the first redoubtable English victory at sea since before the Norman Conquest.

6. He gave money to religious foundations, to Worcester Priory, for instance. During the Interdict, when John admittedly confiscated a great deal of Church land, the barons had the Pope's backing – the perfect excuse, in fact – to rebel and overthrow John. They didn't do so because they were reluctant to undermine their control over the Church in their own territories. In the end, it was of course the Pope who overturned Magna Carta.

7. In summary, the case for the defence is that John was simply trying to professionalise government, the administration of justice and the military. He was sometimes overly aggressive in this. So it was inevitable that his actions should bring him into conflict with the barons whose semi-independence and near-equality with the monarch had been guaranteed by the old feudal system. So Magna Carta didn't herald a new age of freedom. It was a trumpet call for a last desperate charge in support of an old cause that was dying on its feet.

Which of these opposing views of John is closer to the truth? To some extent, both are right.

John was certainly a violent man. But it's right to point out that he was no worse than many of his contemporaries. It was an age when summary justice often meant having a limb chopped off or being burned alive. As the twentieth-century historian J. C. Holt has pointed out, 'John was harsh and cruel, certainly, but a king was more likely to suffer disaster through kindness than through cruelty.'

His best points were that he was industrious and ingenious. He seems to have genuinely enjoyed taking part in the administration of justice, for instance, and would often sit on the bench with his judges. To quote the historian W.L. Warren, John 'possessed the high administrative ability of a great ruler'. This was bound to bring him into conflict with the barons. The more active that royal officials became, the more they dealt directly with knights and those just below the barons in the pecking order, which of course undermined the barons' own authority.

John could be generous. For example, he made sure his first wife never lacked for anything. As for his religious faith, it was fairly conventional for that time. After his coronation he went on a pilgrimage to the shrine of St Thomas à Becket at Canterbury, and later, at the height of the Interdict, he borrowed some spiritual books from the Bishop of Reading. A mobile chapel always travelled with him.

It's too much to say that he was the *victim* of circumstance. But it is true that there were factors against him that were beyond his control. The anarchy that had allowed the balance of power to swing in the barons' favour during Stephen's reign had been reversed largely by the efficient administrative system introduced by Henry II. Richard had used it to raise huge amounts of cash for his overseas adventures. So the barons were already unsettled by the time John came to the throne. And it was a time of monetary inflation, an economic factor unrecognised at the turn of the thirteenth century. So John put the same amount of energy that Richard had devoted to soldiering into improving and extending the reach of the justice system and of his taxation officials. And of course, once Normandy was lost to the French crown, John had less territory from which to raise cash, so a greater burden fell on England.

John's real problem was the way he set about his task of ruling. He was wilful and capricious. You didn't know where you were with him. You didn't want to get on the wrong side of him. So, on top of the problems he inherited, he himself made matters worse.

What drove him? Fear. Fear for his personal security and that of his throne. It made him a control freak. He was obsessed with finding ways to manipulate those who showed signs of independence or just got too big for their boots. This was an age when loyalty to a king was partly a feudal obligation, but was also partly a personal relationship. Put simply, John was no good at this second part. He didn't have the easy manner of a diplomat who could cajole those around him into supporting him. Nor did he possess the heroic reputation of a Henry V or a Richard the Lionheart, which would command the full respect due to a king. So instead, John resorted to the crude methods of a gangland boss. Bribery and extortion were his tools. He tried to buy loyalty and security by heaping land and honours on those of his barons who promised to support him. At other times, he extracted loyalty by means of threats. The barons often had to give up their children to him as hostages, aware of the terrible fate that would befall their offspring if they themselves didn't behave. Sometimes, as with William de Briouze, he used both methods at different times on the same person, rewarding the man generously one year, then stripping him bare and crushing him underfoot like an insect the next. Such callous unpredictability was a warning to all – including the mightiest in the land – to be careful to keep the king's goodwill.

The same worries about security were behind his preference for paid foreign mercenary soldiers over powerful barons, whose independence threatened him. He promoted men like Falkes de Breauté and Gerard d'Athée, who were employees entirely dependent on him. For the barons, of course, this was political heresy. They claimed the ancient right to be at the king's right hand, and seeing themselves replaced by these jumped-up foreign nobodies was an insult to their ancient aristocratic dignity. So when John rewarded his mercenaries with real landed power, it was the last straw. As we have seen, for the barons one of the most attractive elements of Magna Carta was the way it stripped out these new foreigners – and their relatives too.

So was John a tyrant? We have to be careful here not to apply the standards of the twenty-first century. In pure political terms, for us today a tyrant is one who has seized absolute power – trampling on the will of the people – and who then abuses that power for his (or her) own advantage. It's a term which is particularly appropriate in the twenty-first-century western world, where authority is held to stem from the people and is properly held for their benefit. Thirteenth-century England was a very different place. On a spectrum which has absolute monarchy – subject to no restraint – at one end, and constitutional monarchy – entirely subject to parliament – at the other, medieval English kings were somewhere in between. On the one hand, their authority was God-given. On the other hand, they were part of a feudal system and had obligations towards those beneath them in the hierarchy. It was a confusing set-up. John lurched between the two ends: One moment, arbitrary, crushing the de Briouze family; the next, dealing out fair and just decisions in the royal law court. And his character fitted with this confused theory of political extremes. The renowned twentieth-century historian A.L. Poole said of John that 'he was cruel and ruthless, violent and passionate, greedy and self-indulgent, genial and repellent, arbitrary and judicious, clever and capable, original and inquisitive. He is made up of inconsistencies.'

Judged by the standards of his day, John was not an irredeemably evil king. He just stepped over too many lines that defined how a monarch should behave, in particular towards his tenants-in-chief, the barons and towards the Church. Magna Carta tries to define those lines John had strayed over.

But we should leave the final verdict on John to the barons themselves. Not only the verdict they delivered with the Great Charter, but also the opinion of him reflected in their actions. Or rather, their inaction. Why – we have to ask – if their king really was such a despot as his detractors have claimed, did it take sixteen years before just one in four of them took up arms and rebelled against him?

Our primary school teacher in Worcester Cathedral got it right: 'King John wasn't a nice man, but he wasn't an especially wicked one, either.'

★★★

So how did it come about that John has been painted as the devil incarnate? The answer is that he failed to do what all modern politicians strive to do: get the press on their side. The journalists of the thirteenth century had it in for him. We shall meet them on our next stop. They created an image of King John which persisted well into the twentieth century and is often still seen in the popular opinion of him today.

17 THE INTERNET

A BAD PRESS

Once upon a time, there was a handsome count who went on a long journey. When he returned to his castle some years later, he brought with him a beautiful bride. His courtiers remarked that she was obviously of noble birth. She bore him four children, and the family looked set to live happily ever after.

However, as time went by, it was noticed that there was something strange about the countess. No relatives or friends from her past life ever came to visit her, and no one knew exactly where she came from. The other odd thing was that, when the family went to church, she often found an excuse to stay at home, and even on those rare occasions when she did accompany her husband and children to mass, she would always slip away just before the priest consecrated the bread and wine at holy communion. The count became more and more puzzled and troubled by her behaviour, and could get no explanation from her. So he decided to put her to the test, and the next time she came to church, he quietly instructed four of his loyal knights to stay close to her and to stop her from leaving.

The moment arrived when the priest prepared to consecrate the bread and wine, and when as usual the countess turned to head for the door, one of the knights trod on the hem of her dress so she couldn't get away. She struggled, and as the priest raised the Host above his head, she let out a blood-curdling scream. She wrenched and tore her robe free, then, still shrieking, she snatched up two of her children, and like a startled raven clutching its carrion, flew out of the window.

She was Melusine, Satan's daughter. The count was the Count of Anjou. And from the two children she left behind were descended Henry II and his two sons, Richard and John. This ancestry, it was said, accounted for the vile tempers of the Angevin kings and for the way they fought each other. They were the devil's brood.

Richard and John used to banter about the story, saying, 'You can't blame us for the way we are, it's in our genes,' or twelfth-century words to that effect. But they were only half-joking. In the days before Freud, Darwin and the Wright brothers, attributing your bad behaviour to a flying demon who was your great-grand-mother was not so outrageous and would have been believed by many who heard the tale. In the thirteenth century, the logical line between the fanciful and the provable was blurred, and sometimes non-existent. And it was in such a sludgy mix of fact and fiction that the seeds of John's own reputation first took root.

✳ ✳ ✳

From the later historian's point of view, it wouldn't have mattered if the gossip about 'bad King John' had been limited to the rough alehouse or the genteel embroidery circle. But it wasn't. It was written down and preserved for posterity by men of God in their chronicles with every appearance of fact.

Today, medieval chronicles, written in abbeys and monasteries scattered across the land, are all available for the curious reader in one place. Or, should I say in two and a half billion places. Or, to be to be strictly accurate, they're in one place and are capable of appearing at the same time in two and a half billion other places. Rather like the Holy Spirit, in fact. The one place being the Internet and the two and a half billion places the total of downloaded web browsers through-out the world, a concept which would certainly have seemed miraculous and mystical to a thirteenth-century monk.

Of course, a monk, scratching away at his parchment in a cell at St Albans or Coggeshall, had none of the benefits available to a present-day political, social or economic commentator writing about contemporary affairs. The monk's only source of information was usually the guests who broke their journeys to stay the odd night at his abbey, and he couldn't Google or make a quick phone call to check what they told him. And anyway, the monk's objective in writing his chronicle wasn't necessarily to set down an objective account of the day's news for future generations. More likely it was to preach a lesson on how the sinful get their comeuppance, or just to indulge a prejudice against people or institutions that irritated him, or even to make political propaganda on behalf of a favourite party.

The limited perspective of the chroniclers, however, doesn't mean their works are useless fables for the historian. At the very least twelfth- and thirteenth-century writers might reflect what contemporaries felt or thought about kings and lords and popes and their doings. the chroniclers undoubtedly recorded events of note and cast clarifying light upon them. But the danger is that the existence of some undoubtedly reliable information can lure the unwary into mistaking other trumped-up anecdotes or unsubstantiated comments, for the unalloyed truth. It was into this trap that eminent Victorian historians sometimes fell, so bestowing the stamp of academic approval on what we now know to be myths about King John.

★ ★ ★

John was cursed with bad luck when it came to the chronicles. He got a bad press. Worse than he deserved. And it tarnished his image over the centuries, which in turn has made it more difficult for historians to get to the truth about him.

For a start, there were few well-informed and reliable writers at work during his reign. The best of them was a monk called Gervase, who lived in Canterbury. He was well placed there to gather news from the constant stream of travellers crossing back and forth over the Channel, and he seems to have done a fairly objective job as far as it went. But he died in 1210, so was not around to tell us about the dramatic events leading up to Magna Carta, or to pull together any overall assessment of the king's legacy. Typical of the other chroniclers was Ralph, Abbot of Coggershall Abbey in Essex. His was less a chronicle, more jottings, mainly about the weather and harvests in East Anglia. Otherwise, the only contemporary accounts came from monks who were even more isolated from mainstream events and who slipped into their journals the occasional jibe at the king, coloured by their knowledge that his actions had cast the country out of God's grace during the Interdict, that he had been excommunicated, and that he had plundered the Church's property. Then, as now, you can't expect a good write-up from someone whose beliefs and livelihood you've attacked.

For John and his reputation, it was especially unfortunate that no one writing at the time was a loyal friend who knew him personally. His brother Richard had been far luckier on this score. For instance, later generations learned from an anonymous author who accompanied him on his crusade that when he fell ill during the siege of Acre Richard still insisted on being carried on his litter before the walls of the city so he could loose his crossbow at the defenders. By contrast, there was no sympathetic journalist with John when he made his heroic dash to Mirebeau to rescue his mother and capture his arch-enemy, Arthur.

There are, however, two chronicles which deal in detail with the deeds of King John and the dramatic events of his reign. The first attempt at a comprehensive account of John's reign wasn't written until ten years or so after he died. It came from the quill of a monk at St Albans Abbey known to us as Roger of Wendover. Roger had set himself the task of writing a history of the world, and when he reached the years following 1199, he must have despaired at how thin was the reliable information available. But not to be put off, he simply rehashed the tittle-tattle about the dead king, or, where that seemed inadequate, he just sexed up the story a bit. Roger wrote how John threatened the Pope's representatives with having their noses slit or their eyes poked out, and how the king extorted money from a Jew in Bristol by the daily routine of knocking one of his teeth out.

Roger's best anecdote concerned Geoffrey, Archdeacon of Norwich. According to our chronicler, in 1209 Geoffrey declared that it was no longer safe for priests to serve the king. John heard about this, and went into a rage. He had Geoffrey arrested, imprisoned, and chained up with lead weights hung on his body like a cloak. In this agonising state, the archdeacon was then starved to death. The problem with this gripping little tale is that we know for certain that this same Geoffrey, Archdeacon of Norwich, was made Bishop of Ely sixteen years after his own alleged death.

To be fair to Roger and his chronicle, he didn't see himself as a historian. He regarded his writings as more of an extended sermon, a warning to his readers that God's wrath is visited on evil men like John. *We* may see his chronicle as a dodgy dossier. For Roger, it justified a righteous war, against worldly sin.

✷ ✷ ✷

But even more influential in forming John's image throughout history were the writings of Roger's successor as the official chronicler at St Albans, one Matthew Paris. Matthew was even further removed from the events of John' reign – he didn't start his own chronicle until 1235, nineteen years after John's death. And what he wrote was even more trap-ridden for the unwary historian than his predecessor's words. Not only did Matthew embellish Roger's anecdotes even further, he also added a few of his own. What's more, he knew how to entice his readers with a cracking narrative mixed with lively commentary.

Matthew missed no opportunity to blacken John's name. At Christmas 1203, we're told, the king, 'effeminate and dissolved in luxury', spends the night drinking. A year later, when Château Gaillard has fallen, John lazes about, 'indulging his gluttony and luxury with his wanton queen while lying in whose bosom he thought that he was in possession of every joy'. We hear him swearing 'By God's feet,' that 'the sterling money of England should restore everything'. By 1208, he's 'oppressing one or other of the nobles of the kingdom, either by extorting money from them unjustly, or by stripping them of their privileges and properties'. Next, we see him hanging children at Nottingham, before throwing all the country's Jews, of both sexes, into prison. By 1213, he's accusing his barons of treason, calling them 'jealous, miserable idiots, boasting he's violated their wives and deflowered their daughters'. The following year, the Battle of Bouvines is lost because the king has fled 'most disgracefully and ignominiously'. After the Charter with the barons is sealed at Runnymede, John soon reneges on the deal, and when the barons demand he fulfil his promises, he laughs at them. During the subsequent war, he becomes 'a destroyer of his own kingdom, hiring as his soldiers a detestable troop of foreigners such as Falkes de Breauté, a man of ignoble birth and a bastard.' Finally on his deathbed, John – according to Matthew Paris – 'cursed all his barons instead of bidding them farewell. And thus, poor and deprived of all treasure, and not retaining the smallest portion of land in peace, so that he is truly called Lackland, he most miserably departed this life.'

But the most extraordinary story of all those pedalled by Paris is of John's failed attempt to turn England into an Islamic nation. The St Alban's chronicle alleges that in 1213, the king tried to enlist the military help of the Muslim emir of North Africa, offering in return to renounce Christianity himself and convert to Islam, as well as to make his kingdom a dependency of the Muslim ruler. When John's ambassadors arrived at the Muslim court with this proposal, the emir was flabbergasted, and even he disapproved of the Christian king's betrayal of his religion and his people (remember that, as a Muslim and the enemy of crusaders, he was generally regarded as little better than the devil himself). The emir asked one of John's representatives to tell him more about John's character. According to Matthew Paris, the ambassador, a priest named Robert, replied that:

> John was a tyrant not a king, a destroyer instead of a governor, crushing his own people and favouring aliens, a lion to his subjects but a lamb to foreigners and rebels. He had lost the duchy of Normandy and many other territories through sloth, and was actually keen to lose his kingdom of England or to ruin it. He was an insatiable extorter of money. He invaded and destroyed his subjects' property. He detested his wife and she him. She was an incestuous and depraved woman, so notoriously guilty of adultery that the king had given orders that her lovers were to be seized and strangled to death on her bed. He himself was envious of many of his barons and kinfolk, and seduced their more attractive daughters and sisters. As for his Christianity, the King was unstable and unfaithful.

This, then, is the foundation of the myth of the irredeemably evil King John.

✶ ✶ ✶

Why, we may ask, did Roger of Wendover and Matthew Paris paint such a diabolic picture of him? The answer is simple. Both were faithful servants at the right hand of the abbots of St Albans. The abbots were more than high-standing, respected prelates. They were lords of vast estates; in other words they were barons themselves, among the most powerful in the realm. In addition, the abbey of St Albans stood on the main route from London to the north, and its guests frequently numbered the nobility of the realm. So the news and opinions that were bandied about the cloisters and refectory of St Albans Abbey were solidly those of

Matthew Paris, the chronicler of St Albans, kneeling in prayer, a self-portrait. Matthew was a talented artist; the face is unusually personal and expressive for a thirteenth-century drawing.

the baronial party. Roger's and Matthew's chronicles were baronial propaganda, as distorted as anything that Soviet-era information ministries could turn out.

All would have been well, if historians had always understood this. But the great Victorian antiquarians did not, and it's to them that we owe much of the abiding strength of the myths about John.

William Stubbs, the most respected nineteenth-century historian, wrote of King John:

> There is nothing in him which for a single moment calls out for our better sentiments; in his prosperity there is nothing we can admire, and in his adversity nothing we can pity ... He had neither energy, nor capacity, nor honesty ... the very worst of all our kings ... a faithless son, a treacherous brother ... polluted with every crime ... false to every obligation ... in the whole view there is no redeeming trait.

In his renowned *Short History of the English People*, Stubbs's contemporary J.R. Green wrote:

> In his inner soul, John was the worst outcome of the Angevins ... His punishments were the refinements of cruelty, the starvation of children, the

crushing of old men under copes of lead. His court was a brothel where no woman was safe from the royal lust, and where his cynicism loved to publish the news of his victim's shame. He was as craven in his superstitions as he was daring in his impiety. He scoffed at priests and turned his back on the mass, even amid the solemnities of his coronation, but he never stirred on a journey without hanging relics round his neck.

It reads like a paraphrase of Roger of Wendover or Matthew Paris. Green's ultimate damnation of John was one which both of those priests might have wished they had written themselves: 'Foul as it is,' wrote Green, 'Hell itself is defiled by the fouler presence of King John.' He added, 'The terrible verdict of the king's contemporaries has passed into the sober judgement of history', which might prompt us to wonder which dictionary Green was using for his definitions of 'contemporaries' and 'sober'.

The great Victorian writers, like Green and Stubbs, with their view of history as the unstoppable march of progress – industrial, constitutional and moral – seized on the writings of the St Albans chroniclers and made of John a monster. The Victorians needed a medieval villain, one they could see being tamed by their own values, those of democracy and the rule of law. And they had one ready made in King John.

By the judgement of these respected nineteenth-century academics, John's reputation as a tyrannical, vicious, depraved, cowardly, sacrilegious and incompetent king then entered folklore. It spread from the libraries of Oxford to the parlours and pubs of middle- and working-class England.

It wasn't until the mid-twentieth century that this image of John was seriously challenged by historians, when they began to place more faith in the detailed analysis of thousands of documents from the royal archive rather than in the biased opinions of thirteenth-century clergymen. As it happens, many more such administrative documents have survived from John's reign than from those of his predecessors. This fact alone is testament to the thoroughness and comparative efficiency of his government. The judicial and chancery rolls of King John not only tell us about court decisions and the state of the royal finances, they also throw up many personal details about the king too. His laundress was named Florence, for instance; and one night he lost 5s playing games of chance with Brian Delisle.

And so it was that historians like W.L. Warren in the latter half of the twentieth century presented a more balanced view of John, one that showed him as a man of many faults but not the devil incarnate. This more subtle, nuanced, ambiguous King John, however, is not so easy to jeer at and boo off the stage, and so the popular image of bad King John has been slow to catch up with the latest academic research.

★★★

But this is only half the story. The distorted image of John is an important element in producing the impression that has come down through history of the Great Charter. Just as John's role in history had been rewritten to make him a monster, so Magna Carta also been recast as the sword capable of slaying such monsters. From its origins as a medieval feudal document with limited short-term aims, subsequent generations transformed it into the origins of parliamentary democracy, the first British constitution, and the foundation stone of some of our most treasured legal rights.

That transformation occurred during the years between 1215 and the English civil war in the seventeenth century. To see how that happened, we're going to the Palace of Westminster, mother of parliaments, home to the House of Commons, the House of Lords, and a spectacular hall which is more than a century older than Magna Carta itself.

18 THE PALACE OF WESTMINSTER, LONDON

A CHARTER FOR ALL SEASONS

The Palace of Westminster – that elegant jumble of buildings beside the Thames, celebrated across the world on tea towels printed with Big Ben, but more respectfully known as the Mother of Parliaments – has got nothing to do with Magna Carta. And that's official.

Or at least that's what the official guide tells me.

The only way you can see inside the palace – that is, unless you're an MP, a lord, an accredited journalist or the queen – is to join an official tour. And that's what I'm doing. It's no easy job. First, to find the right entrance to the palace I have to brave the eyeless stares of a military dictator and a foreign adventurer (statues of Oliver Cromwell and Richard the Lionheart) who guard the approach from Parliament Square. Next, I go through the real security checks – airport-style X-ray machines and pat-downs. Then I join hundreds of other folk streaming ever onwards in search of the right queue, for the 3 p.m. tour in Japanese, the 3.30 tour in German or, as in my case, the 3.15 English one. Eventually, I find my group, clustered around a balding, portly chap in a sagging blue jacket and faded tie, who looked as though he'd just come from a committee meeting of his local bowls club; he's our guide. I sidle up to him and ask if there is anything here to commemorate Magna Carta.

'No,' he replies without hesitation. 'Nothing. I think there may be a photographic copy of Magna Carta somewhere in the Palace of Westminster. But the fact is Magna Carta's got nothing to do with this place and its history.' And with that, he reminds me and my fellow group members not to chew gum (which we might be tempted to throw on the floor), not to sit on any seats unless he says we can, and not to stray too far while we await our departure.

We can give him two cheers for not mythologising about the Great Charter. But there's something he's missing.

If you were to stop a random selection of people in the street and ask them why Magna Carta is still important today, the odds are that – unless you've stumbled upon a medieval historian – you'll hear one of three answers: (1) because it was the start of parliamentary democracy; (2) because it's Britain's constitution; or (3) because it gave us basic legal rights, like trial by jury and an independent judiciary.

The first of these three myths is probably what our guide was thinking of, and it's the easiest one to dismiss. As we've seen in our examination of its clauses, there's nothing in King John's Magna Carta that remotely resembles an elective parliament.

The second – that the Great Charter was a kind of early constitution – is equally false, but was given credibility by one of the finest brains ever to occupy the building we're in now, the Palace of Westminster.

The third – that Magna Carta was responsible for giving us the fundamental legal rights we so value – is by far the most intriguing of the myths. In one sense it's true that we can trace the origins of an independent legal system and other of our most cherished legal rights back to the 1215 Magna Carta sealed by King John. But it was all something of a misunderstanding. An accident, never intended, and as we shall soon discover, it too happened here in the Palace of Westminster.

✵ ✵ ✵

I've been so wrapped up with finding my tour group and official guide that it's several minutes before I let my gaze rise above the heads of my fellow ground-lings and look around. What I see is a vast hall, not the sort you normally end up in after an airport-style security check, but one with carved stone walls, timber roof and decorated windows reminiscent of a cathedral nave.

This is Westminster Hall, the oldest, the biggest, the most spectacular and the most historically important non-religious, non-military building to have reached us from the Middle Ages. It was already over a hundred years old when King John came to the throne. As other parts of the Palace of Westminster were torn down and rebuilt over the centuries, the hall stood firm. In 1834, it was the only part of the palace to survive a disastrous fire. When German incendiary bombs in 1941 hit both the House of Commons and Westminster Hall on the same night, the firefighters were ordered to save the hall and sacrifice the Commons. It seems to me a humiliating use for such a historic treasure to be little more than an assembly point for tourists.

The hall's glory flies high overhead. Statues of kings grace a line of niches along the top of its cliff-face walls. And far up above me, capping the whole building, is the world's most magnificent medieval hammer beam roof. It was constructed in the 1390s, and was apparently a dangerous job to assemble at such a height. It's little short of magical to know that most of the timber, and its thousands of joints, is still propping up the roof today just as the fourteenth-century carpenters intended it to do. On the tips of its dark wooden braces mystical figures leap out like figureheads on a line of galleons, straining to reach a new world. The whole ceiling is an example of how engineering that works with natural forces can produce a thing of beauty, whether it's a cathedral tower, a cantilevered bridge, a ship on the ocean or even in space.

The origins of this great building over 900 years ago are about as far removed from elective democracy and the rule of law as it's possible to get. It was built on the orders of King William Rufus (William II) in 1097. His aim in creating Westminster Hall was simple: he wanted to impress his new subjects with royal power and the majesty of his authority. It's said that when the hall was finished, and the king came to make his first official inspection, one of his courtiers – not the most diplomatic of attendants – remarked that the hall was a lot bigger than was really needed. The king snapped back that the man was wrong, that the hall was not half large enough, and that it was a mere bedchamber compared to what he had in mind. In fact, it was by far the largest hall in England – and almost certainly the largest in Europe, probably even in the world – at that time, and its purpose was solely to glorify the might of the King of England.

And so it continued. At the conclusion of Richard the Lionheart's coronation across the road in Westminster Abbey, his celebratory banquet was held here. A total of 900 guests – all men – sat at table. But it wasn't just women who were excluded. There were no invitations either for the richest merchants of London, who were relegated for the day to the kitchen. And the common people were, of course, kept out. But as the feasting inside got under way, the honoured guests heard shouting outside. A deputation of wealthy Jews wanted to enter, simply to offer the new king gifts along with their congratulations. The royal guards barred their way, and there was an altercation. A rumour spread that the king had ordered a massacre of the Jews (this falsehood was common currency, as we've seen, and spread to Lincoln and other towns at the time of the Third Crusade). A crowd of ordinary Londoners who had been celebrating in nearby alehouses weighed into the scrum, and soon there was a full-scale riot. By the end of the day, much of the surrounding neighbourhood was in flames and a number of Jews were among the dead. The king and his aristocratic guests remained safe, however, eating their venison and drinking their French wine here inside Westminster Hall.

✵ ✵ ✵

So how did Magna Carta, a largely aristocratic manifesto, and Westminster Hall, with its most undemocratic of origins, manage to come together to produce a system of justice which was independent and available to all?

The answer is an illustration of the law of unintended consequences.

Think of Magna Carta as a blindfolded man standing in the middle of a meadow, who suddenly feels a football land at his feet. He gives it a good kick and thinks no more about it. The ball bounces off a tree, hits a fence, skies into the air, and just happens to land in the middle of a nearby football match. The players are confused. In particular, the captain of the red team is convinced this alien ball is the one they're playing with, and he proceeds to dribble it round the blue team's defence and, in a spectacular move, shoots it past the goalie and into the opponents' net. What connects the blindfolded man (Magna Carta) to the goal (a universal, independent legal system) is a gigantic fluke, a deal of confusion and a downright error. And Westminster Palace is the pitch where the game was played.

We'll look at each stage in turn: fluke, confusion and mistake.

★★★

The first stage, the fluke, brought us an independent judiciary.

To get a feel for the function that this great place fulfilled in the years following the 1215 Magna Carta, I steal away from my group for a moment and make my way through the crowds towards the far end of Westminster Hall, to where a towering stained-glass window floods the whole place with light. Beneath it, a flight of steps, as broad as the building itself, leads up to a higher level, a stone platform from where today I can look down over the madding throng of tourists. This is where the judges sat. During the later Middle Ages, Westminster Hall became a court of law and the place where a royal legal system – set in motion by kings Henry II, Richard and John – was gradually transformed into an independent and unbiased process for delivering justice to all.

The system of royal justice established by Henry II had been strengthened even further by King John. He seems to have been particularly interested in the whole process of legal decision making, and frequently sat alongside his judges. These men were appointed by the king, and he could sack them at a moment's notice. In these early days, there was no question therefore of royal justice being anything but a royal tool. It was the king's prerogative to instruct his judges as to the decision they should reach, and this was an arrangement which was generally acceptable in the early thirteenth century. Of course, there were many cases where the king's interests would not be directly affected by the court's decisions: disputes between the families of two relatively lowly knights, for instance, or, say, the trial of some little-known merchant accused of murdering a commercial rival. So, as we have seen, in these cases where the king didn't care about the outcome, royal judges got a reputation for delivering fair and unbiased judgements.

But what was irritating to many barons, and to the freemen who were their vassals, was that it was often difficult to gain physical access to the royal courts. The king was not wilfully denying justice to litigants, but the problem was that royal judges were part of the king's entourage. Where he went, they went, and kings like John and his immediate successors were constantly on the go, all around the country. In the days before railways delivered national newspapers, or electronic communication, it was pretty much impossible for anyone not part of the royal court to have any idea where the king – and his judges – would be at any one time.

This difficulty explains why the barons got two particular clauses inserted into the 1215 Magna Carta. Clause 17 stated that:

> Common pleas shall not follow our [i.e. the king's] court but shall be held in a fixed place.

Common pleas referred to courts handling civil law, disputes between subjects. Clause 24 provided that:

> No sheriff, constable, coroner, or others of our [i.e. again the king's] bailiffs, shall hold pleas of our crown.

Pleas of the crown meant criminal law. The barons didn't want petty, bribable officials involved in this. Better that criminal law be in the hands of royal judges, who – provided the king had no interest in who was guilty or innocent – would make a better job of it. Again, for the system to work there had to be reasonable certainty where these judges could be found.

Magna Carta hadn't laid down where that should be. It just said, 'in a fixed place'. The capital city would be the most convenient location, and because it was the *king's* justice at stake here, the king's great hall here at Westminster was the obvious place for the judges of the Common Bench, administering civil law, and of the King's Bench, criminal law, to install themselves.

From this simple measure of fixing the courts in one place, a great and glorious principle, that of a judicial system independent of any influence from the most powerful person in the land, the monarch, arose – by accident. It didn't happen overnight, it took several hundred years. But from the thirteenth century onwards, justice increasingly became associated, not with a person – prejudiced by malice, favouritism and foibles, i.e. the king – but with a place. Stones and timber have no bias. That place was Westminster Hall.

And this process – whereby the words 'royal justice' came to mean 'independent justice' – was given a massive boost in the seventeenth century by the words and actions of one man. If the long and tangled history of the Palace of Westminster has only one hero, it would be Sir Edward Coke, of whom more to come.

★ ★ ★

I see my tour group forming up, so hurry back to join it just in time to march off. Our guide leads us straight out of the hall, without stopping to talk about it. 'That's for later,' he says. At first we pass beneath lines of ghostly statues cloaked in milky-white polythene sheeting (they're being cleaned), then along a labyrinth of lobbies looking for all the world like cathedral side chapels which have lost their altars, and through a series of ceremonial rooms, each adorned with ageing portraits and bright tapestries as befit somewhere called a 'palace'. At key points, we pause and the guide entertains us with a mix of hard fact and breezy anecdote. We learn that the Arthurian paintings in the highly decorated Robing Room symbolise the chivalric virtues of hospitality, generosity, mercy, religion and courtesy, and that Queen Victoria was so irritated by Prime Minister William Gladstone that she wrote in her journal: 'He speaks to me as though he's addressing a public meeting.'

No-nonsense our guide may be about Magna Carta, but we soon discover there's also something quaint about him. For instance, when describing the suffragettes' struggle for female emancipation, he keeps talking about 'Votes for Ladies'. It's as though the last hundred years have passed him by. He seems to believe he'll be demeaning 50 per cent of the population by calling them 'women', even though the suffragettes themselves gloried in that title. At the same time, there's an element of old-fashioned laddishness about him, and when we reach the Chamber of the House of Commons, he points up, with a mischievous grin, to the little curtains hung below the rail of the Visitors' Gallery. Do we know why those drapes are there? he asks. Before we can think, he tells us it's so the Members of Parliament down below can't see up the skirts of their colleagues' wives.

The Chamber of the House of Commons, as anyone who's ever been in it will tell you, is tiny. By rough calculation, I reckon you could fit three and a half Houses of Commons inside Westminster Hall, with space left on top for a couple of parliamentary tea rooms.

What historians regard as the first English parliament was convened exactly fifty years after Magna Carta, in 1265, by the baronial rebel Simon de Montfort, and it met at Westminster, not where we're standing now, but back in Westminster Hall. That was a one-off, however. At first, parliaments tended to meet all around the country, wherever was convenient at any particular time, and it was several hundred years before Westminster became established as its permanent home. Gatherings of representatives of what was only a limited section of the king's subjects owed nothing to Magna Carta, and certainly didn't grow out of the council of twenty-five barons which the 1215 Great Charter had tried – and failed – to set up to oversee the king's good behaviour.

However, parliamentarians began to realise that the Great Charter was a useful piece of parchment to wave in front of the king's face whenever he stepped out of line or became too demanding.

And that was how the second stage in the transformation of the Charter from feudal document to heroic symbol took place. It was a confused process.

Every time the king faced revolt or needed to raise cash he would be forced to make a concession. And these concessions were then incorporated into a rewritten Magna Carta. In the thirteenth century alone, the Charter was reissued in 1216, 1217, 1225 and 1297, and it was confirmed, without further change, by various monarchs at least fifty-five times. By 1300, it was parliament that began to take the lead in making the changes to the Great Charter. Soon, it became usual for the first item of parliamentary business to be a reading of Magna Carta. The parliamentary officials, however, lost track of which charter they were dealing with. They would refer to it as if it were the 1225 version, and assume it hadn't been altered much from the original 1215 Charter, when actually they were looking at the text of the 1297 Magna Carta.

Some of the changes to the old document were fundamental and far-reaching. In the fourteenth century, during the reign of Edward III, clause 39 – the one that had promised that no free man should be unlawfully arrested or imprisoned – was transformed into what was much closer to a universal right. As we know, the old version in King John's charter had applied only to the top 12 per cent or so of society, the free men. In the new version, the words 'free man' were replaced by the phrase 'no man, of whatever estate or condition he may be'. That was unambiguous. And if we recognise that the status of women in fourteenth-century society made it unthinkable at that time for them yet to be included, we have what by late medieval standards is protection against the arbitrary exercise of power, made available down to the lowest levels of society. This was a monumental development. The year was 1354.

Other changes were made at the same time, so the clause now read:

No man, of whatever estate or condition he may be shall be dispossessed, imprisoned or put to death except by due process of law.

Due process of law. It's worth repeating. This is the first use of that hallowed phrase, still now quoted across the globe, and especially in the United States, thousands of times a day, whenever an individual's rights are believed to have been infringed in some way. In fact, so often is this mantra recited in the twenty-first century that it's often abbreviated to just two words. 'Due process'. A suspect is questioned without first being read their rights, and their lawyer has only to enquire what happened to 'due process' for the client to be released. Someone is fired from their job on the spot, and they can appeal against the lack of 'due process'. Civil rights campaigners protest that trying Guantanamo Bay detainees before a military commission is not 'due process' and is therefore arbitrary. These two words are one of the most powerful legacies of Magna Carta. Not of the original 1215 Magna Carta issued by 'bad' King John to the 'freedom-loving' barons, but the re-engineered document sealed 139 years later by Edward III.

And there's a certain irony in all this. Most of the principles of personal freedom that were gradually incorporated into the many reissued Magna Cartas were conceded by monarchs in return for parliament's agreeing to some new tax. In 1225, for instance, John's son Henry III put his seal to a re-worked Magna Carta in return for a tax of a fifteenth of the value of movable items. So we could say that the principle of universal freedom under the law was not bought with the blood of our forebears. It was simply bought. With money, like a product in the marketplace.

✯✯✯

Before we leave the House of Commons, our guide reminds us that in 1642 King Charles I marched into this chamber with an armed guard to arrest those MPs who had spoken against him, and dragged them off to prison. This was the age of the great clash between parliament and monarch, resulting in civil war, the execution of a king, an eleven-year republic, and a military dictatorship.

We're now nearing the end of the official tour, and our guide wraps up, leading us back to Westminster Hall, where he tells us about some of the famous people who have stood trial here: William Wallace – Scottish patriot/traitor (delete as appropriate); Sir Thomas More – saint to Catholics, or torturer with complex motives to readers of the best-selling novelist Hilary Mantel; and Guy Fawkes and his co-conspirators for their attempt to blow up the Houses of Parliament. But the most famous person to face justice here was King Charles I himself. His conviction for treason marks our third Westminster stage in the transformation of Magna Carta. It's a stage we might call The Great Mistake.

When we've all thanked the guide, and he has advised us to sample the cakes in the tea room, I go and sit instead on one of the ancient stone benches that run along the side walls of the hall, from where I can admire again the vast magnificence of the place. It's here that the real contest between parliament and king was fought out. Not on the battlefields of the Civil War, which it was clear within a few decades had settled nothing. The war of ideas was what decided the future political direction of the country, and that was fought out in Westminster Hall.

The first Stuart kings – James I and Charles I – declared that they received their authority from God alone and therefore had a divine right to rule. A king's actions needed no other justification than that they were the will of the monarch. To rebut this claim, the opposition needed a powerful argument, something so ancient and venerable that it had almost biblical authority. The parliamentary lawyers found what they were looking for in Magna Carta; or rather, in an anachronistic misunderstanding of it. And this is where we get properly introduced to Sir Edward Coke: the most brilliant jurist of his age, and a man of steely determination. At one time or another, he presided as Chief Justice here in Westminster Hall, over both the civil and criminal courts. Contemporaries described him as 'arrogant' and 'brutal', which were perhaps just the qualities of self-belief that Coke needed if he was to win the intellectual war against monarchical absolutism.

There's no suggestion that Coke (pronounced Cook) and his fellow lawyers deliberately twisted the truth. Their misreadings of the original Great Charter are forgivable because in the early seventeenth century no one fully understood the complexities of society and politics 400 years earlier in King John's day. Nevertheless, honourable as were his motives, Coke's commentaries on Magna Carta were riddled with errors.

First, he claimed that the Great Charter was so-called because of its 'great importance, and the weightiness of the matter', whereas the real reason was far more prosaic. 'Big' rather than 'Great' might have been a more accurate translation of *Magna*, and the Charter was so-called because it had been written on a slightly larger piece of parchment than another document, the Charter of the Forest, issued shortly afterwards.

Then, he changed the name. It was no longer the *Magna Carta Libertatum*, the Great Charter of Liberties, liberties in John's day having the much more limited sense of privileges, such as sheep-grazing or castle-building granted to a particular group of subjects. Instead Coke called it 'The Great Charter of Liberty, because,' he said, 'it maketh free men.' 'Liberty' in the singular implied something much more fundamental, closer to what we might understand as the freedom of the individual. And to claim that Magna Carta had somehow created free citizens was to stand on its head the original Charter, which had actually been limited to the small section of society who already happened to be free.

In effect, the Stuart kings asserted that they were above the law. Charles I claimed 'sovereign' – that is absolute – 'power' to rule the country. Coke, in an eloquent speech to parliament, retorted, 'Take we heed what we yield unto,' adding, 'Magna Carta is such a fellow that he will have no sovereign.'

Coke and his fellow lawyers saw that the parliamentary opposition's strongest counter-weapon lay in two of Magna Carta's clauses. They needed to justify what would become known as the writ of *habeas corpus*, which allowed the courts to enquire into the lawfulness of any imprisonment and – if there were no legal grounds for it – to order the prisoner's release. And so the parliamentary lawyers seized on an almost forgotten clause, number 36 in the 1215 Charter, which stated:

> In future nothing shall be paid or accepted for a writ of inquisition of life or limbs. It shall be given gratis and not refused.

Coke decided that 'a writ of inquisition of life or limbs', was a reference to the right that lay behind *habeas corpus* at work in the early thirteenth century. But we now know that the words have got little to do with the far-reaching protection against illegal imprisonment, as the parliamentarians claimed. It had been inserted into Magna Carta simply to try and stop excessive demands for bail money.

And Sir Edward also misinterpreted the more famous clause 39 of Magna Carta:

> No free man shall be seized or imprisoned, or stripped of his rights or possessions, or outlawed or exiled, or deprived of his standing in any other way, nor will we [i.e. the king] proceed with force against him, or send others to do so, except by the lawful judgement of his equals or by the law of the land.

Coke asserted that one of the great pillars of justice was enshrined in these words: trial by jury. He was wrong. As we've seen, 'the lawful judgement of his equals' in John's day referred to a process usually brought into action when there was some confusion as to which court had jurisdiction in a case. The normal way to test guilt or innocence in the early thirteenth century had still been by obliging an accused to carry hot iron or be plunged into water. These were historic details unfamiliar in the seventeenth century, so Coke's error was understandable.

But it wasn't enough for *habeas corpus* and trial by jury to be tracked back to Magna Carta. If the God-given, absolute power claimed by kings James and Charles were to be defeated then these principles of justice would need to have something almost mystical and primordial about them, as if they were part of the natural order of the world. And that is what Coke claimed for them. The terms of Magna Carta, he wrote, were 'for the most part declaratory of the principal grounds of the fundamental laws of England'. In other words, according to Coke our most treasured legal rights somehow dated back to time immemorial and were first written down in 1215.

Accurate or not, Coke's words were explosive stuff. In 1621, King James I had him seized and thrown into the Tower of London, where he languished for seven months. Sir Edward was by now 70 years old. In the words of the eminent Victorian historian Thomas Carlyle, he was 'tough old Coke, the toughest man England ever knew'. He was not a man to be bullied out of what he believed with all his heart and every sinew in his body.

In 1628, Sir Edward Coke delivered his finest achievement. He secured in written law the rights of English subjects against oppression by the monarch. This was the Petition of Right, approved by both houses of parliament and – under pressure – by King Charles himself. It safeguarded protection against arbitrary imprisonment, freedom from taxation without parliamentary representation, and due process of law. In effect it was an updated version of Magna Carta, as interpreted by Coke. This man of powerful brain, oratorical eloquence, physical resilience, arrogant self-belief and unswerving determination made the two documents – Magna Carta and the Petition of Right – stand together as England's constitution. His voice in these matters was to echo down the centuries. All references to Magna Carta in the courts and in law books until the twentieth century derived from Coke's interpretation of the document.

Erroneous as his understanding of the Great Charter often was, Sir Edward Coke should remain one of our gloried heroes. Trial by jury, *habeas corpus* and due process of law became the inalienable rights that we enjoy today because of Sir Edward Coke's brilliant and determined fight to make Magna Carta live in a new age.

★ ★ ★

Coke himself didn't see the most dramatic result of his commentaries on Magna Carta. In 1649, fifteen years after his death, there came the ultimate example of how a king, like the rest of us, is subject to the law. Charles I was put on trial, here in Westminster Hall. Just as Magna Carta had demonstrated that King John was not above the law, so too it did with King Charles. He was accused of being a 'tyrant, traitor and murderer; and a public and implacable enemy to the Commonwealth of England'. There was, however, an irony in this. The king, unlike his subjects, was not afforded the legal protections which it was believed Magna Carta had provided to all. He couldn't be tried by a jury, because kings don't have twelve social equals to form one. So sixty-eight judges heard the evidence and pronounced the verdict. But unfortunately, there was nothing in English law that specifically defined how a monarch could be put on trial. So the judges resorted to a process devised by a Dutch lawyer quoting Roman law. Charles was found guilty.

In the cold morning air of 30 January 1649, King Charles was allowed to walk his dog in St James's Park – 200 yards down the road from the Palace of Westminster – for one last time. Then he was led to a scaffold in front of a huge crowd that had gathered in the street, outside Westminster Hall. There, after a delay when the executioner backed out at the last minute and a reserve axeman was brought in with a promise of the gigantic fee of £100, King Charles I's head was chopped off.

***

I make my way again to the foot of the flight of steps at the far end of Westminster Hall. There used to be a fence, or bar, right across the inside of the building just here. Its purpose was to keep the public back from the raised level where the judges of the King's Bench and of Common Pleas used to preside. People would come into the hall in huge numbers to watch and listen as the courtroom dramas unfolded, and to rub shoulders with the lawyers, litigants and their supporters. When an advocate's turn came to question witnesses and to plead his client's case, he would be summoned to the other side of the bar, where the jury and judge were stationed. This gave rise to the strange title of 'barrister', by which a court advocate is still known in England today. I take childish pleasure in noting that the American Bar Association gets its name from a piece of wooden fencing erected here in Westminster Hall as an accidental consequence of Magna Carta.

So Westminster Hall, which had been born to glorify the power of kings, ended its working life as the embodiment of justice for the ordinary citizen. The hall continued as England's premier court of law until 1882, when the Royal Courts of Justice were re-sited in the Strand, a mile to the east. The word 'royal' had come to signify, not a justice system biased towards the interests of the monarch of the day, but one that is patently free from outside influence.

It's true that Magna Carta marked the beginning of that transformation. Not intentionally, by requiring King John to adopt trial by jury and *habeas corpus*, as seventeenth-century parliamentary lawyers and later some Victorian historians believed. In part, it was the accidental consequence of the rebellious barons' desire for something far less grand: they just wanted to be sure they could always know where to find the king's judges. And partly it was the result of the confused horse-trading between later generations of parliamentarians and the king. And, most of all, it was due to some overenthusiastic misunderstandings by Sir Edward Coke and his colleagues. We can safely say that it was Magna Carta that had set the ball in motion in the first place with a blind kick that by a series of flukes, confusions and errors gave us the prized goal of universal, impartial justice.

***

With the establishment of parliament and a respected judicial system, we might expect that Magna Carta would become redundant as a weapon against arbitrary and oppressive power, and fade into the background. For a time it did; or rather, it did in England. But the age of Coke was also the age of discovery, of colonising new worlds beyond the oceans. It was the age when greed for gold and silver prompted people to set sail in small ships to make a new life in Virginia and along the eastern seaboard of what we know as the United States. Those first settlers took with them not only canons, ploughshares, cattle, sheep and bibles, but also Magna Carta. Not

Sir Edward Coke, 'the toughest man England ever knew', turned to Magna Carta to combat the Stuart kings' claim to be absolute rulers.

the physical parchment, and not just the feudal privileges detailed in the Charter agreed by King John and the barons at Runnymede in 1215, but the fundamental rights defined in Magna Carta as interpreted by Sir Edward Coke.

Magna Carta, in its new form, was given a fresh, vigorous life in a New World. There was something about the Great Charter and its capacity to limit the executive power of government that was to make it peculiarly attractive to the independent spirits of those who were to found America. That's where we're going next, to the site of the first permanent English colony established in the New World, on an island in the estuary of the James River in Virginia.

19 JAMESTOWN, VIRGINIA, USA

THE GENTLEMEN CANNIBALS

Jerome paces in front of us, his face lit up with joy and excitement. 'You see what a beautiful place this is?' he asks, casting an expansive arm out towards the wide, still waters of the James River estuary. 'You see that? Is it not a place of beauty?' This is no rhetorical question. It demands confirmation.

The woman in front of me – short, plump, with grey hair quivering like magnetised wire – responds in a dreamlike voice, 'Yes, yes we see.' Others take up the chant, 'Yes, it's beautiful.'

Jerome stops and, as though in a trance, looks up at heaven, then, shaking his head in slow disbelief, says, 'Those folk arriving here after four and a half months crossing the ocean, through storms and gales, with no fresh water, confined in the darkness below decks in small ships. Why, they stepped ashore here on this island in the spring of 1607, and they truly believed they had come to …' (here he slows right down) 'A land of milk and …'

It's our turn again, and the magnetised hair woman leads us in our response, 'Milk and honey.'

'That's right,' declares Jerome. 'They thought this was a land running with milk and honey.' And he bends, eyes wide, and looks round at us as if about to share a sly secret. 'But this was no land of milk and honey.' He claps his hands. We jump. He races on, 'This was to be a land of hard work, of manual labour, of extreeeeme weather.' He claps again. His eyes narrow. 'A land of death. Death from disease. Death from starvation. And death from what they called –' (he pauses) '– the "naturals", that is the native tribe of Powhatan Indians who had been living in this region for 10,000 years.' He straightens up, and with a tone that implies astonishment at life's surprises, he adds, 'This was no paradise. It was more like a hell.' Then he slowly moves his head looking around at each one of us in turn. 'But despite all these terrors, despite all these trials, despite all their suffering, though many, many of these people who had come here in their little ships would die, enough of these folks, enough of them surviiiiiived to make …', he raises his hands in the air, looks up, and says in slow triumph, 'the first … permanent … settlement … by the English … in … *America!*'

'Allelluia!'

Actually, we don't call this out, but I swear we nearly do.

'And now, folks,' says Jerome, looking satisfied with the effect of his delivery, 'if you'll be so kind, just follow me and we'll find out more about these early Americans.' And we, his flock, gladly walk at his heels.

I'm on a tour of Historic Jamestown. There are around two dozen of us in our group, mostly senior citizens in baggy shorts and baseball caps. Once our guide had introduced himself – his full and respectful title is Ranger Jerome Bridges, 'Ranger' because Historic Jamestown is part of the US National Park Service – we'd had to say where we're from: Tennessee, Idaho, Michigan, Florida, California, Maine, two from Australia and me. 'Ah-ha,' says Jerome. He adjusts his ranger's hat so he looks less like a boy scout and more like a Canadian Mountie, then, singling me out, says, 'Now, if you don't mind, you're going to get the American version of what you English did here.' I nod.

I don't know whether, on a Sunday, Ranger Bridges is a preacher at his local Baptist church, but his style of oratory is in keeping with the subject matter. There's something Old Testament about the hopes, sufferings and triumphs of the Jamestown story.

✮ ✮ ✮

The first group of 104 Englishmen – they were all men – to set foot on this shore on the sunny spring day of 14 May 1607 could not have anticipated what lay ahead of them. They had the misfortune to arrive here during what historical climatologists believe was the worst drought in 800 years. The venture came close to failure many times in many ways.

The settlers knew the region was inhabited by hostile native tribes. From a distance of four centuries, we might think that colonists armed with guns would have a clear advantage over Powhatan 'naturals' with nothing more than bows and arrows. But, as Ranger Bridges explains, with his usual charismatic accompanying actions, 'it took a well-trained settler thirty seconds to load and fire a matchlock musket, during which time a Powhatan warrior could fire off ten arrows with deadly accuracy. 'Oh, and,' he adds with a mischievous grin and a hand-clap, 'there were 15,000 Powhatans against 104 settlers, a number which would soon be getting fewer by the day!'

So the colonists' first task was to build themselves a wooden fort. And we can see here exactly what that meant. 'Historic Jamestown', where we are, is an archaeological site, not to be confused with 'the Jamestown Settlement' a mile up the coast, which is more of a theme park with replica houses and guides in seventeenth-century costume. The actual site of the old colony is here at Historic

A recreation of the stockade built by the first settlers at Jamestown to defend themselves against the Powhatan tribespeople.

Jamestown, where archaeologists have meticulously explored and traced out the exact footprint of the old buildings and of the palisade that formed the defensive wall around the first settlement. In order for us to appreciate what the fort would have looked like, historians have gone through the same labours that the colonists did in building it. With axes they have chopped down oak and walnut trees, then split them into 15ft-long poles, which they hauled by hand to the shoreline – the 1607 settlers had no horses. With shovels resembling those in the early seventeenth century, the archaeologists dug out holes 5 feet deep, into which they set the wooden posts. The result before us now is a crude fence 10 feet high. The ground plan of the original fort was a triangle with sides 300 to 400 yards long with a 'bastion' – essentially a rounded bay sticking out – at each corner. The settlers finished the job in nineteen days, a remarkable achievement.

But the most savage killers were not ones that could be kept out with a defensive stockade. One of those who survived what happened next, a 'gentleman' by the name of George Percy, wrote an account of the tribulations he and his fellows encountered:

Our men were destroyed with cruel diseases as swellings, fluxes, burning fevers, and by wars, and some departed suddenly, but for the most part they

213

died of mere famine. There were never Englishmen left in a foreign country in such misery as we were in this new discovered Virginia ... Our food was but a small can of barley sod in water to five men a day; our drink cold water taken out of the river, which was at flood very salty, at a low tide full of slime and filth, which was the destruction of many of our men. Thus we lived for the space of five months in this miserable distress, not having five able men to man our bulwarks upon any occasion. If it had not pleased God to have put a terror in the savage's hearts, we had all perished by those wild and cruel pagans, being in that weak estate as we were ... If there were any conscience in men, it would make their hearts to bleed to hear the pitiful murmurings and outcries of our sick men, without relief, every night and day for the space of six weeks, some departing out of the world, many times three or four in a night, in the morning their bodies trailed out of their cabins like dogs to be buried.

Of the 104 men who had come ashore in May 1607, only thirty-eight were still alive eight months later. It's likely that even these few would not have survived if it had not been for one man.

Today, alongside the split timbers of the stockade stands a tall, square stone plinth beneath a statue of a cloaked figure with bushy beard, in billowing bloomers and floppy-topped boots, his left hand on his sword hilt, a Bible in his right. There's no evidence that John Smith was particularly religious, but he was a soldier of some fame. Before coming to Jamestown, he had fought in Hungary, Turkey and Transylvania; he was once captured by the Turks and made a slave but escaped by murdering his jailor. Smith did not suffer fools in any wise, and in his view there were a few too many fools in Jamestown. Around half of the settlers were men who liked to describe themselves as 'gentlemen'. And it's reported that one day their representatives swaggered up to Smith and complained that their delicate hands were not made for hauling logs or digging trenches, and that such work should be left to the other, inferior sort of colonists. Smith was blunt with them. 'If ye do not work,' he told them, 'nor shall ye eat.' We can assume that, reluctant or not, they chose food over idleness.

In December 1607, Smith was ambushed and captured by the Powhatans, and this led to his name being associated with its own set of myths. The story is that he was about to be sacrificed by having his skull crushed, when the 12-year-old Powhatan princess Pocahontas saved his life by placing her own head between his and the executioner's club. Whether this actually happened, we have only Smith's own account to go by. The popular notion that he later married her is, in Ranger Bridges' words, 'a lie and a falsehood. I bet you've seen the film, with your grandkids,' he adds. 'Yes? Well, Walt Disney made that story up. That's what moviemakers do.' What is true, though, is that Smith established friendly relations with these 'wild and cruel pagans' who presented bread, corn, fish, and meat to the starving English.

In October 1609, John Smith was badly injured when a boat carrying gunpowder exploded. 'Hhmm, I wonder if that was really an accident,' says our guide, scratching his chin and peering thoughtfully into the distance. Smith returned to England, where he lived on a further twenty-two years, writing his memoirs.

By the time John Smith left, further contingents of settlers had sailed into the Jamestown estuary, and numbers had swelled here to around 600, now including women and even children. They had arrived just before the blackest hours – or rather months – in the colony's fragile life. The winter and spring of 1609–10 was known, with chilling simplicity, as the 'Starving Time'. The settlers ate their horses, then killed their dogs and cats for food. When these ran out, they trapped rats, mice and snakes, and devoured them. Such pitiful straits were not unknown in time of famine even back in England. But what came next showed a new depth of desperation. People tried to find nourishment by boiling their boots and shoes then drinking the water and chewing on the leather. Then, in their craving for meat, any meat, they began to dig up the corpses of their dead fellows and to consume them. And even more terrible things were done.

George Percy again writes:

One of our colony murdered his wife, ripped the child out of her womb, and threw it into the river, and after, chopped the mother in pieces and salted her for his food. The same not being discovered before he had eaten part thereof, for the which cruel and inhuman fact, I adjudged him to be executed, the acknowledgement of the deed being enforced from him by torture, having hung by the thumbs with weights at his feet a quarter of an hour before he would confess the same.

Of the 600 colonists at Jamestown in the summer of 1609 before the Starving Time, only some sixty were still alive by May 1610.

Later generations have cast doubt on the accounts of cannibalism among the first settlers. But at a point almost in the very centre of the triangular fort, during the early part of 2014, archaeologists here unearthed the bones of a 14-year-old girl. The grave itself has been left exposed for us to see today. Her skeleton was gashed with crude chop-marks that showed her flesh had been stripped for food. Mercifully, the archaeologists were able to deduce that she was already dead when the amateur butcher got to work. In the museum a few yards from the excavations, her skull is on display, along with a reconstruction built up from it of her head and face. It's disquieting to look on her calm beauty and imagine how this young girl must have suffered. We don't know who she was. A servant girl, perhaps. Or a defenceless orphan whose parents had already joined the hundreds who starved to death. The archaeologists called her Jane.

★ ★ ★

I thank Ranger Bridges for his dramatic presentation of Jamestown's history, and decide to visit the other Jamestown attraction just up the coast, the Jamestown Settlement. My route takes me over a low footbridge that links Jamestown Island with mainland Virginia – in the seventeenth century there was a causeway here. On each side of the bridge, virulent green marsh grass sprouts from equally green, slimy water. I hurry across as horseflies with wings the width of a hand zip around my face. From the trees at the swamp's edge, the screech of cicadas is almost deafening as it reaches its crescendo before dying away again.

From the car park on the far side, it's a short ride. After Historic Jamestown's immediacy (a strange word, I know, for an archaeological excavation, but you can't beat the very place where things happened), the Jamestown Settlement seems contrived and even a little Disneyfied. Its recreated houses, with thatched roofs and smooth walls of pink plaster, are as neat and cute as the ones we saw near the beginning of our journey at Abbot's Ripton and Wennington in the English fens. The Jamestown Settlement's own mock-up of the fort has stockade posts that look like they've just come off a factory production line. The reconstructed Powhatan village is a particular disappointment. I ask the bespectacled young woman in fringed smock and moccasins standing at the entrance to a domed mud hut if she is herself a Powhatan. 'No,' she says, 'they're all westernised now.' Which seems to me an odd answer coming from a westerner pretending to be a Powhatan. If, for instance, there was to be a recreated slave colony, it would be unthinkable to black up a few white folks to represent the slaves, so why are the Powhatan native Americans to be treated differently?

There is, however, a glittering gem at the Jamestown Settlement. Or I should say, three gems. Alongside the jetty, with magnificent views to the low forested hills half a mile away across the still water of the estuary, three ships lie at anchor. The word 'ships' to us conjures images of ocean liners as high as an office block and the length of three football fields. But ships in the seventeenth century meant small wooden boats. These three are topped with masts, furled sails and a network of rope rigging. They represent the three ships that set sail from London in December 1607 to bring those first 104 colonists here. They're called the *Susan Constant*, the *Godspeed* and the *Discovery*. The *Susan Constant* is an exact replica of the original, and the biggest of the three at just 116 feet long, barely more than one and a half times the length of an English canal boat. The other two are even smaller. The journey from London to Jamestown could take up to six months. Passengers were confined below decks – so they wouldn't get in the way of the crew – except when they were allowed up to empty their chamber pots. Water was undrinkable after a week – algae grew in it. Weak beer was drunk instead. Food was usually limited to gruel – oats or wheat boiled in water.

In such boats as these, in such conditions, through violent storms, more and more settlers came to Jamestown, and increasingly to other colonies along the east coast of what we know as America.

So who were these people? And why were they here? The Virginia venture was a mix of social engineering, religious piety and commercial enterprise. As we've seen, some were 'gentlemen'. But in part the colonies were regarded as a way of ridding London of some of its criminals, the so-called 'human offal', who were rounded up and shipped off to Virginia. Other, more high-minded settlers saw themselves with a mission to save the 'naturals' from the devil and convert them to Christianity.

But above all, Jamestown was about corporate greed. The venture was organised by the Virginia Company of London with the intention of finding gold and silver in the New World and of setting up trading operations to return riches to the company's investors back in England. In order to fulfil this role, the Company was given a royal charter, signed and sealed by King James I in 1606. This charter was more than an official grant of the land to be colonised by the settlers on the east coast of the American continent. It also did something which would have a lasting influence on the government of the future United States.

The chief draftsman of the Jamestown Charter was none other than the great proponent of Magna Carta, Sir Edward Coke himself. Among its clauses was one which provided for the protection of the colonists' fundamental rights. It stated:

Every person, and their children … shall have and enjoy all liberties, franchises and immunities within any of our other dominions, to all intents and purposes, as if they had been abiding and born within this realm of England.

The Virginia Company collapsed and went out of business in 1624. No glittering minerals were found here on the east coast. But the colonists did discover another kind of gold, grown in the earth by the Powhatan and other native tribes. The settlers called it the 'golden weed'. Tobacco, which was to have a burgeoning market back in England. So the colony thrived, and the English settlers here were allowed to continue enjoying the guarantee of their rights as free English subjects.

There was, however, a practical problem. The ultimate authority which could interpret how these personal 'liberties, franchises and immunities' would apply to any particular case, was not easily accessible. In fact, it was further away than anything we can imagine in our age of instant communication. It would take so long to appeal to the judges in Westminster Hall or to raise a complaint in the Westminster Parliament and for the decision to be conveyed back via months of ocean voyaging that it could well be too late to correct any injustice.

The solution in the end was simple. Over the next hundred years, as more and more colonists arrived, they decided they needed a sort of legal bible, something that would set out the fundamental principles of the law in a way that would be beyond dispute. In other words, a charter or a constitution which could be consulted for an immediate decision on a citizen's rights. When these first English settlers formed themselves into provinces, commonwealths and states, one of their first acts was usually to draw up their own charters, statements of their citizens' basic rights. In drafting these new documents they wanted to show that they had their roots in ancient, inviolable law. So they turned to Magna Carta; of course, it was not the obscure medieval customs of King John's 1215 Magna Carta that inspired them, it was Sir Edward Coke's interpretation of Magna Carta they turned to, enshrining trial by jury, *habeas corpus,* and the requirement for 'due process of law'.

In 1639, for instance, the leaders of the colonists in Maryland 160 miles north of Jamestown met in General Assembly and passed an Act for the Liberties of the People. It stated that, 'slaves excepted', the inhabitants of the province:

Shall not be imprisoned nor disseissed or dispossessed of their freehold goods or chattels or be outlawed, exiled or otherwise destroyed, forejudged or punished except according to the laws of this province.

In other words, clause 39 of Magna Carta as interpreted by Coke.

The words 'Magna Carta' became a slogan that summarised the political and legal identity of the new Americans. In Massachusetts about the same time, the settlers decided to appoint some men from among them who would:

Frame a body of grounds of law, in resemblance to a Magna Carta, which being allowed by some of the ministers and the General Court, should be received for fundamental laws.

The result was an act entitled 'The Body of Liberties' which in 1641 became Massachusetts law, and again included a clause modelled on number 39 of the Great Charter. Six years later, the Governor of Massachusetts instructed his representative to bring back from England two copies of Coke's commentary on Magna Carta, 'to the end that we may have better light for making and proceeding about laws'.

It's no exaggeration to say that the early American leaders looked to two ancient documents as their spiritual and temporal guides: the Bible and Magna Carta. Thus, in 1687, William Penn, the great Quaker founder of Pennsylvania, published a book, a small volume just 6 inches tall by 3.5 inches wide with patchy print and peppered with typographical errors. But its physical make-up belies its importance. It was called *The Excellent Privilege of Liberty and Property* and was designed by Penn as a handbook for his judges and lawyers. It began on Page 1 with the full text of Magna Carta, as confirmed and reissued by Edward I in 1297, followed by sixteen pages of commentary on the Great Charter.

In fact, all thirteen American colonies incorporated something of Magna Carta into their means of government and administration of the law. Rhode Island adopted clause 39 in 1647, for instance. So did New York in 1683, and New Jersey in the same period, with South Carolina following suit in 1712. Subscribing to Coke's anachronistic views, the settlers held Magna Carta to be the guarantee of their ancient liberties.

It would be no surprise then that when, in the mid-eighteenth century, the issue was not the liberty of an individual citizen but the liberty of a whole emerging nation Magna Carta would again play a key role. Americans came to regard the king in England and Parliament at Westminster as jointly tyrannical. To support their case for breaking away and governing themselves, the Americans needed to appeal to some principle of law that stood above both king and parliament. They found it in Magna Carta, which they claimed as a kind of primordial justification for independence from what they now regarded as foreign tyranny.

To tell this next part of Magna Carta's story, and to understand why Americans – more than any nation on earth – still revere its name today, we're driving three hours north from Jamestown to the federal capital of what was to become the United States of America, Washington DC.

✫ ✫ ✫

But before we leave Jamestown, we have to note something shocking. The very future of the place is in doubt. It's not threatened with being reduced to a ruin, like so many of the places we've visited. Jamestown, this treasured milestone on America's, England's, and Magna Carta's journey, is threatened with total destruction.

Throughout its history Jamestown has been subject to extremes of weather. In 2003, Hurricane Isabel scoured the flat, low-lying landscape around the old settlement. Jamestown Island was flooded and thousands of historic artefacts which archaeologists had unearthed here were destroyed. Many others were so badly damaged that the work to restore them was still going on more than ten years later.

But there are two other, even more devastating, threats. The Tidewater of Virginia and parts of Chesapeake Bay are among the most vulnerable places in the world to fluctuations in sea levels. If climate change raises the Atlantic Ocean by just 18 inches, then 60 per cent of the island would be underwater. Global warming may or may not be something we humans could slow down or reverse. However, the other catastrophe on the horizon cannot be escaped. The whole region is – slowly but inexorably – sinking as result of a meteor that gouged out Chesapeake Bay 35 million years ago.

Visit Jamestown while you can.

20 WASHINGTON DC

TEMPLES AND TYRANTS

At first I think it's just another protest. A parade of brightly dressed young women, all wearing sashes to proclaim their cause, marching along the traffic-free road in front of the White House. If you want to protest in Washington DC, this is the place to do it. There's a half-naked young guy with the puzzling words 'CHANCEprose.com' written across his bare chest, and a sign hanging from his shorts that says, 'We all have our own super-power. Mine is the ability to be annoying.' There's a tiny elderly woman apparently living here in a tent decked with signs saying things like, 'Stop Israel's slaughter in Gaza.' Next to her a battered billboard announces, '24 hrs a day anti-nuclear peace vigil since 1981 maintained by Concepción & W. Thomas.' There's no sign of Concepción herself. She must be on a break.

As the young women start to form up in front of the White House railings, I notice there's a remarkable uniformity about them. They're all in tight mid-thigh skirts, look comfortable on 8-inch heels and are sporting the kind of make-up and hairstyling normally seen in ads for beauty products. The cops leaning on their patrol cars, marked 'Police Secret Service', turn to watch. Curious as to the exact nature of the protest, I move closer to read the slogan on the sashes. The nearest young woman – auburn hair, a dark blue dress – is taking a selfie with the tall white columns of America's highest seat of power in the background. It's only when she lowers her smartphone that I see the words 'Miss Minnesota' stretching from her right shoulder down to her left hip. Then along comes Miss Nevada, followed by Miss Alaska who's chatting to Miss Oregon. And yes, there must be about fifty of them. But what are they doing here? I turn to ask a stout, middle-aged woman (definitely not Miss Anything) who is attempting to marshal them into some sort of alphabetical order.

'It's the Miss America Pageant,' she replies, before instructing her flock, 'Now guys, get in a line for the camera.'

'But why the White House?' I persist.

She takes a cigarette from a silver case, lights it, puffs a plume of smoke over her right shoulder, and replies, 'They're here in our nation's capital for a policy briefing and a session with Women-in-Leadership. To become Miss America,' she adds, tossing the barely smoked cigarette to the ground then grinding it into the tarmac with a ruthless foot, 'these ladies have to advocate for their personal platforms.'

'Oh,' I say.

And while the camera pans the length of the line, from Miss Alabama to Miss Wyoming, as one, they wave.

★ ★ ★

So here's a question. What is it that links attractive young women, the White House and Magna Carta?

The answer is a court case that grabbed headlines around the world, when Magna Carta nearly – and some might say 'should have' – brought down the President of the United States himself.

On 6 May 1994, an employee of the state of Arkansas named Paula Jones filed a sexual harassment case against President Bill Clinton. Three years earlier, when Clinton was state governor, she'd been helping at a management conference at the Excelsior Hotel in the state's capital, Little Rock. Paula Jones claimed in court that a member of Governor Clinton's security staff approached her and told her that the governor would like to meet her. Minutes later, she took the elevator to Clinton's hotel suite. There, according to her account, which was disputed in court, Clinton made a series of increasingly aggressive moves, culminating in his dropping his trousers, exposing himself, and then asking her to 'kiss it'. Ms Jones claimed that she told the governor, 'I'm not that kind of girl.'

As she left, Clinton stopped her by the door and said, 'You're a smart girl, let's keep this between ourselves.' A witness reported that she seemed pleased when she left the hotel room, and that anything that happened inside appeared to be consensual.

When the Arkansas judge ruled against Ms Jones, she appealed to a higher court. Clinton and his lawyers then argued that the Jones case would distract him from the important job of being president, and that the trial should be delayed until he was no longer in office. A federal district judge dismissed this defence on the grounds that the president, in a court of law, is no different from any of his fellow citizens, adding by way of justification: 'It is contrary to our form of government, which asserts, as did the English in the Magna Carta and the Petition of Right, that even the sovereign is subject to God and the law.'

There's no doubt, as we have seen, that Magna Carta was the first written document that placed the king, like his subjects, beneath the law. In 1990s America,

Magna Carta did not have the force of law. But here it was being cited by a judge as more than a symbol. It was evidence of time-honoured, fundamental justice.

Like it or not, President Clinton was in the same boat as King John.

The US Supreme Court went on to rule that the case against the president could go ahead. Evidence was brought forward of other sexual indiscretions, including lurid details of the president's affair with Monica Lewinsky. For only the second time in US history a sitting president was impeached – that is, was put on trial before the Senate. He was not accused of sexual harassment or extramarital affairs, but of lying, i.e. perjury and obstruction of justice. Unlike King John, however, President Clinton managed to get enough of the most powerful magnates in the land to support him: the Democratic party majority in the Senate, voting pretty much on party lines, threw out the charges.

Nevertheless, Magna Carta had played its part in pushing the most powerful man on earth to the edge of ruination.

And this case was no exception. Magna Carta is regularly cited in US courts. More than 900 legal cases have sought guidance from the Great Charter, over 400 of them in the highest court in the land.

The US Supreme Court is housed in a huge neo-classical building next to the US Congress on Capitol Hill. If you go there in the early morning before Washington's attorneys and judges turn up with their laptop bags and cardboard coffee mugs, you can admire its massive bronze doors, still shut at that time. They're decorated with embossed images illustrating key events in the development of the rule of law. In the middle of the right portal, there's a picture of Sir Edward Coke barring King James I from entering the 'King's Court' at Westminster, and thereby asserting the court's independence. Just below it – in the most prominent position – the founders of America's highest judicial forum have chosen to show King John granting Magna Carta to the barons.

And the range of such cases has been enormous. In 1940, the Supreme Court relied in part on Magna Carta to overturn death sentences on four young black men whose confessions of murder had been extorted from them by police during five days of terror and isolation. In 1989, it was used to argue against a $6 million fine in a trade monopoly case. The Great Charter was called on in 1991 to prevent a young man being sent to a detention centre, and in 2005 in support of trial by jury. Over the years, Magna Carta has turned up in court cases concerned with private property, commerce, capitalism and slavery – in 1857 the Charter was quoted in defence of the slave owners' rights! According to at least one analysis, during recent decades, the Great Charter has been cited more and more often in criminal and civil actions in the USA.

But it's not just during complex arguments in courts of law that Magna Carta makes an appearance. As historian H.D. Hazeltine, notes, 'The history of Magna

Carta in America has a meaning far deeper than the influence of a single constitutional document … its spirit is inherent in the aspirations of the race.'

✷ ✷ ✷

For the story of how and why the Great Charter has taken such pride of place in the judicial system and at times in the daily lives of Americans, we need to go next to a building exactly halfway between the White House and the Supreme Court. It occupies a block on the corner of 9th Street and Pennsylvania Avenue. It's the US National Archives. The word 'archives' – unless you're an enthusiastic librarian – may prompt you to yawn. But believe me, you should stay awake, because this building is packed with surprises.

I first catch sight of it from the open top of a double-decker hop-on-hop-off bus as we cruise down Constitution Avenue. The bus's pre-recorded commentary blares out, 'This temple of a building was constructed to revere the birth certificates of our nation.' And a temple is what it looks like. Think of the Royal Exchange in London, at the very start of our Magna Carta journey, then triple in size its wide flight of steps, its towering columns and its triangular pediment on top, and you'll get some idea of the grandeur of the National Archives. I balance down the stairs from the bus's top deck, and hop off to find those 'birth certificates' of a nation.

On the ground floor, directly opposite where all visitors enter the National Archives, there it is, the only exhibit immediately visible. Magna Carta, on permanent display. It's not of course one of the Great Charters sealed by King John

The United States National Archives building in Washington DC. It houses the original US Constitution, the Bill of Rights and a 1297 Magna Carta. (by kind permission of US National Archives)

– they're all in England. But it is an original 1297 Magna Carta, as reissued by Edward I. Some constitutional historians regard this version as more important than the 1215 one, because it was accompanied by a declaration that any decision taken by a judge or royal official which was at odds with Magna Carta 'shall be undone, and holden for nought'.

The parchment sits here in a sealed glass case. Just like the Magna Carta we saw in the British Library it's no bigger than a page of a tabloid newspaper and its continuous, faint tiny brown scratchings, even if we could see them properly, would make no sense because they're in abbreviated medieval Latin.

I have to wait to get a close look at it, because there's a young guy, rucksack on his back, bending over studying it. I'm surprised at how long he devotes to it, a good five minutes. So when he steps back, I ask if maybe he's a specialist in deciphering ancient manuscripts.

'Oh no,' he says, smiling. 'Actually I've just graduated in Economics and Business Administration.'

'So how come you're so interested in Magna Carta?' I ask.

'It was a big deal at school,' he says. 'We learn about it in eighth grade and again later in high school.' I nod approvingly. 'We're taught about it as part of the first lessons in American history,' he goes on. 'It's the foundation of the Constitution and the Bill of Rights. I've always been fascinated as to why such a really old document can still be so important.'

'So have you seen it before?' I ask.

'Yes, my folks brought me here when I was a kid,' he replies. 'I always remembered it. So I'm just down in DC for the day and thought I'd come and take another look.'

I'm impressed, and I tell him so. He says *he's* impressed to meet an Englishman alongside this old English parchment. We laugh and shake hands before parting.

A sign on the wall reads:

> Magna Carta remains a powerful symbol
> of mankind's eternal struggle against oppression

I make my way upstairs to the floor above. Here in the centre of the building is a large hall. It's a cross between a cathedral chancel and the concourse of a very exclusive bank. You enter through gigantic bronze gates. Inside, I find myself in semi-darkness as if the place were lit by candles. At the far side of its vast marbled floor stands a line of what look from a distance like altars. There are three of them. The central one is flanked by uniformed guards. A handful of devotees occasionally whisper to each other, our steps faintly echoing as we move to and fro. Above the altars, the upper walls are covered with long and sumptuous murals depicting what must be the saints of this cult. We are in a shrine to the most hallowed of treasures. The impression is deliberate. As the archives guidebook says: 'The majestic domed ceiling, rising 70 feet above the floor, and the 40-foot-tall bronze doors contribute to the feelings of awe and reverence experienced by visitors to this magnificent space.'

It's called the Rotunda for the Charters of Freedom. It's not a temple, of course – not in the strictly religious sense, anyway. The saints in the paintings are in fact America's founding fathers. The altars are display cases. The central one holds the Constitution. To the left is the Declaration of Independence. On the right is the Bill of Rights. The worshippers are, like me, visitors. The guards … well, they are actually guards, overseeing the security of the most revered documents in America.

I make my way over to look closer. I don't expect to be able to read what's written on them any better than I could on Magna Carta. That's certainly so with the Declaration of Independence – it was once kept in a shop window exposed to sunlight for thirty years and is badly faded. The Constitution itself is a little clearer. I step gingerly over to the right, giving a friendly smile to the guard as I pass – his face remains stony – to examine the Bill of Rights. By peering very near to its glass cover, I can decipher some of its faint brown words in slanting copperplate writing.

These then are the 'birth certificates' of the American nation. The Constitution is basically a job description. It set out in simple clear language the functions of the three bodies that hold power in the United States – President, Congress and the judiciary. The Bill of Rights is the name given to the ten articles that were attached to the Constitution to define the rights of citizens. Rather confusingly, these articles were called 'amendments' though they were additions rather than corrections. It was in framing this document, in 1791, that America's founding fathers took their inspiration from Magna Carta.

To understand how Latin words on an ancient piece of English parchment came to be at the heart of American law, and in fact at the centre of America's devotion to liberty, we need to remind ourselves about the labour pains that led to the birth of the nation. They were momentous and bloody events.

✶ ✶ ✶

The clash between Britain and its American colonies in the mid-eighteenth century was not David versus Goliath. Both had become giants in their own right. By 1759, the British found themselves ruling an empire of which the American colonies formed only one part, as big as any the world had seen since the Romans.

That status sometimes led to ill-informed arrogance among Britain's leaders. The Earl of Chatham remarked: 'The Americans must be subordinate. This is the Mother Country. They are children. They must obey, and we prescribe.' Not a statement likely to go down well across the Atlantic. The fact was the Americans now lived in one of the fastest growing and richest places on earth. Intensive immigration and a high birth rate had combined with seemingly endless supplies of land and natural resources to produce in the colonies booming economies and relatively high living standards. The Americans chafed under patronising and oppressive rule from London.

What tipped discontent into war was taxation.

Westminster introduced a tax that applied only to the American colonies. Its very bizarre nature was enough to expose it to ridicule. By the Stamp Act, many printed materials commonly used in America had to be produced on a special paper manufactured in London and embossed with a revenue stamp to show the tax had been paid. These printed materials included not only legal documents but also magazines, newspapers and – puzzlingly – playing cards. To make the whole exercise even more ham-fisted, among those hit by it were two groups of Americans who had every opportunity to whip up a sense of grievance among their fellow countrymen: innkeepers, who had to use the paper in applying for their licences, and journalists. The result was rioting in the streets, usually culminating in a ceremonial bonfire of the stamped paper. One of the special tax collectors, a man named Zachariah Hood, was chased off by a righteous mob in Massachusetts. He rode without stopping till his horse collapsed and died under him. At this period, a new slogan was heard, 'No taxation without representation.'

Then the rift between the two sides was further deepened by the opposing constitutional arguments they each put forward. In England, following the so-called Bloodless Revolution of 1689, parliamentary democracy rather than Magna Carta increasingly came to be regarded as the ultimate guardian of liberty. The Americans, on the other hand, held that Magna Carta and English common law were the restraint on all arbitrary power, whether that be the king, the House of Lords, or – if it behaved in a despotic fashion – the House of Commons.

In early 1775, more taxes brought more violence. In Massachusetts this amounted to open rebellion, and there was skirmishing between American militiamen and the British redcoats. Massachusetts chose this moment to design a new official seal. It showed a colonist with Magna Carta in his left hand and a sword in his right, ready to fight for his liberties. The other colonies, divided in their opinions and actions on so many matters, also started to rouse themselves against British rule. In the Virginia House of Burgesses, one elected representative, Patrick Henry, decided a bit of theatrics might galvanise opinion. He got down on his knees, imitating a manacled slave, and in a steadily rising voice, intoned, 'Is life so dear, our peace so sweet, as to be purchased at the price of chains and slavery? Forbid it, Almighty God!' Then he threw himself flat on the floor, before suddenly jumping to his feet, and shouting, 'Give me liberty!' And he made as if he were holding a dagger to his breast, adding, in funereal tones, 'Or give me death!'

★★★

By May, fighting between the colonists and the British was widespread. War had broken out.

One year into that conflict, on 4 July 1776, the thirteen American colonies, after some pushing and shoving, unanimously declared their independence in a document that – unlike Magna Carta – began with a masterful statement of fundamental principle. 'We hold these truths to be self-evident,' wrote its authors, 'that all men are created equal, that they are endowed by their Creator with certain inalienable rights, that among them are life, liberty and the pursuit of happiness.' They have been described as the most potent words in American history. However, just like clause 39 of Magna Carta, which had said that free men should not be punished except according to the law, the opening words of the Declaration of Independence too were flawed. Just as 'free men' in the 1215 Magna Carta meant a limited section of the population, so did the words 'all men' in the Declaration of Independence. It excluded 600,000 black slaves. The matter had been debated by the founding fathers, and to preserve unanimity, it had to be agreed that slaves, though human, were – by some perverse logic – neither created equal nor had the same inalienable rights as free white Americans. It would take more than two centuries of bloody struggle before the Declaration of Independence, like Magna Carta before it, would be reinterpreted to become all-inclusive.

The War of Independence was a war of attrition. It took eight years for the two sides to wear each other down. In the end there was no appetite among the British to fight on, and when General Cornwallis surrendered at Yorktown, America achieved her aim and was free of the imperial yoke. Now it had to define how it would govern itself.

The man who more than any other shaped the new US Constitution hardly looked a hero. He was physically frail and, unusually for a politician, rather reticent. But he had the brain of a genius. He understood the opportunity now presented to forge a new political, legal and social order. He was James Madison.

The heart of the new system of government framed by Madison was the separation of powers. In Britain, the three great institutions of the state – the executive arm of government, the lawmakers and the judges – were mingled together in what to outsiders looked like a tangled hotchpotch (and still does).

James Madison, the frail genius who turned to Magna Carta when framing the American Bill of Rights. (Library of Congress)

The Lord Chancellor, for instance, sitting as tradition dictates on a sack of wool in the House of Lords, manages to be one of the leaders of the government, a member of the legislature and a prominent judge, all at the same time. Not so in the new American constitution. Madison and his colleagues saw such confusion as a recipe for madness, an invitation for some corrupt leader to take all the reins of power in his hands and to assume absolute authority. Instead under the new

American Constitution, the three powers – the executive, that is the President, the legislature in the form of Congress, and the judiciary – would be entirely separate. The force of each one would counterbalance the other two.

But the Constitution said nothing about the rights of individual citizens. And for a while it looked as though they might get overlooked amid the frenzy of tasks facing the government of the new nation. Madison himself even thought that what he called 'parchment barriers' against a tyrannical government were unnecessary. But eventually he changed his mind. The man who was known for his shyness then – in the words of one of his contemporaries – 'hounded his colleagues relentlessly' till the ten amendments, known as the Bill of Rights, were ratified by Congress in 1781.

Central to the document is the Fifth Amendment, perhaps best known in the phrase 'Plead the Fifth' when some politicians is accused of an abuse of office by a Senate Committees, or when a mafia boss faces a criminal trial, and by pleading the Fifth Amendment, they reserve their right not to give testimony against themselves and so refuse to answer questions. But there's much more to the Fifth Amendment than that. Its final few words state a fundamental comprehensive civil right:

> No person shall be deprived of life, liberty, or property without due process of law.

This of course was a repeat of what the thirteen original colonies had, with minor variations in the wording, copied from Magna Carta under the influence of the writings of Sir Edward Coke. It was Coke's interpretation of the Great Charter too that led to the inclusion in the Bill of Rights of trial by jury, a provision that fines should not be excessive, as well as the right of citizens to join, or leave, an association such as a trade union or a political party, and the right to petition the government without fear of reprisal.

In the late nineteenth century, America's most celebrated jurist, Judge John Forest Dillon, wrote:

> This was not new language, or language of uncertain meaning. It was taken purposely from Magna Carta. It was language not only memorable in its origin, but it had stood for more than five centuries as the classic expression and as the recognized bulwark of the ancient and inherited rights of Englishmen to be secure in their personal liberty and in their possessions … It will hereafter, more fully than at present, be regarded as the American complement of the Great Charter, and be to us – as the Great Charter was and is to England – the source of perennial blessings.

✦✦✦

Of course, America's love affair with Magna Carta does not mean that elective democracy has had no place in the nation's government. John Smith himself had been elected president of the Jamestown council as early as September 1608, the earliest example of democracy at work in the New World (followed – significantly – eight months later by the earliest example of London overruling the colonists' wishes, when it, in effect, removed him from office). It is only in the ballot booth that ordinary citizens can choose their leaders. But the American attitude has always been to distrust 'Washington', by which they mean the people in power, who can be corrupted. So throughout history, from the Jamestown Charter, through the colonial constitutions to the US Constitution itself and the Bill of Rights, Americans have made pieces of paper rather than institutions the ultimate authority for their civil liberties. And all of these documents have, to a greater or lesser extent, looked to Magna Carta as their model and as their historic justification. The Great Charter runs through the American body politic like a pumping vein.

But that doesn't wholly explain why Magna Carta has spread beyond the law libraries to become an icon for ordinary Americans. It seems there's a quality about the Great Charter that answers a deep need in the national consciousness. That something is Magna Carta's central role as a defence against tyranny. The USA has never had its own Stalin or Hitler. Yet the fear – not just of tyranny but of any overmighty government – runs through the national psyche like a recurring nightmare. Throughout their history, Americans have felt the need to be vigilant for the merest sign that despotism may be taking root. To this day, the state flag and official seal of Virginia still have an image of the figure of Virtue with her foot on the neck of Tyranny.

Part of the reason for this obsession dates to the American experience during the struggle for independence. British imperial tyranny almost triumphed then. That was a lesson, and was the logic behind Madison's separation of powers in the constitution itself, so that an over-ambitious, self-serving president could be checked by an elected Congress and by an independent judiciary.

This obsession has its roots in what's sometimes called 'the American Dream', the ideal (that often falls short in real life, but is a national aspiration nevertheless) that even a baby born in a log cabin can grow up to be president or a millionaire. Such values as self-reliance and the worth of the individual – forged in Jamestown and the rest of America's pioneering settlements – could be cramped by an interfering government, and would certainly be killed stone dead by an absolute dictator.

This sentiment can surface in the most innocent of circumstances. At election time, for instance, when candidates campaign against Big Government. That's partly of course about a reluctance to pay taxes, but it also reflects a worry that government might become so powerful that its citizens' liberties would be threatened.

But fear of tyranny can also, on occasions, burst forth with violence in the darkest moments of America's history. This is exactly what happened just a ten-minute walk from the National Archives, on 10th Street, five blocks east of the White House. Just along from the Hard Rock Café, there's a small playhouse called Ford's Theatre. A billboard outside advertises today's production, *Driving Miss Daisy*, a gentle drama about race and friendship. Visitors are allowed inside during those hours between productions and rehearsals. The auditorium is small and charming, its white stuccoed walls, red velvet seats and brass railings, all kept much as they were on the evening of 14 April 1865 when one of those dark moments in history occurred.

It was five days after the end of the American Civil War, a conflict that had seen the worst casualty rate per serving soldier of any war the world has ever known. It had rent the nation in two. That evening, Ford's Theatre had famous guests in its audience. President Abraham Lincoln, the first lady, and their friends Major Henry Rathbone and his fiancée Clara Harris were watching a performance of the play *Our American Cousin*.

At a little after 10.25 on that evening, a celebrated actor and Confederate supporter named John Wilkes Booth slipped into the presidential box. In one hand he held a .44 calibre Derringer pistol, and in the other a knife. He shot Lincoln in the back of the head. Then as Major Rathbone stepped forward, Booth stabbed him. Eyewitnesses say he then leaped on to the stage. Once in front of the footlights, he raised his knife and shouted to a shocked audience, '*Sic semper tyrannis*', the words attributed to Brutus when he killed Caesar and roughly translated as 'it is ever thus for tyrants'.

From the circle, where I'm standing, I get a clear view of the presidential box, to the right of the stage. Since that day it has remained empty. This afternoon it's draped in two huge Stars and Stripes flags. It dominates the little auditorium. From the balcony of the box down to the boards below I would estimate to be a 15-foot drop. The theatre's guide who is standing nearby can see my puzzlement.

'That was one fearsome leap,' I say to her. 'Did he really do that?'

'Oh yes,' she replies, 'Booth was a well-known athlete. And I guess his adrenaline had kicked in too.'

Lincoln died the following morning at a house across the road. Booth escaped, but twelve days later was caught and shot dead by a soldier.

THE ASSASSINATION OF PRESIDENT LINCOLN,
AT FORD'S THEATRE WASHINGTON.D.C.APRIL 14TH 1865.

The assassination of President Lincoln in 1865 in a box at Ford's Theatre in Washington DC. On the left, Major Henry Rathbone steps forward to restrain the killer. Next to him his fiancée, Clara Harris, alongside the First Lady. John Wilkes Booth, the assassin, has a knife as well as the gun. After shooting the president, he stabs Rathbone before leaping onto the stage. (Library of Congress)

This was perhaps the most extreme example of that American fear of tyranny. But it's far from unique. In total, four American presidents have been assassinated. There have been attempts on the lives of six others.

We may regard it as a vile slander to label Abraham Lincoln a tyrant. His memorial in Washington – one of the most famous landmarks in the world – is inscribed with the words, 'In this temple, as in the hearts of the people, for whom he saved the Union, the memory of Abraham Lincoln is enshrined for ever.' Nevertheless, in the heated era of the Civil War, 'tyrant' was what his enemies branded him. So perhaps we can understand that violent attacks on presidents and a reverence for Magna Carta have something in common. Although they're at the opposite extremes of what is acceptable in American society, both stem from the same sentiment: a wariness of overmighty political leaders. It was this sentiment that made the original thirteen colonies adopt the Great Charter as the model for their constitutions, and it was the same sentiment that inspired James Madison when he drafted the Bill of Rights. True or not, Magna Carta in the United States has been the seen as the first constitutional weapon to defeat tyranny. It's a sentiment that permeates the everyday lives of Americans.

Today in the twenty-first-century United States, Magna Carta surfaces all over the place, in TV interviews, Congressional debates, in high school and college curricula, in newspaper articles. The imprisonment without trial of suspected terrorists at Guantanamo Bay has brought a slew of recent references to the Great Charter. On 14 November 2013, a columnist in the *Chicago Sun-Times* wrote:

> Once rights are eroded, the slope is steep and slippery. The idea that a fair trial is central to all other rights was recognized more the 2000 years ago in the Roman Republic, in the 13th century in the Magna Carta, and again in the U.S. constitution. The denial of a fair trial to anyone today is a threat to all of us in the United States in the future.

If we count the phrase 'due process' as a reference to Magna Carta – which is a direct quote by the Fifth Amendment from the 1354 reissued Great Charter – then barely a second goes by but that someone somewhere in the USA isn't using Magna Carta to challenge their boss when he threatens to fire them, to complain about some over-officious bureaucrat, or to object to a parking fine.

From defender of the privileges of a handful of feudal aristocrats, to the watchword of Mr, Mrs and Ms Middle America, what a wondrous journey Magna Carta has trodden.

But what of the Great Charter's future? Can it sustain its position as the bastion of freedom and justice, not just in the USA, but in the country of its birth and in the rest of the world? It's time to take stock back at the place where the Great Charter was born one June day eight centuries ago.

21 BACK TO RUNNYMEDE

MAGNA CARTA'S FUTURE

uring the great British floods of January 2014, nature reclaimed the meadow at Runnymede. To our medieval ancestors, such an event would have been a near-normal winter occurrence. To us, it was shocking front-page news. Thousands of people had to flee the comfort of their damp-coursed, draft-proof insulated homes. In north-west Surrey, the River Thames overflowed and turned the fields below the official American Magna Carta memorial into a lake. The main Windsor to Egham road was under 3 feet of water.

But then, something magical happened. Magical for historians, that is. As the flood waters receded, Runnymede – for a few days – reverted to what it must have looked like during the average thirteenth-century summer, before the days of land drainage and flood prevention schemes. The lake disappeared, but left parts of the meadow a swamp of filthy, treacherous, sucking mud. The Windsor to Staines road poked up above it by just a foot or so, and formed a link between odd stretches of similarly slightly higher, drier ground. For those few days, Runnymede revealed itself as the place where, in the Middle Ages, enemies could meet and negotiate – without fear of ambush or night-time assault – on a dry island of land, isolated by impassable marshland and accessible only by the narrow raised causeway road between Windsor and Staines.

★ ★ ★

Today Runnymede – all dried out again and safe by twenty-first-century standards – is getting a facelift.

I received an email from the American Bar Association announcing that the official, American, Magna Carta memorial here is being refurbished ahead of the 800th anniversary of the Great Charter on 15 June 2015. It's being spruced up ready for the arrival of several thousand US lawyers who will participate in a special rededication ceremony here. Even the Magna Carta Tea Room is under new management and has been given a paint-job inside with stripped pine tables replacing the old Formica ones.

Not everything, however, is changing at Runnymede. It seems the myths linger on. At the car park entrance there's still a small silver plaque on a pole, which announces:

> Runnymede
> the birthplace
> of modern democracy

I want to write underneath, 'No it isn't! Magna Carta's got nothing to do with democracy', but there isn't room.

And that's not all. A couple of hundred yards away is one of the most desirable properties in this desirable neighbourhood. Not just a house, but a house on its own island in the Thames. It's called Magna Carta Island. This is the spot that Jerome K. Jerome in *Three Men in a Boat* claimed – without a sliver of evidence – was where the Great Charter was born. It's up for sale. And if you have a £4 million budget for your new home, you can get 3.72 acres of mid-river privacy, containing not only the old cottage (which now has an outdoor swimming pool and boat mooring), but also, says the current owner, 'the stone on which Magna Carta was signed.' A bunch of baloney is halfway round the world before the truth has got its boots on.

★★★

A hundred yards or so along the field path that leads from the tea room to the American memorial stands a small oak tree, not much more than a sapling. It's difficult to imagine that one day it may grow to 100 feet high and have a stout trunk that five people together couldn't hug. For now, it's so insignificant that I'd missed it on our first visit here, and would have done so again if I hadn't noticed a small plaque on a post in front of it. This is what it says:

> This oak tree, planted with soil from Jamestown, Virginia, the first permanent English settlement in the New World, commemorates the bicentenary of the constitution of the United States of America. It stands in acknowledgement that the ideals of liberty and justice embodied in the constitution trace their lineage through institutions of English law to the Magna Carta, sealed at Runnymede on June 15th, 1215.
> Planted December 2nd 1987, by John O. Marsh jr, Secretary of the Army of the United States of America.

The words are perfect. Perfect not just for those who idolise Magna Carta, but also for those who want to see beyond the myth to the true story of the Great Charter. There are no flamboyant, unsubstantiated claims about the 1215 Magna Carta being the birth of democracy or a constitution that defines how a nation is to be governed. The statement manages to put Magna Carta on a pedestal without flouting historical accuracy, and it does so in a couple of handfuls of resounding words: 'the ideals of liberty and justice embodied in the constitution [that is, the constitution of the United States] trace their lineage through institutions of English law to the Magna Carta'. Historians and worshippers of Magna Carta across the globe can unite in intoning this sentence.

Magna Carta has been described as 'England's greatest export.' It now belongs to the world. Not only was it shipped out to the American colonies in the seventeenth century to become the foundation of the constitution and to be relied upon in more and more cases where civil liberty is at stake, but also, when the British empire was broken up in the twentieth century, many of the new nations of the Commonwealth, such as Canada, India and Australia, recognised the influence of the Great Charter on their own systems of law and government. At the end of the Second World War, Germany and Japan, the nations which had suffered at first hand the arbitrary power of dictatorship, began to teach their children about the history and political significance of Magna Carta as part of the school syllabus. And in 1948, when the United Nations formulated its Declaration of Human Rights, the Great Charter was marked out as its inspiration. Eleanor Roosevelt told the UN General Assembly, 'We stand today at the threshold of a great event both in the life of the United Nations and in the life of mankind. This Declaration may well become the international Magna Carta for all men everywhere.'

The Great Charter has gone global.

✳ ✳ ✳

At the end of the field path, two men are at work with pressure washers on the memorial itself. It's a sunny day and I decide to sit on the grass a little further up Cooper's Hill. From here, I can see beyond the circle of classical columns now being scoured of their grime, and out across the flat grassy meadow to where speeding vans and cars drone along the old causeway road which 800 years ago brought together the armies of King John and the rebel barons. There's a sudden screech. It's the noise of a cherry picker, the motorised lifting platform the workmen are using to reach the roof of the memorial, its stonework still a grubby grey contrast to the stark white of the columns now gleaming in the sunlight.

It's the end of our journey. We've gone from cloudy myth to shining beacon. Along the way, we've discovered that history, like life itself, is never a child's fairy tale of good and evil.

King John was not, as the Victorians believed, the tyrant whose foulness would defile even hell itself. We should judge him not by our own standards, but by those of the thirteenth century. By that light, he failed as a king because he didn't win personal glory on the battlefield, and he roused opposition because he, like his father and brother before him, was changing the old feudal relationship with his mightiest subjects. Yes, he was unpredictable and vengeful, but we shouldn't forget that an inoffensive monarch in the Middle Ages was seen as weak and was more likely to be humiliated or overthrown than a brutal one. It was dog-eat-dog. At the end of the day, though, one of the most fascinating things about John is that – from whatever point of view we analyse him – we can never quite pin down the contradictions in his character.

The motives of the barons of England during the crisis of 1215 are just as elusive. The 170 or so earls and other lords of high rank had a range of grudges and loyalties. Most of these barons took no direct role in the creation of Magna Carta. Of the minority who did, few probably thought beyond the benefits to themselves, their families and their class.

Then what of the Charter itself, sealed here at Runnymede on 15 June 1215? It's time to ask the question that – for fear of being thought a spoilsport, a nit-picker or guilty of treason – you perhaps haven't dared utter till now.

Was Magna Carta all it's cracked up to be? After all, it didn't do much for one half of the population, women – in fact, it set out to limit their legal rights – and the other half, the men, didn't do so well out of it either – not the overwhelming majority, anyway, who were near-slaves. It doesn't sound like much of a beacon of fairness, does it?

We could say that the lasting value of the 1215 Magna Carta lies in the fact that three of its provisions are still on the Statute Book in England today 800 years later. They're the ones guaranteeing the ancient customs of the City of London and promising freedom for the English church, plus clause 39 granting to 'free men' the right not to be punished except by 'the law of the land'. In 1970, Parliament decided to cull from the Statute Book all dead and useless old laws. These three Magna Carta clauses were spared the axe, but I can't help thinking that was more on sentimental grounds, rather than in any expectation that prosecutions would follow their breach.

But there is at least one reason why we should today still revere the original Magna Carta, in the form as agreed and sealed by King John. That is because it shows us that even a king must obey the law. The Great Charter doesn't spell this out in so many words. But many of its clauses are examples of how the law of the land applies to the monarch as well as to his subjects. That was a breakthrough in the early thirteenth century. The 1215 Magna Carta therefore can rightly be quoted to show that any ruler – a twenty-first-century American one like President Bill Clinton, just as much as a thirteenth-century English one like King John – is no different from the rest of us in a court of law. A wonderful principle, given to us 800 years ago by the original Magna Carta.

The Great Charter, however, is much more than the words scratched in parchment here at Runnymede in 1215. Unlike the king and the barons, who were dead and buried centuries ago, it lives on. And like all living things, it's grown over the years into something that – while it has resemblances to its appearance at birth – looks a lot different from the way it did in 1215. So the very words 'Magna Carta' have come to embrace both the original Charter and what it became over subsequent centuries.

The most striking example of this broader definition is clause 39 itself. It was an acorn from which a mighty oak could grow. It doesn't matter that 'free men' – protected by Magna Carta from illegal and arbitrary action – made up only a small proportion of the population. What matters is that a principle was established: that arbitrary punishment is wrong. Extend this same principle to the wider population, as later generations did, and you have yourself a fundamental and *universal* civil liberty. The idea behind that right was clearly laid out in 1215.

Magna Carta's growth was, as we've seen, haphazard, often based on error, and at times it stalled and almost died. Kings routinely kept reissuing and reconfirming the Great Charter, often tweaking it here and there to head off the latest grievances which otherwise might fester into rebellion. Heroes, such as England's Sir Edward Coke, and America's James Madison, refashioned it further to meet the changing nature of their own conflicts with overmighty rulers. And, over many centuries, Magna Carta came to be regarded as the ancient and hallowed record of rights so fundamental they attained the force of morality itself: the right to trial by jury; the writ of *habeas corpus* requiring the release of a prisoner whose detention could not be justified before a judge; and the most comprehensive of all our rights, the need for due process of law before any of us can in any way be punished. With age, the Great Charter has established itself as – in the words of the most celebrated English judge of the twentieth century, Lord Denning – 'the foundation of the freedom of the individual against the arbitrary authority of the despot'.

***

It is inevitable when speaking of such a venerable document that we tend to have eyes on its history. But what of the Great Charter's future?

The 800th birthday of Magna Carta is boosting both our understanding and our reverence for the old document. As well as the rededication of the memorial at Runnymede attended by American, British and Commonwealth lawyers, there are a vast range of other celebrations. The BBC is broadcasting peak-time programmes about the Great Charter on both TV and radio. The British government is sponsoring a Global Legal Forum with the theme of Magna Carta – over two thousand judges and lawyers are expected from more than a hundred nations. The British Library is holding its biggest ever exhibition featuring the two 1215 Magna Cartas; special coins and stamps are being issued.; and the British Council is organising commemorations in over 100 countries worldwide. Magna Carta certainly won't be forgotten in the lifetime of anyone reading this book.

But could it become no more than an antiquarian relic, something to be marvelled at and treasured, like an Egyptian mummy, but of no practical use any more? In one sense, that has happened already.

Magna Carta cannot stop bad things happening. It can't topple a dictator. It cannot shut down torture chambers. Faced with a prison gate that needs to be prised open to free those who have been thrown inside without a fair trial, we'd be better off with a crowbar than a copy of Magna Carta. It cannot do anything on its own. But what Magna Carta can do is inspire us to fight against arbitrary power wherever we can – whether that's in a court of law, in an elected assembly, or in the columns of a newspaper. It may mean no more than simply standing up to be counted, or, if all else fails, it may mean doing what freedom fighters have sometimes had to do – take to the hills or to the streets.

At least part of the Great Charter's inspiration comes from the thought that we are not alone. To battle against injustice in the name of Magna Carta is to do what Coke and the Parliamentarians did in their war against the Stuart kings. It's what Madison and the founding fathers did in their battle for independence, and what the English Chartists did fighting for working-class rights in the early nineteenth century. It's following in the footsteps of brilliant lawyers and respected judges. And it's doing what thousands of people do every day when they claim the protection of 'due process of law'. Whenever we cite Magna Carta in defence of our rights, we are making ourselves part of a long and honourable tradition. It inspires us and at the same time it strengthens our cause.

The need for such an ancient and hallowed weapon against injustice is not going to go away, unless – as seems unlikely – human beings become universally peaceful, loving and kind. Recent news headlines show no sign of a let-up in the number of outrages that accompany the exercise of arbitrary power: the return of military dictatorship to Egypt; the suppression of minorities in China. Imprisonment without trial in Burma; the illegal seizure of property and countless other violations of human rights in Zimbabwe; summary executions and religious persecution in the IS caliphate. Not all – in fact, few – of the victims on this woeful and ever-changing list will actually call on Magna Carta as the inspiration for their fightback. Many will have never even heard of the Great Charter. But their resistance to despotism will nevertheless be part of the same battle that Coke and Madison and millions of others have fought in the name of Magna Carta. What unites all those engaged in such struggles are basic human instincts for fairness, security and freedom from oppression, instincts that have their roots in a time long forgotten. Those roots emerged as the green shoots of a political philosophy right here on the meadow at Runnymede, when King John bought off his rebellious barons one June day in the year 1215 by agreeing to abide by certain rules.

There will always be Magna Carta. After the parchments have perished and Runnymede is permanently drowned, the Great Idea that Magna Carta represents will live on.

When the last human beings on earth face subjugation by an alien tyrant and some among them choose not to bow but to fight, there'll be an Englishman surveying them from his heaven, Sir Edward Coke, who will shout down two medieval Latin words that forever mean justice and freedom.

Magna Carta!

APPENDIX

THE TEXT OF MAGNA CARTA

JOHN, by the grace of God King of England, Lord of Ireland, Duke of Normandy and Aquitaine, and Count of Anjou, to his archbishops, bishops, abbots, earls, barons, justices, foresters, sheriffs, stewards, servants, and to all his officials and loyal subjects, Greeting.

KNOW THAT BEFORE GOD, for the health of our soul and those of our ancestors and heirs, to the honour of God, the exaltation of the holy Church, and the better ordering of our kingdom, at the advice of our reverend fathers Stephen, archbishop of Canterbury, primate of all England, and cardinal of the holy Roman Church, Henry archbishop of Dublin, William bishop of London, Peter bishop of Winchester, Jocelin bishop of Bath and Glastonbury, Hugh bishop of Lincoln, Walter bishop of Worcester, William bishop of Coventry, Benedict bishop of Rochester, Master Pandulf subdeacon and member of the papal household, Brother Aymeric master of the knighthood of the Temple in England, William Marshal earl of Pembroke, William earl of Salisbury, William earl of Warren, William earl of Arundel, Alan of Galloway constable of Scotland, Warin fitz Gerald, Peter fitz Herbert, Hubert de Burgh seneschal of Poitou, Hugh de Neville, Matthew fitz Herbert, Thomas Basset, Alan Basset, Philip Daubeny, Robert de Roppeley, John Marshal, John fitz Hugh, and other loyal subjects:

(1) FIRST, THAT WE HAVE GRANTED TO GOD, and by this present charter have confirmed for us and our heirs in perpetuity, that the English Church shall be free, and shall have its rights undiminished, and its liberties unimpaired. That we wish this so to be observed, appears from the fact that of our own free will, before the outbreak of the present dispute between us and our barons, we granted and confirmed by charter the freedom of the Church's elections – a right reckoned to be of the greatest necessity and importance to it – and caused this to be confirmed by Pope Innocent III. This freedom we shall observe ourselves, and desire to be observed in good faith by our heirs in perpetuity.

TO ALL FREE MEN OF OUR KINGDOM we have also granted, for us and our heirs for ever, all the liberties written out below, to have and to keep for them and their heirs, of us and our heirs:

(2) If any earl, baron, or other person that holds lands directly of the Crown, for military service, shall die, and at his death his heir shall be of full age and owe a 'relief', the heir shall have his inheritance on payment of the ancient scale of 'relief'. That is to say, the heir or heirs of an earl shall pay £100 for the entire earl's barony, the heir or heirs of a knight 100s. at most for the entire knight's 'fee', and any man that owes less shall pay less, in accordance with the ancient usage of 'fees'.

(3) But if the heir of such a person is under age and a ward, when he comes of age he shall have his inheritance without 'relief' or fine.

(4) The guardian of the land of an heir who is under age shall take from it only reasonable revenues, customary dues, and feudal services. He shall do this without destruction or damage to men or property. If we have given the guardianship of the land to a sheriff, or to any person answerable to us for the revenues, and he commits destruction or damage, we will exact compensation from him, and the land shall be entrusted to two worthy and prudent men of the same 'fee', who shall be answerable to us for the revenues, or to the person to whom we have assigned them. If we have given or sold to anyone the guardianship of such land, and he causes destruction or damage, he shall lose the guardianship of it, and it shall be handed over to two worthy and prudent men of the same 'fee', who shall be similarly answerable to us.

(5) For so long as a guardian has guardianship of such land, he shall maintain the houses, parks, fish preserves, ponds, mills, and everything else pertaining to it, from the revenues of the land itself. When the heir comes of age, he shall restore the whole land to him, stocked with plough teams and such implements of husbandry as the season demands and the revenues from the land can reasonably bear.

(6) Heirs may be given in marriage, but not to someone of lower social standing. Before a marriage takes place, it shall be made known to the heir's next-of-kin.

(7) At her husband's death, a widow may have her marriage portion and inheritance at once and without trouble. She shall pay nothing for her dower, marriage portion, or any inheritance that she and her husband held jointly on the day of his death. She may remain in her husband's house for forty days after his death, and within this period her dower shall be assigned to her.

(8) No widow shall be compelled to marry, so long as she wishes to remain without a husband. But she must give security that she will not marry without royal consent, if she holds her lands of the Crown, or without the consent of whatever other lord she may hold them of.

(9) Neither we nor our officials will seize any land or rent in payment of a debt, so long as the debtor has movable goods sufficient to discharge the debt. A debtor's sureties shall not be distrained upon so long as the debtor himself can discharge his debt. If, for lack of means, the debtor is unable to discharge his

debt, his sureties shall be answerable for it. If they so desire, they may have the debtor's lands and rents until they have received satisfaction for the debt that they paid for him, unless the debtor can show that he has settled his obligations to them.

(10) If anyone who has borrowed a sum of money from Jews dies before the debt has been repaid, his heir shall pay no interest on the debt for so long as he remains under age, irrespective of whom he holds his lands. If such a debt falls into the hands of the Crown, it will take nothing except the principal sum specified in the bond.

(11) If a man dies owing money to the Jews, his wife may have her dower and pay nothing towards the debt from it. If he leaves children that are under age, their needs may also be provided for on a scale appropriate to the size of his holding of lands. The debt is to be paid out of the residue, reserving the service due to his feudal lords. Debts owed to persons other than Jews are to be dealt with similarly.

(12) No 'scutage' or 'aid' may be levied in our kingdom without its general consent, unless it is for the ransom of our person, to make our eldest son a knight, and (once) to marry our eldest daughter. For these purposes only a reasonable 'aid' may be levied. 'Aids' from the city of London are to be treated similarly.

(13) The city of London shall enjoy all its ancient liberties and free customs, both by land and by water. We also will and grant that all other cities, boroughs, towns and ports shall enjoy all their liberties and free customs.

(14) To obtain the general consent of the realm for the assessment of an 'aid' – except in the three cases specified above – or a 'scutage', we will cause the archbishops, bishops, abbots, earls, and greater barons to be summoned individually by letter. To those who hold lands directly of us we will cause a general summons to be issued, through the sheriffs and other officials, to come together on a fixed day (of which at least forty days notice shall be given) and at a fixed place. In all letters of summons, the cause of the summons will be stated. When a summons has been issued, the business appointed for the day shall go forward in accordance with the resolution of those present, even if not all those who were summoned have appeared.

(15) In future we will allow no one to levy an 'aid' from his free men, except to ransom his person, to make his eldest son a knight, and (once) to marry his eldest daughter. For these purposes only a reasonable 'aid' may be levied.

(16) No man shall be forced to perform more service for a knight's 'fee', or other free holding of land, than is due from it.

(17) Ordinary lawsuits [the court of common pleas] shall not follow the royal court around, but shall be held in a fixed place.

(18) Inquests of *novel disseisin, mort d'ancestor,* and *darrein presentment* shall be taken only in their proper county court. We ourselves, or in our absence abroad

our chief justice, will send two justices to each county four times a year, and these justices, with four knights of the county elected by the county itself, shall hold the assizes in the county court, on the day and in the place where the court meets.

(19) If any assizes cannot be taken on the day of the county court, as many knights and freeholders shall afterwards remain behind, of those who have attended the court, as will suffice for the administration of justice, having regard to the volume of business to be done.

(20) For a trivial offence, a free man shall be fined only in proportion to the degree of his offence, and for a serious offence correspondingly, but not so heavily as to deprive him of his livelihood. In the same way, a merchant shall be spared his merchandise, and a villein the implements of his husbandry, if they fall upon the mercy of a royal court. None of these fines shall be imposed except by the assessment on oath of reputable men of the neighbourhood.

(21) Earls and barons shall be fined only by their equals, and in proportion to the gravity of their offence.

(22) A fine imposed upon the lay property of a clerk in holy orders shall be assessed upon the same principles, without reference to the value of his ecclesiastical benefice.

(23) No town or person shall be forced to build bridges over rivers except those with an ancient obligation to do so.

(24) No sheriff, constable, coroners, or other royal officials are to hold lawsuits that should be held by the royal justices.

(25) Every county, hundred, wapentake, and tithing shall remain at its ancient rent, without increase, except the royal demesne manors.

(26) If at the death of a man who holds a lay 'fee' of the Crown, a sheriff or royal official produces royal letters patent of summons for a debt due to the Crown, it shall be lawful for them to seize and list movable goods found in the lay 'fee' of the dead man to the value of the debt, as assessed by worthy men. Nothing shall be removed until the whole debt is paid, when the residue shall be given over to the executors to carry out the dead man's will. If no debt is due to the Crown, all the movable goods shall be regarded as the property of the dead man, except the reasonable shares of his wife and children.

(27) If a free man dies intestate, his movable goods are to be distributed by his next-of-kin and friends, under the supervision of the Church. The rights of his debtors are to be preserved.

(28) No constable or other royal official shall take corn or other movable goods from any man without immediate payment, unless the seller voluntarily offers postponement of this.

(29) No constable may compel a knight to pay money for castle-guard if the knight is willing to undertake the guard in person, or with reasonable excuse to

supply some other fit man to do it. A knight taken or sent on military service shall be excused from castle-guard for the period of this service.

(30) No sheriff, royal official, or other person shall take horses or carts for transport from any free man, without his consent.

(31) Neither we nor any royal official will take wood for our castle, or for any other purpose, without the consent of the owner.

(32) We will not keep the lands of people convicted of felony in our hand for longer than a year and a day, after which they shall be returned to the lords of the 'fees' concerned.

(33) All fish-weirs shall be removed from the Thames, the Medway, and throughout the whole of England, except on the sea coast.

(34) The writ called *precipe* shall not in future be issued to anyone in respect of any holding of land, if a free man could thereby be deprived of the right of trial in his own lord's court.

(35) There shall be standard measures of wine, ale, and corn (the London quarter), throughout the kingdom. There shall also be a standard width of dyed cloth, russet, and haberject, namely two ells within the selvedges. Weights are to be standardised similarly.

(36) In future nothing shall be paid or accepted for the issue of a writ of inquisition of life or limbs. It shall be given gratis, and not refused.

(37) If a man holds land of the Crown by 'fee-farm', 'socage', or 'burgage', and also holds land of someone else for knight's service, we will not have guardianship of his heir, nor of the land that belongs to the other person's 'fee', by virtue of the 'fee-farm', 'socage', or 'burgage', unless the 'fee-farm' owes knight's service. We will not have the guardianship of a man's heir, or of land that he holds of someone else, by reason of any small property that he may hold of the Crown for a service of knives, arrows, or the like.

(38) In future no official shall place a man on trial upon his own unsupported statement, without producing credible witnesses to the truth of it.

(39) No free man shall be seized or imprisoned, or stripped of his rights or possessions, or outlawed or exiled, or deprived of his standing in any other way, nor will we proceed with force against him, or send others to do so, except by the lawful judgement of his equals or by the law of the land.

(40) To no one will we sell, to no one deny or delay right or justice.

(41) All merchants may enter or leave England unharmed and without fear, and may stay or travel within it, by land or water, for purposes of trade, free from all illegal exactions, in accordance with ancient and lawful customs. This, however, does not apply in time of war to merchants from a country that is at war with us. Any such merchants found in our country at the outbreak of war shall be detained without injury to their persons or property, until we or our chief justice

have discovered how our own merchants are being treated in the country at war with us. If our own merchants are safe they shall be safe too.

(42) In future it shall be lawful for any man to leave and return to our kingdom unharmed and without fear, by land or water, preserving his allegiance to us, except in time of war, for some short period, for the common benefit of the realm. People that have been imprisoned or outlawed in accordance with the law of the land, people from a country that is at war with us, and merchants – who shall be dealt with as stated above – are excepted from this provision.

(43) If a man holds lands of any 'escheat' such as the 'honour' of Wallingford, Nottingham, Boulogne, Lancaster, or of other 'escheats' in our hand that are baronies, at his death his heir shall give us only the 'relief' and service that he would have made to the baron, had the barony been in the baron's hand. We will hold the 'escheat' in the same manner as the baron held it.

(44) People who live outside the forest need not in future appear before the royal justices of the forest in answer to general summonses, unless they are actually involved in proceedings or are sureties for someone who has been seized for a forest offence.

(45) We will appoint as justices, constables, sheriffs, or other officials, only men that know the law of the realm and are minded to keep it well.

(46) All barons who have founded abbeys, and have charters of English kings or ancient tenure as evidence of this, may have guardianship of them when there is no abbot, as is their due.

(47) All forests that have been created in our reign shall at once be disafforested. River-banks that have been enclosed in our reign shall be treated similarly.

(48) All evil customs relating to forests and warrens, foresters, warreners, sheriffs and their servants, or river-banks and their wardens, are at once to be investigated in every county by twelve sworn knights of the county, and within forty days of their enquiry the evil customs are to be abolished completely and irrevocably. But we, or our chief justice if we are not in England, are first to be informed.

(49) We will at once return all hostages and charters delivered up to us by Englishmen as security for peace or for loyal service.

(50) We will remove completely from their offices the kinsmen of Gerard de Athée, and in future they shall hold no offices in England. The people in question are Engelard de Cigogné, Peter, Guy, and Andrew de Chanceaux, Guy de Cigogné, Geoffrey de Martigny and his brothers, Philip Marc and his brothers, with Geoffrey his nephew, and all their followers.

(51) As soon as peace is restored, we will remove from the kingdom all the foreign knights, bowmen, their attendants, and the mercenaries that have come to it, to its harm, with horses and arms.

(52) To any man whom we have deprived or dispossessed of lands, castles, liberties, or rights, without the lawful judgement of his equals, we will at once restore these. In cases of dispute the matter shall be resolved by the judgement of the twenty-five barons referred to below in the clause for securing the peace [§61]. In cases, however, where a man was deprived or dispossessed of something without the lawful judgement of his equals by our father King Henry or our brother King Richard, and it remains in our hands or is held by others under our warranty, we shall have respite for the period commonly allowed to Crusaders, unless a lawsuit had been begun, or an enquiry had been made at our order, before we took the Cross as a Crusader. On our return from the Crusade, or if we abandon it, we will at once render justice in full.

(53) We shall have similar respite in rendering justice in connexion with forests that are to be disafforested, or to remain forests, when these were first afforested by our father Henry or our brother Richard; with the guardianship of lands in another person's 'fee', when we have hitherto had this by virtue of a 'fee' held of us for knight's service by a third party; and with abbeys founded in another person's 'fee', in which the lord of the 'fee' claims to own a right. On our return from the Crusade, or if we abandon it, we will at once do full justice to complaints about these matters.

(54) No one shall be arrested or imprisoned on the appeal of a woman for the death of any person except her husband.

(55) All fines that have been given to us unjustly and against the law of the land, and all fines that we have exacted unjustly, shall be entirely remitted or the matter decided by a majority judgement of the twenty-five barons referred to below in the clause for securing the peace [§61] together with Stephen, archbishop of Canterbury, if he can be present, and such others as he wishes to bring with him. If the archbishop cannot be present, proceedings shall continue without him, provided that if any of the twenty-five barons has been involved in a similar suit himself, his judgement shall be set aside, and someone else chosen and sworn in his place, as a substitute for the single occasion, by the rest of the twenty-five.

(56) If we have deprived or dispossessed any Welshmen of lands, liberties, or anything else in England or in Wales, without the lawful judgement of their equals, these are at once to be returned to them. A dispute on this point shall be determined in the Marches by the judgement of equals. English law shall apply to holdings of land in England, Welsh law to those in Wales, and the law of the Marches to those in the Marches. The Welsh shall treat us and ours in the same way.

(57) In cases where a Welshman was deprived or dispossessed of anything, without the lawful judgement of his equals, by our father King Henry or our brother King Richard, and it remains in our hands or is held by others under our warranty, we shall have respite for the period commonly allowed to Crusaders, unless a lawsuit

had been begun, or an enquiry had been made at our order, before we took the Cross as a Crusader. But on our return from the Crusade, or if we abandon it, we will at once do full justice according to the laws of Wales and the said regions.

(58) We will at once return the son of Llywelyn, all Welsh hostages, and the charters delivered to us as security for the peace.

(59) With regard to the return of the sisters and hostages of Alexander, king of Scotland, his liberties and his rights, we will treat him in the same way as our other barons of England, unless it appears from the charters that we hold from his father William, formerly king of Scotland, that he should be treated otherwise. This matter shall be resolved by the judgement of his equals in our court.

(60) All these customs and liberties that we have granted shall be observed in our kingdom in so far as concerns our own relations with our subjects. Let all men of our kingdom, whether clergy or laymen, observe them similarly in their relations with their own men.

(61) SINCE WE HAVE GRANTED ALL THESE THINGS for God, for the better ordering of our kingdom, and to allay the discord that has arisen between us and our barons, and since we desire that they shall be enjoyed in their entirety, with lasting strength, for ever, we give and grant to the barons the following security:

The barons shall elect twenty-five of their number to keep, and cause to be observed with all their might, the peace and liberties granted and confirmed to them by this charter.

If we, our chief justice, our officials, or any of our servants offend in any respect against any man, or transgress any of the articles of the peace or of this security, and the offence is made known to four of the said twenty-five barons, they shall come to us – or in our absence from the kingdom to the chief justice – to declare it and claim immediate redress. If we, or in our absence abroad the chief justice, make no redress within forty days, reckoning from the day on which the offence was declared to us or to him, the four barons shall refer the matter to the rest of the twenty-five barons, who may distrain upon and assail us in every way possible, with the support of the whole community of the land, by seizing our castles, lands, possessions, or anything else saving only our own person and those of the queen and our children, until they have secured such redress as they have determined upon. Having secured the redress, they may then resume their normal obedience to us.

Any man who so desires may take an oath to obey the commands of the twenty-five barons for the achievement of these ends, and to join with them in assailing us to the utmost of his power. We give public and free permission to take this oath to any man who so desires, and at no time will we prohibit any man from taking it. Indeed, we will compel any of our subjects who are unwilling to take it to swear it at our command.

If one of the twenty-five barons dies or leaves the country, or is prevented in any other way from discharging his duties, the rest of them shall choose another baron in his place, at their discretion, who shall be duly sworn in as they were.

In the event of disagreement among the twenty-five barons on any matter referred to them for decision, the verdict of the majority present shall have the same validity as a unanimous verdict of the whole twenty-five, whether these were all present or some of those summoned were unwilling or unable to appear.

The twenty-five barons shall swear to obey all the above articles faithfully, and shall cause them to be obeyed by others to the best of their power.

We will not seek to procure from anyone, either by our own efforts or those of a third party, anything by which any part of these concessions or liberties might be revoked or diminished. Should such a thing be procured, it shall be null and void and we will at no time make use of it, either ourselves or through a third party.

(62) We have remitted and pardoned fully to all men any ill-will, hurt, or grudges that have arisen between us and our subjects, whether clergy or laymen, since the beginning of the dispute. We have in addition remitted fully, and for our own part have also pardoned, to all clergy and laymen any offences committed as a result of the said dispute between Easter in the sixteenth year of our reign [i.e. 1215] and the restoration of peace.

In addition we have caused letters patent to be made for the barons, bearing witness to this security and to the concessions set out above, over the seals of Stephen archbishop of Canterbury, Henry archbishop of Dublin, the other bishops named above, and Master Pandulf.

(63) IT IS ACCORDINGLY OUR WISH AND COMMAND that the English Church shall be free, and that men in our kingdom shall have and keep all these liberties, rights, and concessions, well and peaceably in their fullness and entirety for them and their heirs, of us and our heirs, in all things and all places for ever.

Both we and the barons have sworn that all this shall be observed in good faith and without deceit. Witness the abovementioned people and many others.

Given by our hand in the meadow that is called Runnymede, between Windsor and Staines, on the fifteenth day of June in the seventeenth year of our reign.

INDEX

Aaron of Lincoln 117–18

Acre, Israel 39, 41–52, 191

Adam, mayor of Lincoln 115

administrative efficiency of King John 121, 185, 186, 195

Alexander II, King of Scotland 170, 249

American Bar Association 150, 151, 208, 235

Angoulême 45, 52, 53–61

Anjou, Count of 189

Arthur of Brittany 51, 60, 67–8, 70–1, 92, 184, 185

Assize of Clarendon 37–8

Australia 237

barons

    before King John 15, 17–27, 32–3, 36–8, 45–6

    and King John 9–12, 49–50, 79, 84–5, 88–93, 95–6, 106–7, 123, 125, 128, 133, 152

    at Runnymede 10–11, 146, 153, 154–5, 156, 167–8, 170

    in Welsh Marches 88–9, 91–3

Becket, Thomas à 36–7, 186

Berwick, Northumberland 170

Bill of Rights, United States 225, 226, 230, 231, 233

Bogis (French soldier at Château Gaillard) 82

Booth, John Wilkes 232, 233

Bouvines, Battle of 136–8, 142, 152, 153, 192

Bouvines, France 130, 131, 132–44

Brayford Pool, Lincoln 112

Breay, Dr Claire 158

Briouze family see de Briouze

British Library 157–68, 240

Burwell, The Fens 23, 25

Cambridge 22

Canada 237

Canterbury, Archbishop of 10, 36, 37, 118, 119, 123, 153, 165, 242

Carlyle, Thomas 207

Charles I, King 204, 205, 207–8

charters 9–10, 114, 115, 218, 247

Château Gaillard 502–1, 73–85

Chatham, Earl of 227

Chesney, Bishop of Lincoln 117

Chester, Earl of 26

Christian, Reverend Paul 122, 126–7

Church and King John 123–5, 185–6

Church and Magna Carta 37, 120, 165, 238, 242, 250

clauses of Magna Carta 12–13, 37, 39, 95–6, 118–20, 160–2, 163–7, 177, 201, 206, 239–40, 242–50

    clause 39 162–3, 166, 203–4, 206, 218, 219, 238, 239, 246

Clifford, Rosamund 66

Clinton, Bill 222–3

Coke, Sir Edward 202, 205–7, 217–19, 223, 230, 239, 240, 241

commoners in medieval England 96, 97–108, 110, 125, 166

constitution, Magna Carta's actual influence on 13, 150–1, 167, 196, 236–7

constitution, Magna Carta's perceived influence on 12, 198, 207

Constitution of United States 225–31, 233–4, 236

Constitutions of Clarendon 37

Cooper's Hill, near Runnymede 146, 237

Cornwallis, General 228

cottars 103–4, 108

Court Leet 101, 107

Croxton, Abbot of 175, 176

crusades 45–51, 152, 170

Damme, Belgium 129

d'Athée, Gerard 92, 94, 95, 187

de Breauté, Falkes 91, 176, 187, 192–3

de Briouze, Matilda 92, 93, 184

de Briouze, William 85, 88–9, 91, 92–3, 94, 95, 187

de Caux, Robert 105

de Clare, Isabel 155

de Lacey, Roger 77–8, 79, 82, 83

de Lusignan family see Lusignan family

de Mandeville, Geoffrey 18–26, 23

de Mauléon, Savary 176

de Montfort, Simon 202

de Roches, Peter (Bishop of Winchester) 122–3

de Vesci, Eustace 154

Declaration of Human Rights 237

Declaration of Independence 226, 228

democracy, Magna Carta's actual influence on 13, 151, 167, 196

democracy, Magna Carta's perceived influence on 12, 147, 165, 197, 236

Denning, Lord 239

des Barres, William 138

Dickens, Charles 7

Dillon, Judge John Forest 230

Dovecote Inn, Laxton 100, 101, 107

due process of law 203–4, 207, 218, 230, 234, 239, 240

Edward I, King 224–5

Edward III, King 203, 204

Edward the Confessor, King 152

Eleanor of Aquitaine 49, 61, 64–8, 70–2, 185

Elizabeth I, Queen 9

Ely, Bishop of 24

Ermine Street 112

farming in medieval England 99–100, 102–3, 107

Fens, Cambridgeshire 15, 17–27

feudalism and Magna Carta 12, 13, 160, 161–5, 196, 209

feudalism in medieval England 17–18, 38, 45–6, 93, 133, 163, 186, 187, 188

Fifth Amendment 230

Fitzwalter, Robert 154, 185

Flanders 112, 135, 135

Fosse Way 112

Foul Anchor, The Wash 172, 172

free men in Magna Carta 108, 162–3, 203, 228, 238, 239, 242, 244

free men in medieval England 37, 103, 201

freedom, Magna Carta's actual influence on 13, 39, 108, 120, 149–50, 151, 161–3, 167, 204, 236–7, 239, 241

freedom, Magna Carta's perceived influence on 8, 12–13, 96, 145, 164, 205, 227, 239

Fritel, Pierre 141

Geoffrey, Archdeacon of Norwich 192

Germany 237

Gervase of Canterbury 191

Great Charter see Magna Carta

Green, J.R. 180, 194–5

Guantanamo Bay 204, 234
guilds 113–14, 115

habeas corpus 206, 208, 239
Hazeltine, H.D. 223–4
Henry I, King 152
Henry II, King 12, 26–7, 31–3, 35–9,
    66–7, 117, 142, 163, 167, 184, 186,
    189, 200
Henry III, King 175, 176–7, 204
Henry, Patrick 227–8
Henry VI, Holy Roman Emperor 49–50
Henry VIII, King 20, 182
High Bridge, Lincoln 111
Hindley, Geoffrey 152
Hiothhere, King 158
Holt, J.C. 152, 186
Hood, Zachariah 227

India 151, 237
Innocent III, Pope 122, 123–5, 128, 130,
    152, 170, 185, 186
Interdict 122, 124–5, 128, 182, 183,
    185–6, 191
Internet and King John 189–96
Isabella of Angoulême (then Queen
    Isabella) 55, 57–9, 60, 105
Islam and King John 193

James I, King 205, 207, 217, 223
Jamestown Charter 217, 231
Jamestown, Virginia 211–20, 231, 236
Japan 237
Jerome, Jerome K. 145, 236
Jews in Medieval England 116–18, 191,
    192, 199
John, King
    administrative efficiency 121, 185,
        186, 195
    death of 171, 175–6
    images of 10, 11, 183, 184, 223
    medieval reputation 189–94

modern reputation 12, 184–6, 190,
    194–6
at Runnymede 10–11, 153, 154–5,
    156, 167–8
tomb of 180–3, 184
Jones, Paula 222–3
jury, trial by 12, 37–8, 162–3, 198, 206,
    207, 208, 218, 223, 230, 239
justice
    before Magna Carta 34–5, 36–8, 39,
        153, 186
    Magna Carta's actual influence on 13,
        163–4, 167, 185–6, 199–202, 208,
        236–7, 241
    Magna Carta's perceived influence on
        12, 164, 206, 222–3
    see also law

King's Lynn 169, 171, 172
Knights Templars 126, 127–8

Langton, Stephen 123, 128, 153, 165, 242
law
    due process of 203–4, 207, 218, 230,
        234, 239, 240
    habeas corpus 206, 208, 239
    see also justice; trial by jury
Laxton, Nottinghamshire 97–108
Leopold, Duke of Austria 48, 49
Lewinsky, Monica 223
liberties in Medieval England 161, 205
liberty and Magna Carta see freedom
Lincoln 33, 109–20, 164–5
Lincoln, Abraham 232, 233
Llewelyn, Prince of Wales 90–1
London and King John 9–10, 110, 114,
    119, 152, 164, 170–1, 238, 244
Longchamp, William 49
Longsword, William (Earl of Salisbury)
    129, 132, 138
Louis, Prince of France (after, Louis VIII)
    133, 170–1, 177

Louis VII of France 64–6
Lusignan family 57, 59–60
Lusignan, Guy de 47
Lusignan, Hugh de 57, 59, 71, 133

Madison, James 228, 229–30, 231, 239, 240
Magna Carta
   copies of 109, 156, 159–60, 167–8, 224–5
   future of 235–41
   reissues 166, 176–7, 203, 204, 219, 224–5, 234, 239
   text of 242–50
   see also clauses
Magna Carta Tea Room 148, 235–6
Maidford, Northamptonshire 106
Manvers, Lord 100
Marches, Welsh 88–96, 236
Marshall, William (Earl of Pembroke) 155–6, 176–7
Maryland 218
Massachusetts 218, 227
Matilda, Empress 18–19, 26
Melusine, Satan's daughter 189
merceneries
   and King John 74, 91, 92, 93, 94, 95–6, 133, 136–7, 161, 170, 176, 184–5, 187
   and King Richard 46, 95
   in Magna Carta 247
Mirebeau-en-Poitou 60, 63–4, 68–72
Mowbray, William 153

National Archives, USA 224–6
navy under King John 129, 185
Newark Castle 175
Normand, Ernest 10–12, 154
Normandy 50, 60, 77, 84, 132, 143, 184–5, 187, 193
   see also Château Gaillard

Otto of Brunswick 132, 136, 137–8, 142
Oxford 33

Palace of Westminster 197–209
Pandulf 122, 126–7
Paris, Matthew 174, 192–4,
parliament and Magna Carta 165, 196, 197–8, 202–3, 204–7, 208–9, 227, 238
Penn, William 219
Percy, George (Jamestown settler) 213–14, 215
Peter of Blois 32
Petition of Right 207, 222
Philip Augustus (King of France) and King John 49–50, 51, 59–60, 77–84, 125, 128–9, 132–3, 136–8, 142, 170
Philip Augustus (King of France) and King Richard 47–8, 49–50
Pitt the Elder, William 12
Pocahontas 214–15
Poole, A.L. 170, 188
Powhatan Indians 211, 212, 214–15, 216, 217

Ralph, Abbot of Coggeshall 174, 191
Ramsey 19–22, 23, 24, 25–6
Rathbone, Major Henry 232, 233
Raymond of Poitiers 65
Richard the Lionheart
   as King 39, 45–51, 67, 95, 114, 155, 186–7
   in Magna Carta 248
   reputation of 11, 12, 45, 187, 191
Richard the Villein 111
Roger of Wendover 174, 191–2, 193–4
Roos family, Laxton 100
Roosevelt, Eleanor 237
Roosevelt, Franklin D. 12
Rose, Edmund and Stuart 100, 101–3, 104, 105, 107

Royal Exchange 7–15, 8
Runnymede 7, 142, 144, 145–56, 235–7, 241
Runnymede-on-Thames Hotel and Spa 145, 146
Ruskin, John 120

Salisbury, Earl of (William Longsword) 129, 132, 138
scutage 133, 152, 164
seal of King John 150
serfs in medieval England see commoners; cottars; villeins
Short History of the English People 194–5
Smith, John (Jamestown settler) 214–15, 231
St Albans, Abbots of 193–4
St Mary's Guidhall, Lincoln 113–14, 115
St Pierre church, Bouvines 134, 141
Steep Hill, Lincoln 109, 112, 116, 117, 227
Stephen, King 18–19, 22, 24, 26, 186
Stubbs, William 12, 194
Supreme Court, USA 223
Sutton Bridge, The Wash 172,
Sverre, King of Norway 112
Swineshead Abbey 175

taxation and Richard the Lionheart 46, 49–50, 51
taxation in Medieval England 104, 106, 110, 114–15, 116, 184, 204
Temple Ewell, Kent 121–2, 126–9, 182

Thatcher, Margaret 100
Three Men in a Boat 145, 236
tournaments 155, 170
trade in medieval England 110, 112–14, 115
trial by jury 12, 37–8, 162–3, 198, 206, 207, 208, 218, 223, 230, 239

United Nations 237
United States 38, 203–4, 211–34, 236–7

Victoria, Queen 9
villeins 103–4, 108, 111, 166, 245
Virginia 209, 211–20, 227, 231, 236

Warren, W.L. 93, 186, 195
Wash, The (Lincolnshire) 169–77
Washington DC 221–34
Welsh Marches 88–96
Wennington, The Fens 17, 23
White Castle, Welsh Marches 94–5
Wigford, Lincoln 113–14
William Rufus, King 199
William the Breton 78, 79, 80, 83
Witham, river 112
women and Magna Carta 162, 166–7, 203, 238
women in medieval England 34, 71, 103–4, 108, 203
Worcester Cathedral 176, 179–88
Wulfstan, St 183

York 118

If you enjoyed this book, you may also be interested in…

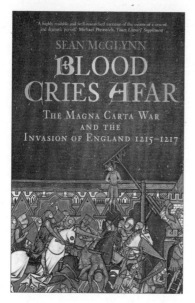

Blood Cries Afar: The Magna Carta War and the Invasion of England 1215–1217

SEAN MCGLYNN

978 0 7509 6391 6

Exactly 150 years after the Norman Conquest of England in 1066, history came extremely close to repeating itself when another army set sail from the Continent with the intention of imposing foreign rule on England. This time the invasion force was under the command of Louis the Lion, son and heir of the powerful French king Philip Augustus. Taking advantage of the turmoil created in England by the civil war over Magna Carta and by King John's disastrous rule, Prince Louis and his army of French soldiers and mercenaries allied with the barons of the English rebel forces. The prize was England itself.

The invasion was one of the most dramatic episodes of British history. This specially updated edition of *Blood Cries Afar* contains new material on the importance of the Magna Carta and the conflict that surrounded its birth. It tells a dramatic and violent but overlooked story, with a broad appeal to those interested in the history of England and France, and war in an age of kings, knights, castles, battles and brutality.